Confessions of a Coach

Confessions of a Coach

Norman Sloan
with Larry Guest

Introduction by Al McGuire

RUTLEDGE HILL PRESS
Nashville, Tennessee

Published in Nashville, Tennessee, by Rutledge Hill Press,
513 Third Avenue South, Nashville, Tennessee 37210

Typography by Bailey Typography, Inc., Nashville, Tennessee

Library of Congress Cataloging-in-Publication Data

Sloan, Norman, 1926–
Confessions of a coach / Norman Sloan, with Larry Guest : introduction by Al McGuire.
p. cm.
ISBN 1-55853-130-0
1. Sloan, Norman, 1926– . 2. Basketball—United States—Coaches—Biography. I. Guest, Larry, 1942– . II. Title.
GV884.S53A3 1991
796.323'092—dc20 91-31246
[B] CIP

Printed in the United States of America
1 2 3 4 5 6 7 8—97 96 95 94 93 92 91

Contents

Foreword: Al McGuire *7*
Raped *13*

Chapter 1 • Some Rules Cry to Be Bent *19*
Chapter 2 • Who Is Stormin' Norman? *39*
Chapter 3 • Fighting for Respect in the Bigs *59*
Chapter 4 • Wolfpack Wonders *79*
Chapter 5 • From Dominant to Downer *103*
Chapter 6 • Don't Call Me "Boy" *121*
Chapter 7 • Drugs and Dunks *145*
Chapter 8 • Captain Loose Screws *165*
Chapter 9 • University of Investigations-Gainesville *183*
Chapter 10 • Halloween Massacre *201*
Chapter 11 • Undue Process in the Rockies *221*
Chapter 12 • Battling Woodward, Bernstein, and the Zebras *239*
Chapter 13 • Storm Clouds at Seven-Feet-Two *259*
Chapter 14 • Rating My Fellow Asylum Inmates *277*
Chapter 15 • In Retrospect *295*

Epilogue *313*

Foreword

Norm Sloan and I go back to when he was the coach at The Citadel in South Carolina and I was the coach at little Belmont Abbey College just across the state line in North Carolina. I had a pretty good small-college team, made up mostly of tough guys off the playgrounds of greater New York, and Norm had a good team at The Citadel.

We'd get together for preseason scrimmages. It was during one of those particularly spirited scrimmages that I came to know Norm in a hurry. When things started to get a little physical, Norm waved his hands for everything to stop. He twisted his face into an angry turnip and shouted, "Listen, if we're going to fight, let's just stop and goddam fight for a few minutes! Then we'll get back to playing basketball!"

Naturally I shouted back, and suddenly we were in a shouting contest. The kids, both amused and dumbfounded, stopped and watched. Norm and I had to take turns yelling because if we yelled at the same time, the windows probably would have blown out.

Hello, Norm Sloan. I loved him from the start.

You see, the one thing anyone like me with any moss on them appreciates about Norm is you always knew where you stood with him. He didn't have to say anything. You could look at him and know by his face whether he was in your corner or an opponent. The guy has never been a chameleon, one of those reptiles that changes color. His attitude is, "This is me. You take all of me and no bullshit." Some people might find that hard to take because the bluntness becomes offensive if you are not secure within yourself. Secure people never had any trouble with Norm's M.O. (modus operandi). But I think there were times in his career, because of this macho attack or leading with his chin, that he made important people ill at ease.

In my world, it never bothered me. I see in Norm a lot of the same qualities that Bobby Knight has. They both come at you strong, but strip away the gruff veneer and underneath you find a marshmallow.

Norm is too hard on himself. He candidly admits that he spent too much time envying Dean Smith, when he could have taken notes on how to be a smoothie. Dean has been under the fingernails of all the other ACC coaches for the past thirty years because of his unbelievable success. Obviously, Norm has never had the complete package to compete year in and year out that the Tar Heels had.

In fact, I don't think Norm has ever been at a school where he could select players. Some coaches (for instance, at Notre Dame, North Carolina, UCLA, Indiana) enjoy the luxury of selecting their players. They recruit, then select. But at Presbyterian, The Citadel, North Carolina State, and Florida, the places where Norm coached, it was recruit, recruit.

His first job has always been just to get a top recruit to pick up the phone. A coach at Notre Dame, Arizona, or Syracuse may not get a given player, but that player is more likely to pick up the phone and listen to what he's got to sell. Norm never had that advantage. The fact that he has won six hundred-plus games and has lasted thirty-eight years in this business at smaller colleges is an accomplishment that shouldn't be taken lightly.

Norm thought my M.O. was more to stage street fights than basketball. On the Friday before we both played in the 1974 Final Four—Norm at North Carolina State and me at Marquette—all four teams were allotted one-hour practice sessions in the arena. We had the third hour, right ahead of Norm. His team came in and watched the last few minutes of our practice, which was, let's say, "spirited," as usual. When my players and I were through yelling, I passed Norm as we were leaving the floor. I stopped and shook a finger at him, warning him not to take advantage of being last up and practicing longer than his allotted hour. He laughed and offered to give us some of the time in his hour if we would continue yelling. He said that he and his kids were enjoying the show.

Norm, and other coaches, thought my coaching style was an act. A lot of people thought it was a publicity stunt. But that's the way I coached. I coached by instinct, by feeling. Coach Norm was in love with basketball—still is. I was not. To me, basketball was just a means to an end. But it was Norm's whole world. To a certain degree, basketball was his social life, his religious life.

There were two occasions when I bumped into Norm in off-season that reveal his true character.

The first came in San Francisco not long after he beat us for the national title. We were in one of those hotels out there that are trying not to slide down a hill. I grabbed him, and we went for a long walk, long talk.

It was the first of many times that I suggested that I had helped him out in the championship game by getting a couple of technicals. It also was the first of many times that he reminded me that North Carolina State won by twelve points, therefore the two or three points I contributed were inconsequential. Which was true. He had the better ball club.

What struck me was that he had just won the big one, but he wasn't showing any facial joy or glad-handing. There was no gloating or lobby-walking. When my club won the championship in 1977, I didn't want to go to bed at night. I'd walk the streets and go to the watering holes to enjoy it, to smell the roses. It seems that in coaching, the great ones take an evening to celebrate and that's it. Then they're back in the hunt, whether it's scheduling or recruiting or whatever.

That brings me to the later encounter. I had a speaking engagement somewhere in Florida, just a few years ago. I bumped into him in a hotel lobby, while he was on his way to see some recruit on behalf of the Gators. It was a living flashback to when I first met him some thirty years earlier. The same fervor, the same dedication, the same passion were all there. Only the lines in his face were different.

I like to consider the assets and liabilities of a friend. Whether it's Saturday night when they're at their best, or Monday morning with their hair in curlers, you have to take them both ways. And I take Norm both ways. He's always been like an island, a fighting city-state. When it got down to short strokes, he never had cultivated safety nets. I would guess that he never gave the president of Florida any time, not to be rude but simply because that was his M.O. That's the way he operates—this rigid drive toward roundball. That's why I compare him to Bobby Knight. But Bobby has softened, and I don't know that Norm ever did. I don't know that

Norm ever landed in a position of comfort. I think every place that he coached, he was taking over a problem or taking on an evacuation of Dunkirk. There was always a mission that became the challenge. And he stayed on one side of the street, and the administration stayed on the other side.

If he had tried to be a Dean Smith or more of a diplomat, he wouldn't have been as successful a coach, because that wasn't his natural way. I've got a good instinct about people, and I know Norm is a good person, morally and ethically excellent. But I don't know if the coaching world wants you to be that way any more. His style made it easy to gang up on him in a time of crisis. I would bet the president at Florida didn't really know Norm.

—Al McGuire
Coach, 1977 NCAA Champion Marquette

Confessions of a Coach

Raped

Recently my wife and I were watching an episode of "In the Heat of the Night" in which a black detective's wife was raped by a white man. The actress did a wonderful job of portraying how a woman must feel after she has been raped and violated.

Even though she was the victim and had not been responsible for what happened, she was gripped by shame and guilt. Her dignity had been stripped away like a candy wrapper. The man who attacked her had taken away the things that were important to her, and she kept taking baths in a futile attempt to cleanse her self-esteem.

Several times she expressed doubts about whether her husband believed her. She was unsure about what her friends were thinking, wondering if they privately felt she might not have been so innocent after all.

As I listened to her describe her feelings, it struck me how closely her anxieties paralleled my own after what happened to my wife, Joan, and me at the end of my thirty-eight-year career as a college basketball coach. I felt as if our dignity had been stripped from us, as if we had been raped. We experienced the same emotions the actress had portrayed: guilt and shame. But, I kept asking myself, "Guilt and shame for what?"

That's exactly how I was feeling. When I mentioned this to Joan, she said she had experienced the same sort of emotions. Having had time to think about it, I believe the best way I can describe what happened to us starting on Halloween 1989—my sudden and unscheduled retirement orchestrated by University of Florida administrators and other mysterious forces and the resulting "unethical" brand from the NCAA—was that we were raped of our dignity and raped of our reputations. We were left adrift in a pool of shame and guilt when we didn't do anything that merited either.

Viewing that television episode has given me better ability to express the emotions Joan and I felt after what was done to us by a collegiate athletic system that we had loved so dearly and still care about very much.

I've been married to a very strong, fine lady for forty-three years. We've gone through a rough time here at the abrupt end of my coaching career, but I don't want any sympathy. The business that I was in—and still have not removed myself from emotionally—is a very difficult one. It is a life that affords a great deal of pleasure and some pain. It all goes with the territory. Athletics are very important in this country, and they have a rich place in all our lives.

But what Joan and I went through starting in late October 1989 has been very traumatic, and it hurt my family and some of my closest friends. What should have been a great final year and an orderly retirement from the University of Florida became a complete disaster, an unfortunate and unnecessary experience for fans, coaches, athletes, and a lot of other people who suffered because of it.

Five months afterward, I thought I was pretty much over the trauma. On the Sunday afternoon in March when the NCAA pairings were announced, Joan and I were at our place on Daytona Beach. It was a strange day. I felt the depression coming on Saturday. At first, I didn't realize what was bothering me, then it hit me. Normally, this would be an exciting weekend; this was the big Sunday in college basketball. We would wait, hoping to see our school's name flashed up on the screen and waiting for which regional we would draw and who we would play. For college basketball coaches, this day is about as close to Christmas morning as life gets. We normally were as excited about it as a seven-year-old boy anticipating a toy train under the Christmas tree. But on this melancholy day, none of these feelings would be ours.

When I had coached at North Carolina State, I took three teams to the NCAA tournament, even though at the time the Atlantic Coast Conference could send only one team. At Florida I had three teams chosen for the tournament. On Selection Sunday 1990, however, none of that would happen. Without realizing what was going on, Joan and I both became ill-tempered.

One scene kept flashing in my mind: the first time we were invited at Florida. It was the 1987 NCAA tournament. We had sat in our living room in Gainesville, and the wait had seemed interminable. It was Dwayne Schintzius's freshman year, and we were 21-10, finishing second in the Southeastern Conference. I was near panic, fearful that we were going to be left out. Finally, "Florida" popped on the screen. Who were we paired with? North Carolina State, my former school!

We didn't care who our opponent was. Florida had never made it to the NCAA tournament, and now we were in. We broke into giggles and danced around the room laughing. That was the beginning of the good times for us at Florida.

Now, just three years later, Selection Sunday had become Somber Sunday. We had become conditioned to it being a happy day, with the phone ringing and friends and boosters sharing the excitement. Now we felt marooned, like Napoleon on Elba. It caught me by surprise because I thought we had healed enough that the day wasn't going to be a problem.

The months and years since then have given me the chance to step back and look at college basketball—and my career—from a distance that gives me a new perspective. I've been able to reflect on the warm memories and the uncomfortable moments. This book is about both of those: the human triumphs on and off the court that still give our hearts a lift and the misplaced values taken for granted by me and by others coaching and administering college basketball. Much about college basketball—and all college athletics—needs to be mended, for the moral integrity of those of us who make our living from it and, especially, for the sake of the student-athletes who are being exploited so shamelessly.

When Florida's 1,100-page response to NCAA allegations came out in July 1990, the new president, Dr. John Lombardi, who was hired after I was gone, likened me to someone who intentionally cheats on his income taxes, referring to me by name. Pam Bernard, the university's legal counsel, declared the school had now ridded itself of the "last of the renegades" in the athletic program. I'll trust you to decide if you think those descriptions of me, my staff, and the basketball program were justified. I obviously do not think they were.

Monte Towe, my head assistant, and I grew weary of reading where Steve Spurrier, the new football coach, continued to say that the people who were responsible for all the problems are gone, that it's now a new situation. Yet, we discover that one of the first things that happened after he came on board was that he and one of his assistants, John Reaves, were found recruiting at an illegal time in an illegal place. During a no-contact recruiting period, they went to a church in Middleburg, near Jacksonville, where an outstanding quarterback prospect just happened to attend. The official reaction was "human frailty," and the university stood behind Spurrier and Reaves, reasoning to the NCAA that this was an unintentional mistake.

Well, what they ran me out on the plank for was no more serious than that, probably less. The violations they hung around my neck had nothing to do with recruiting.

Louisville's Denny Crum made a contact bump at an illegal time, and the NCAA forbid him to recruit that player. Bobby Knight did the same thing, but the NCAA accepted Indiana's sixty-page explanation that Bobby and his coaches didn't understand the rule. That's what bothers me, how inconsistent my own athletic director, Bill Arnsparger, was and how selective the NCAA can be in saying, "Oh, we understand, Bobby, you made a simple mistake." But "No, Denny, you should know the rules."

"Well yeah, Steve, we understand it was human frailty." As opposed to, "Okay, Norm, you did this on purpose. Go hire a lawyer and strap on a legal pad, buster."

The blight and public perception thus created are the kinds of things you can never shake. I could write six books explaining, exposing, and documenting the injustices that happened to me and to my staff at Florida, and there still would remain a huge segment of the population steadfastly convinced that Norman Sloan is a scumbag who needed to be squashed. Nothing will ever change that in some people's minds.

The day Joan and I got the news that unseen forces wanted me out, it was a total shock to us. We were completely unprepared for it, and our first reaction was to fight. Joan and I were fully prepared to do that, but we had good advice. We could have won the fight—I knew it then, and I know it now—but in the process we might have lost our retirement and might have been destroyed before the battle was over. Continuing the fight just wasn't the thing to do. I got caught up in something I never dreamed would happen, a baffling situation in which I would not be able to stand up toe-to-toe and fight my way through.

Nobody in administration at the University of Florida would talk to me, so I never knew what they were upset about. I knew what I read in the papers, and that would have upset me, too, if it had been true. Much later—after I had been pushed out—I began to find out about some of the meetings that took place and about some of the conversations that went on. Then I began to understand what happened.

To this day, though, Joan and I still don't understand much of it. Why would the federal government stay after us for all that time when we hadn't committed any crimes? We hadn't done anything contrary to the law of the land. What was their interest in us? Though much of the legal terrorism is detailed in this book, I'm without even a theory as to its motivation. It is frustrating to grasp for those ghosts. What is particularly painful, however, is the perception it created.

If the feds were threatening me with an unspecified indictment, and if administrators at Florida chose to get rid of me mere days before the start of the season and to change coaches at such an inopportune time, then it figures that Norman Sloan must have been guilty of scads of terrible and unspeakable acts. The piddling allegations produced by a two-year NCAA investigation must have just been the tip of the proverbial iceberg.

Unfortunately, that is the portrait Florida interim president Bob Bryan and athletic director Bill Arnsparger painted when they immediately disassociated themselves from me like I was a leper. That is the portrait that Joan and I must now live with for the rest of our days, unjust as it is.

CHAPTER 1

Some Rules Cry to Be Bent

As a college player, I accepted cash from my coach. As a college coach, I gave cash to players.

The occasion when I took money from my college coach, the late and beloved Everett Case, came in December 1947. I was a sophomore at North Carolina State and was anxiously approaching a trip home to Indiana for Christmas. I had received my regular monthly stipend of eighty-five dollars on the GI Bill and had stuffed the money in my watch pocket just before our final practice prior to the holidays.

After practice, the money was gone.

I was crushed. All primed to make the journey home, suddenly I didn't have two nickels to rub together. I went in to see Coach Case with my tale of woe to doggedly plead my case. Finally, he agreed to give me fifty bucks. Christmas 1947 was saved for Norman Sloan, NCAA rules notwithstanding.

I never offered to give the fifty dollars back, and Coach Case never asked for it. At the time I just appreciated what he did for me. He made me convince him that I was in a genuine tight spot and that I hadn't merely squandered my money. It was a moment when human kindness and need superseded the NCAA's unfeeling regulations.

More than three decades later, one of my players sat in front of my desk spilling his own wintertime misfortune, one more serious than my endangered holiday junket. He was from a single-parent home of little means. This was during a cold snap when the temperatures were dipping below freezing every night. The player said his mother was out of heating oil and didn't have enough money for a new supply.

I checked out his story to make sure the claim was valid. She was a nice lady. "Coach, this isn't going to be an ongoing thing," she said. "But I need help."

I gave her and her son a hundred dollars for heating oil.

At that moment I wasn't concerned about violating an NCAA rule. I felt I was helping someone in need, and I felt darned good about it. Her son was already in my program. It wasn't like I was trying to entice him to come with me.

On another occasion at North Carolina State, one of my players—Phil Spence—had a unique problem. His father was dead, and his mother was in ill health with a serious heart condition. I knew she had been in and out of the hospital. They needed money for medication.

I interrogated Phil to be certain they had exhausted all social services and other possible sources of money, then went to visit his mother. It was near Christmas time, and I had received a lot of fruit from friends and supporters. So I took her a bag of oranges, for which she was outspokenly appreciative, and for about four months I made sure that people helped her purchase the medication she needed to help keep herself alive. That was a violation of NCAA rules, but I felt very good about it. I was proud about helping her.

One year a player and his girlfriend came into my office with a grave problem. He was in his freshman year, and they were obviously distraught when they arrived. They soon told me the problem: she was pregnant and they had decided they couldn't have the child. I know that the pro-life and pro-choice argument rages to this day, but my own feelings had to take a back seat at that moment. Here were a couple of kids who were like family to me, and they needed help. I knew they didn't have support from home.

They wanted money for an abortion. The figure that sticks in my mind is 150 dollars, although I'm not sure that's right. I grilled them to make sure they had a plan. Was it safe, or were they going into somebody's butcher shop? Were they sure they were not going to look back on this and regret their choice? Those are the kinds of questions I asked them, the same questions I suppose any of us would ask our own children. I was concerned whether they were doing the right thing.

But they were adamant. One way or another, they were going through with it. So I gave them money. That was a violation of NCAA rules.

When Tom Burleson, the great center, arrived at North Carolina State, the first thing required of him was a forty-dollar dorm deposit, but he had been sent off to college with only twenty dollars in his pocket. Well, I loaned him the other twenty dollars. Another violation of NCAA rules.

In a more publicized incident, I provided a 240-dollar plane ticket from athletic department funds for Florida star guard Vernon Maxwell to attend a Boston Celtics summer camp after his junior season so he could receive much-needed drug counseling from Red Auerbach and K. C. Jones. That was a violation, too, although I didn't realize it at the time.

When I first started in coaching, it was a happier, uncomplicated time. Now, the rules are complex and hard to understand, and they overlap in many areas. It's almost impossible today to conduct business and operate a program without unwittingly bruising an NCAA rule.

At the outset, I adopted a simple precept that basically never changed. In relation to the NCAA's ever-expanding rules, I've primarily been concerned with illegal aid, offered or given, as an inducement to get an athlete to attend my school. If I went out and tried to buy him, that was cheating.

But to me, once a kid gets there, he's family, particularly if it's a kid without a family that can take care of his basic human needs. When you go in a home to recruit now, one of the first things the father or the mother—or both—will say is, "I just want to make sure you will take care of my son. I want to make sure that when he has problems, there is someone he can go to and talk to." That's something a coach tells the parents he will do and something I feel he should do.

Everett Case did that for me, and I tried—when I felt it was warranted—to do that for my players. But don't get the idea there was any truth to those exotic claims Vernon Maxwell made to drug investigators probing in his sudden affluence, that he could walk into my office and get a thousand dollars anytime he wanted. That never happened.

But until the NCAA allows a fair and equitable scholarship, I find it very difficult to hold the player or the coach as responsible as we have to hold them now for violating NCAA rules. The way we're treating these kids only creates a very fertile ground for cheating.

Months after I was pushed out and as the trauma began to subside, I began to start watching the games on television again, listening to the commentators promoting the game like it was a religion. One of the things I had thought about doing was commentary work, and I was tempted by several feelers. I have a lot of experience, representing different conferences and coaching internationally in Olympic-type competition. It seemed a natural for me to become a color analyst.

But the more I watched, the more I realized that the telecasts and the commentators have become a part of the whole hypocritical process and the more I questioned whether I wanted to be a party to that. It was a terrible feeling. I love college basketball. Other than my family, it's been the biggest thing in my life.

Now I find myself really not wanting any part of it.

Announcers are being forced to mouth stupid statements, ask stupid questions, and say things that aren't true. I get the feeling they're actually afraid to raise the serious questions that should be asked, for instance, why the NCAA sends an Alabama out to the West Coast to play its NCAA tournament games.

Look at the NCAA. Look at their facilities. Look where they have their meetings. Have you heard of an NCAA or conference meeting being headquartered at a Day's Inn? Hell, Holiday Inn doesn't qualify anymore. If a resort doesn't have thirty-six championship holes of golf or a beach and spacious rooms where they place fancy chocolates on your pillow each night, it doesn't need to waste its time applying to host a Southeastern Conference meeting. The NCAA has given no-interest or low-interest personal loans to Walter Byers, the former executive director, and to his successor, Dick Shultz, who now hops around the country in a private jet when he's not in the NCAA's plush new offices. It is hypocritical to reward NCAA staffers with lavish salaries and perks at a time student-athletes can't accept a free pizza or a ride across town without violating the rules.

The whole thing is out of kilter. It has become entertainment. It has more in common with big business than intercollegiate competition. When I was working in it, I didn't want to admit that and often didn't even see it. But when I had months to sit back and watch television and read the newspapers, to back off and take a good look, I didn't like the view. I was almost ashamed of what I had spent a lifetime doing.

When I was in college, I had extra income. I was a World War II veteran and thus had those monthly stipends from the GI Bill. Also, we were allowed to take advantage of part-time work, like selling football programs at home games. Today, an athlete can have only room, board, and tuition—basic educational expenses—but no spending money of any kind. The NCAA even eliminated the "laundry money" allowance of fifteen dollars a month and part-time work opportunities. I never have understood why the NCAA considers it a problem to have basketball players selling programs at a football game or football players selling basketball programs.

But then, understanding the arrogance and hypocrisy of the NCAA has become the Rubik's Cube of our athletic times. My first introduction to the shameful ways of the NCAA came when we were placed on probation for one year at North Carolina State as a result of the so-called David Thompson investigation.

The cloud that resulted and still lingers over David's name because of that probation is one of the great injustices in college basketball history. David Thompson's recruitment was one of the sweet memories I'll cherish from my career.

Joan, my wife, was with me the first time I went to David's home. I had thought he lived in Shelby, North Carolina, where he attended Crest High School. Actually, he lived outside of Shelby in an unincorporated area called Lattimore. The Thompsons lived in the middle of a pasture in a structure that formerly had been an animal shelter of some sort. When built, it was not intended to be a house. There was no road, just ruts across the field leading to their front door.

When we arrived, David was out playing basketball and Mrs. Thompson was the only one there. She welcomed us inside. It was an education for Joan and me. The flooring boards literally were on dirt, and the walls were open studding—two-by-fours and cross beams.

But on the cross beams were body talc, deodorant, toothpaste, other items of personal hygiene. That told us a lot about the pride of these people, despite their modest lot in life.

We sat there trying to start a conversation. Ida Thompson had a silk stocking in her hand and beads of perspiration on her brow as big as the end of your finger. Extremely uncomfortable with us sitting there, she was so nervous that she literally was shredding that silk stocking.

Joan, bless her heart, tried to find a common ground to start a conversation and asked Mrs. Thompson if she worked. She did, in a hosiery mill. "Oh, I should have a job there," Joan mused. "My two daughters just go through hose left and right."

Mrs. Thompson smiled and raised her eyebrows at this dainty little white girl sitting there before her. "Oh, honey," she said. "You couldn't handle it. The work's too hard for you."

David was the youngest of eleven children. Vellie and Ida Thompson were far and away the finest parents I've had the joy of working with.

But before David's freshman year was over, we began to be investigated. I wasn't concerned about it. I knew we had done nothing wrong in recruiting him.

As we later put it together, an enthusiastic fan from Shelby who was a supporter of the program at Gardner-Webb University had hoped he could sway David into going to Gardner-Webb. Although he was close to David, David never seriously considered going to Gardner-Webb. At any rate, this man apparently turned in assorted allegations to the NCAA. One charge was that a booster had built a road to David's house. Upon closer inspection, it turned out that a local mill owner, Charles Dover, persuaded a friend in the construction business to grade down the ruts in the dirt road near the Thompsons' house. Dover, who had no connection to North Carolina State, became irate over the suggestion that he built a road for David Thompson and was indignant when NCAA investigators came calling.

Rumors were also printed that we had built David a 35,000 dollar house, had given him money, and had bought him clothes. The NCAA's visit to the Thompson's home promptly shot down the first allegation. They lived in that same ramshackle house until David built his parents a nice home the first year he was in the pros. The NCAA never asked us about the other charges. They had dismissed them on their own.

In short, illegal aid was never given or offered. David signed with us in May 1971, and we had a basketball camp in July. Two of David's close friends from Shelby—Jerry and Larry Hunt—came to our camp, and David came with them, putting a mattress on the floor of their room so he could sleep with them.

We knew he was there. We talked to him every day, and he shot baskets and worked out in the gym. We didn't think there was anything wrong with him moving in with his friends during those two weeks, but the NCAA found us guilty of failing to charge him the then-standard eight dollars a week for using a dorm room.

The second violation occured during a pickup game that summer at Carmichael Gym, our practice facility. David was involved in an impromptu game when one of my assistants, Eddie Biedenbach, walked in. They needed a player, so Biedenbach joined in the game. Although this took place in July and David had signed with us in May, the NCAA called the game an illegal tryout.

The third violation was in relation to Charlie Bryant, a former assistant on my staff who was then in the banking business in Gastonia, not far from David's home. At that time, schools could bring a prospect in for two official visits, one paid for by the school and one by the alumni. We had David in on the school-paid visit; for the other, Charlie Bryant picked him up and drove him to North Carolina State for his two-day visit, then drove him home. Because Charlie had been in the coaching business, the NCAA called his actions those of a scout, which was illegal under its rules.

The fourth violation concerned Tom Burleson. Tom had worked in my summer camp right after he finished high school. I thought prospects couldn't work at a school or coach's summer camp, but Nelson Isley, another kid in our camp, said, "Coach, Tom can come work in your camp. I got a ruling on that." I called Jim Weaver, then commissioner of the ACC, and asked if it were possible for Burleson to work in my summer basketball camp since he had already signed with us. "Yes," said Weaver. "He has undergone a change of status, and he can do that."

I asked him to send me a letter confirming that, and he did.

When I showed the letter to the NCAA, they told me I had gone to the wrong authority.

Those are the four actions that the NCAA used to put North Carolina State on probation. Yet some people continue to talk as though we blatantly purchased David Thompson.

We went on one-year probation—David's sophomore year when we went 27-0 and were ranked number 2 in the nation behind UCLA. The next year, 1974, we beat Bill Walton-led UCLA in the semi-final game of the Final Four, and UCLA's athletic director was quoted in the papers as saying, "Well, if I'm not mistaken, North Carolina State went on probation for the recruitment of David Thompson." (Ironically, Walton later said in his book that he was given $6,000 by infamous UCLA booster Sam Gilbert, though the Bruins didn't go on probabtion for that.)

Yet that's the kind of innuendo and cloud that came out of this. Digger Phelps, the former Notre Dame coach, later wrote a book in which he declared that North Carolina State won a national championship with a kid whose recruitment put them on probation. That was just totally unfair. The infractions that put us on probation were administrative missteps that came *after* David Thompson had chosen North Carolina State and had signed his scholarship. They had absolutely nothing to do with inducing David Thompson to come to State.

What few remember is that Duke also went on probation as a result of the same investigation. Duke had a strong alumnus in Shelby who had befriended David, who didn't even have a suit or jacket in which to graduate from high school. The guy took David down to Belk's department store and bought him a blue blazer for fifty dollars as a graduation present. The NCAA put Duke on probation for one year over that incident.

NCAA procedure is that just before you go off probation, they send an official around to make sure you have completed any corrective actions they had recommended. The guy they sent to see us was Bill Hunt, a man I liked and respected. At that time, Bill was an investigator for enforcement. He later became assistant executive director for legislative services until he resigned from the NCAA in early 1991.

During his visit, I expressed my feelings about the injustice that had been done in our case. I told him that for years and years, in the rest of my coaching career and the rest of David Thompson's life, we would be lumped in with all the notorious cheaters in NCAA history, guys who gained an advantage by violating recruiting rules. We had made four administrative mistakes—none of which was an advantage in recruiting—and I didn't feel they had justified a year's probation.

Hunt said, "Yeah, Norm, I know what you're talking about. You're talking about guys like Tarkanian."

I was sitting behind my desk, and Bill was sitting on the couch on the other side of the room. He jumped up, suddenly red in the face, and said, "I'll tell you about Tarkanian. We're not only gonna get him, we're gonna run him out of coaching."

Some time went by and I was doing a clinic in Joliet, Illinois. Between sessions, a discussion broke out in a small group that included Tarkanian, Joe Dean (now the athletic director at LSU), and Bill Wall, then head coach at Millikin College and later president of the National Association of Basketball Coaches. Wall declared that any time a coach was caught violating any rule, he should be run out of coaching—permanently. Well, since I had just been through probation, I took issue with him.

"You don't know what you're talking about," I snapped. "You need to sit through one of those investigations and talk to some people who have. Things can happen to you beyond your control, or you can violate rules you're not aware are rules, not really trying to get away with anything."

Apparently I became very animated because Joe Dean tried to calm me down. Wall said something, and I jumped him again. This time Tarkanian spoke up and sort of took Bill Wall's side.

So I told Tark, "Well, I've got news for you. You're going to see this whole thing in a different light before long, based on what I've been told by Bill Hunt of the NCAA. He tells me they're not only going to get you, but they're going to run you out of coaching."

Tark just shrugged it off.

That next October, I got a phone call from Tarkanian.

"Norm? It's Tark. Remember when we had that conversation in Joliet?"

"Yeah."

"Well, I'm supposed to appear before the infractions committee here in a couple of weeks. Do I have your permission to tell them what you told me Bill Hunt said?"

I said, "Oh, no! You can't do that. If you do, they'll turn around and come after me again. That's the kind of power they have, and that's the way they think. Do you agree with that?"

Tark said "Yeah."

A couple of weeks went by, and Joan told me one evening that Warren Brown was trying to reach me by telephone. I had basketball on my mind and the name didn't click, although it should have because he was the head of NCAA enforcement.

The phone rang and a voice said, "Norm. It's Warren. Warren Brown. How'ya doin', buddy?"

"Oh, yeah," I said, remembering that the last time we had spoken was during our appearance before the NCAA infractions committee. Warren and I had gotten into such a heated exchange that day, my school president grabbed me by the coattail to restrain me. Now I was Warren's "buddy."

He related that Tarkanian had just appeared before the infractions committee and had repeated what I had told him about Bill Hunt's threat to run Tark out of coaching. He said, "I know that would never have happened, right?"

I said, "No, no, Warren. However, had it been true, that Bill had said that, that's exactly what I would have told Tark. Because I believe you people operate that way."

"Oh, Norm, you don't believe that," he responded.

"Warren, I believe it with every bone in my body."

Another year went by, and I got a phone call from a guy who identified himself as a United States marshal. I didn't even know what a subpoena was, but this guy told me he had a subpoena for me to appear before the oversight committee in Congress on a certain date to testify in the matter concerning Tarkanian and the NCAA.

I said, "Oh, no. I don't want to have anything to do with that."

He said, "Ooooh, Coach, I think you don't understand. I didn't call to ask whether you wanted to go or not. I'm giving you the choice of flying first-class and having a couple of drinks on us or riding back in the tourist section handcuffed to me."

"Send me the first-class ticket," I answered. See how we big-time coaches can handle instant decisions?

Before the oversight committee, with Bill Hunt sitting in the room and a battery of microphones in my face, I repeated what Bill had said about running Tark out of coaching.

The sort of kangaroo court vindictiveness that has become more publicly visible in the recent handling of the UNLV case began to come into focus earlier, when I first appeared before the infractions committee in the summer of 1972. Our North Carolina State delegation consisted of our school president, Dr. John Caldwell, athletic director Willis Casey, and me. At one point during the hearing, the committee brought up the frivolous allegation about Charlie Bryant being a scout. I said I didn't understand how they could consider that a violation or consider Bryant a scout. I reiterated that Bryant was in the banking business at the time of the incident.

Warren Brown broke in and stopped me. "I am the official rules interpreter here," he declared very officiously. "I say it's a violation."

Twice more, Brown and I went at it during the hearing. At the very end, I stood up and said, "I really object to the way this entire thing has been conducted. We haven't intentionally violated any rules. I think that's obvious here. I think it's despicable the tactics your people use to intimidate kids." Brown barked at me again, and I barked back, this time using some profanity.

John Caldwell, who is a Christian Scientist, tugged on my coat and ordered me to sit down.

As I cooled off in the taxi on the way to the airport, I realized I might have some big-time problems with my president. He hadn't said a word all the way to the airport. When we arrived, he asked Willis if our seats on the plane were together. Willis told him two of the three were, and Dr. Caldwell said he wanted the two together so he could talk to me.

My career flashed before my eyes.

We settled into the two seats, and Dr. Caldwell didn't say a word. We taxied out onto the runway, and he still hadn't said a word. Five minutes into the flight, he was still mum. I was growing more nervous by the second.

Finally, Dr. Caldwell turned to me and said, "Warren Brown is a narrow-minded, evil man."

The color began to return to the face of one Norman Sloan!

That's an example of where I've made mistakes in my life because of my openly combative nature. John Caldwell wouldn't go head-to-head with Warren Brown. But I jumped up and started yelling and screaming at him. Dr. Caldwell obviously felt the same way I did, but he handled it in a different way, no doubt the right way.

The next contact I had with Warren Brown was when he called me at my house about Tark and said, "Hey, Norm, buddy. . . ." Buddy my ass!

After years of experience in recruiting, I think there are more exaggerations than truths about illegal actions. Most of it is dorm talk, players trying to one-up one another. In the last decade of my career, just about every year two or three players came in and said they wanted the things—cars, cash, whatever—the other players were getting.

A specific incident will illustrate this pattern.

Andrew Moten, a starting guard for us at Florida, came in and said, "Hey, Coach, I want a car."

"What are you talking about?" I asked.

"Well, you promised Maxwell a car. So I want a car."

"Andrew, that is untrue," I said. And it *was* untrue. "You go get

Maxwell and bring him in here, and we'll all three sit here and get this thing washed out."

I later confronted Maxwell and asked him why he would say such a thing. "Coach, I didn't tell him that," Maxwell said in his sweetest tones of blushing innocence.

I'm sure that at events like the Pizza Hut Classic and the McDonald's All-American game there are more stories like that exchanged between the top recruits, many of them claiming they had been offered this or that as a way of expressing their own importance. When some kid hears those things, he will manufacture a payoff bigger and more exotic to hold his ground against one he just heard. He doesn't want to admit no one offered him anything. I think this is particularly true among the kids who are products of the inner-city playgrounds. For them, the only status they have is when they put their sneakers on and get the basketball in their hands.

Oh, sure, there has been a certain amount of outright player purchases, often due to the advent of self-styled advisers who are, in truth, nothing more than unscrupulous flesh brokers. I remember when recruits started saying, "I have to talk to my *Man.*" The "man"—a guy in town who fronts for him—buys him hamburgers or new sneakers because this kid is *his* status symbol. The kids use them, and they use the kids.

While recruiting Sidney Green (now with the San Antonio Spurs) in New York, I kept getting phone messages from a guy who would identify himself as "Coach Bob." Finally, we hooked up and he said he was Coach Bob Leonard and that he lived in New Jersey. I went there and sat down with Leonard, who wasn't a coach at all but rather a scummy white character with rotten teeth. He began telling me what it would take to get Sidney Green. I asked what he had to do with the decision, and he said he was Sidney's adviser.

Bob Leonard said he also advised another player named Edgar Jones, who signed with the University of Nevada-Reno. He said, "When the Reno coach came to talk to us, he offered us 25,000 dollars. He took the money out and stacked it up on the table in cash. Edgar looked at me and I looked at him, and I told the coach that Edgar and I needed to talk. The coach walked out and left the money on the table. I turned to Edgar and said, " 'Now you realize if we do this, what we're doing? If you take this money you become just a plain whore who has sold himself for money.' "

According to Leonard, Edgar decided to take the money—fifteen thousand for Jones and ten thousand for lovable Coach Bob. Now here he was talking to me about Sidney Green. I really don't think he had that much influence over Sidney's decision. But that was his claim.

I don't know that Sidney and I ever talked about Bob Leonard, but Bob Leonard sure talked about Sidney Green. Sidney has turned out to be a fine young man, a caring individual. In at least two of the NBA cities where he has played—New York and Orlando—he personally bought a block of season tickets to give to underprivileged children in a program that has come to be known as "Sid's Kids."

But there are people out there like Bob Leonard, particularly in the tough areas of big cities, who like to say, "This is my kid. I'm representing him. He listens to me."

Sometimes, the broker is a member of the family. In the early 1980s there was an outstanding prospect at Riviera Beach, Florida, named Richard Rellford. This was not long after I had gone back to Florida to begin my second stint there. We regarded Rellford as the best prospect in the state. In the course of recruiting, we got to know about his older brother, Cecil, who had played at St. John's. According to Richard's high school coach, Cecil was going to have a lot of input in Richard's decision.

So we got in touch with Cecil, who indicated that he would like to be on our staff. At the time, he was working on his masters degree at St. John's and was something of a father figure for Richard. I really didn't think we had much of a chance because the St. John's connection appeared too strong. But Cecil said he would like to get out of New York, get back to Florida, and come to work in our program. I had an opening as a part-time coach, so we hired him, naturally hoping that we would get Richard, too.

Shortly after Cecil arrived, he came to my office and said we needed to talk about what it would take to get Richard to sign with Florida. I remember saying, "I would hope that Richard would be anxious to come and be associated with his brother. Further, I would hope that you have now seen enough of our program that you could recommend it to him. What are we talking about—'What it would take to get Richard'?"

"Well, it's going to take money," he said and proceeded to outline a series of payments totaling $150,000. He broke it up something like $50,000 the first year, $75,000 the second year and then dropped way down to $20,000 the third year and finally just $5,000 the final year.

"You're crazy," I said. "You really think these kinds of things are going on?"

"Oh, yeah, Coach. They're going on."

He proceeded to claim that Michigan had given Anthony Carter, the great football wideout who also played at Riviera Beach, $125,000 and airline tickets anytime he wanted to come home. He mentioned exotic payments to other college stars at St. John's and elsewhere. I told him I didn't believe any of it. I figured he was just trying to make a case for payments to the Rellford family.

My relationship with Cecil deteriorated very rapidly from that point, and it wasn't two months before he moved back to Riviera Beach. Needless to say, we never even got a visit by Richard Rellford, who wound up signing for Michigan.

The incident was a lesson for me. It was the only time in my thirty-eight-year career that I hired somebody, hoping they would influence a friend or a relative into signing with us. I had no more interest in that kind of package deal from then on.

Perhaps a more unfortunate trend has been the increasing misuse of summer basketball camps as an unabashed recruiting tool and, in some instances, a circumvention of certain NCAA restrictions. When they first came into prominence, camps were primarily intended to help youngsters and to build general interest in basketball. But as they grew into a burgeoning business in their own right, camps became a moneymaker for coaches and, worse, a nefarious tool in the gray area of recruiting.

To have key prospects in your camp—to expose them to your campus and facilities—became absolutely vital during the last decade.

I had James Worthy in my camp when he was in the seventh grade. One of my assistants came in and said, "Coach, we've got a 6–7 kid out here who's awfully talented. We can't get him to play inside. He wants to be a guard."

I watched him a few minutes and told our coaches Worthy was better than any of our North Carolina State guards. I talked to James and explained that he should become a part of the inside drills to help broaden his game. He had exceptional skills.

Worthy came to us accidentally, but before long we started going after the James Worthys, trying to get them to come to our camp. It turned into this: an alumnus would call and say, "Coach, we've got a kid in our area who is 6–5 and only in the seventh grade. Looks like he's going to have a lot of talent." You'd have the alumnus encourage the kid to come to your camp.

But in many cases the kid's family couldn't afford the several hundred dollars to send him. We could not pay his way to our camp and neither could we waive his fee. The alumni can't sponsor him, either. So what happened in many programs is that they sidestep the rules. Supporters of the program donate the camp money to the prospect's high school booster club with the understanding that the club will use that money to sponsor him in your summer camp.

In the late 1970s we escalated into team camps. Everybody was trying to get a leg up, and by having a whole high school team at our camp, we could schmooze the kid we wanted, plus his high school coach who typically has considerable influence in the prospect's eventual choice of colleges. In essence, we were giving the high school coach's team a week or two weeks of extra practice they are not otherwise permitted within high school rules.

With team camps now, the job is to get enough money for a whole team, asking a friend or supporters to contribute $1,500 to such-and-such high school booster club so they can send their basketball team to your camp. All of this, basically, is to get one guy—the team's star player—on your campus. In addition to that, you hire the high school coach to be one of your camp counselors. If you didn't, then your rival school would, and where would that leave you on the totem pole when you went back around to woo him the next winter?

We had a situation at Florida in which a booster contributed the money to send coach Willie Jones and his Orlando Jones High School team to our summer team camp every year. But one year the Jones crew was a barrel of very talented, albeit very bad, apples. We had so much trouble with them in camp, we had to send them home at midweek. They were staying out late, wouldn't adhere to curfew, and made a mockery of the drills and games because they were so much better than most of the other camp teams.

The sticky part was calling the booster and explaining why that team was back home on Wednesday after he had paid for them to be there the whole week. I told him I was sorry and appreciated his help but couldn't handle the situation in any other way.

Technically, all of this is legal. But what schools are doing is dodging the rules.

Finally, I closed down our team camp at Florida. I'd had all I wanted of competing with other schools and trying to do different things to entice high school coaches there by tiptoeing around the regulations. In my last two years at Florida, we went back to using the camps as they were first intended. We worked basically with young kids. We'd have two weeks for kids twelve and under and only one week open to kids of high school age. We were back to teaching and having fun. The kids loved it. The parents loved it. I loved it.

The camps with high school stars had gotten to where the star would come to me halfway through the week and say he was ready to go home. They'd get bored. They really weren't part of camp in most cases. You were wining and dining them, showing them around the campus, and introducing them to impressive people, hopefully making the sort of impression that would entice them to later sign with your school.

College coaches get tired of trying to keep the prima donna happy and the high school coach happy. You don't like it, but you have to go along with the program if you want a chance to sign top prospects. As hypocritical as the whole camp thing was, it became a huge risk to turn your back on it.

I'd love to see a survey done on how many kids on scholarship at various Division I schools did not attend a summer camp on that campus or attend an independent camp with an assistant coach from that school serving as a counselor. In the last several years at Florida, I can't think of a single player.

It was amazing what happened to our camp at North Carolina State after we won the 1974 national championship. Every kid wanted to come to our camp and get a T-shirt signed by David Thompson.

That spring, a coach in South Florida got in touch, saying he wanted to send six kids to our camp. He said the parents who had gotten the money up and wanted to know if we could take them and keep them together as a unit. That was before team camps. I said it would be no problem.

As I remember, it was about eight hundred dollars total for the six kids. When they arrived, they didn't have the money. We assumed it would arrive later and went on about our business. But when the money wasn't forthcoming after a few weeks, I called the coach. He said he didn't have anything to do with that. I called the parents, and they said they collected the money and gave it to the coach.

Obviously, the coach kept the money.

I had to show on my books, though, that we were actively trying to collect. I sent bills to parents. If I didn't, the NCAA could come in and accuse us of willingly letting those kids come to our camp free of charge. But none of the parents paid me. They had already paid. I told them I understood, but that unless I dunned them, I was subject to serious NCAA charges.

Ironically, when I moved back to Florida, this same coach had one of the top prospects in the country. So I went to him to recruit his team for our summer camp. We worked it out so that Gator fans in his area contributed money to his booster club, which in turn would sponsor his team in our camp. Coincidentally, the amount was eight hundred dollars.

I never saw that money, either. I billed the principal of that school, but to no avail. This same coach burned us twice for a total of sixteen hundred dollars.

That next school year, we were in the process of trying to recruit that star player and dealing with the same coach. The prospect was a fine young man who indicated he wanted to come to Florida. We really thought we were going to get him. He had friends at Florida, and he said he wanted to stay in the state.

But during the recruiting process, the coach suddenly became aloof and let us know in no uncertain terms that he would control the situation. We had our official home meeting, and the player's mother confirmed the ground rules: the coach was going to be the one to help her son make the decision.

So I went down and had a meeting with the coach to talk about the player's recruitment. I told him I didn't feel things were going well, and I wanted to know why. I wanted to know what was the concern.

It was midmorning, and he led me into the school cafeteria. We were the only ones in there. He said, "I'm just going to tell you how it's going to be. I'm going to control the whole thing. Everything comes through me." He said this kid had to have something in the way of ten thousand dollars a year from a summer job in order to make it. He had responsibilities at home and so forth, the coach reasoned. Well, I had been in the business a long time, and I had never had someone just come out and confront me with a flat figure like that.

Often, parents will talk about the need of a summer job, but in many cases the kid winds up not working in the summer at all. He ends up having to go to summer school to stay eligible, and if he's an outstanding player he'll wind up on some pre-Olympic team or something. But they make it a big issue. It's their way of getting around to the question of whether it is going to cost them anything for this kid to go to school. So you try to show them ways they won't have to come up with any money for their son to play college ball.

I went to a good friend in Miami—Monty Trainer—who owned a marina at the time. I had known Monty from my first stint as coach at Florida. As a student, he was a sharp young man who managed a motel in Gainesville to help work his way through school. In the interim, he had become a successful businessman in Miami. I explained that if we were going to get this kid, he would have to have a summer job making about ten thousand a year. I said, "It's going to have to be a job that the NCAA would judge legitimate for that salary."

In the past, if you were a top prospect being recruited by Kentucky, you might become an apprentice trainer at a Thoroughbred farm. That enabled them to loosely justify a handsome salary when, in fact, the main thing the student did on the job was to shoot baskets on the goal erected out beside the barns.

Monty suggested he could hire the kid as an assistant dockmaster and justify that kind of salary. I was thrilled. I went back to the coach and told him we had gotten the thing worked out. The coach says to me, "You know, the money has to go through me." I said it couldn't work that way. The marina would cut the kid a paycheck during the time he was working there.

He again insisted the money would have to work through him and raised the price. I guess when he realized I was able to work out something worth about forty thousand dollars over the kid's four-year college career, he raised the ante to sixty-five thousand.

I told him that was unworkable.

Needless to say, we didn't get the kid. He signed with a rival SEC school.

During the recruitment of this same kid, there was an assistant coach at Louisville named Bob Dotson. Louisville wanted him too.

After the recruiting was over, I was at Dr. Phillips High School in Orlando watching Team Florida, an AAU squad, and Dotson was there. He got me off to one side and asked what had happened with the player we had recruited. I told him about the marina job and how we thought we were going to get him but were shot down by the coach. "Well, you know, when they told us we were out of it," said Dotson, "I told the coach, 'That kid's worth fifty thousand dollars, and you ought to get the money up front.'"

At that moment, my good feelings toward college basketball hit yet another sour note. Here was a kid who wasn't allowed to make the choice of where he would attend college. The kid left the SEC school because he wasn't happy. It wasn't where he wanted to be, and he went on to an outstanding career at another southern school. Later he told one of our assistants that he regretted what had happened and resented how his high school coach had hijacked one of the most important decisions of his life.

CHAPTER 2

Who Is Stormin' Norman?

Over the course of my career, a lot of people have attempted to paint a picture of who I am and what I stand for. I've seldom agreed with the portraits.

Obviously, we're all products of our environments. We're human tapestries woven first with the threads of parental influence, then shaded by the hues of those around us.

Understanding the late Norman L. Sloan, Sr., goes a long way toward understanding Junior, or "Whitey," as I was known around our modest home in Indiana. Of all the people who have contributed to my life, my father easily had the largest impact. He was a very tough, demanding, honorable individual, and many of the lessons he dispensed were anything but subtle. I didn't have to read between any lines.

Two examples have remained in sharp focus throughout my adult life.

I was in the second grade in Huntington, Indiana, when a big, tough kid chased me home. I ran right up the steps and into the house with a clatter. When Dad said, "What's this all about?" I whined that so-and-so had run after me, wanting to fight. Dad asked why, and I admitted that I had been mouthing back and forth with the kid.

"Well," said my father, "you're just going to have to fight him then."

The next thing I knew, I was out in the front yard doing a great imitation of a punching bag for the bigger kid. After what seemed about an hour of getting my tail thrashed, Dad sent him away, took me inside, helped me clean up, and drove me into town for a consolation ice cream cone. On the way he outlined the lesson of the day just to make sure I hadn't missed the point: "Son, you don't run your mouth and then run away. If you disagree with someone, you stay there and disagree, and if they want to fight, you fight. If you're not willing to do that, then you keep your mouth shut and come on home."

I've never forgotten that. So I never allowed my own kids to whimper and whine. It was ingrained in me.

Some years later, when I was in high school, I thought I was big enough to declare my independence and establish my manhood with my father. I suppose everybody has gone through that. I had gone out on a Saturday night, and, living on a farm, I had certain morning chores. Cows to milk, hogs to feed, and so forth. But while I was out on Saturday night with the guys, I made up my mind that the time had come that I could stay out overnight without bothering to clear my adjusted itinerary through Sloan Central. Only little kids did that, and here I was a worldly man of sixteen. I went home with a friend, Pete Bracken, and figured somebody else could take care of my chores the next morning.

At about 9:00 A.M., I was awakened in Pete Bracken's bed by a strong hand shaking my arm. Guess who. "Okay, boy, let's go," my father ordered. I got up, scowled, and got in the car. As we made our way home, I began hearing what a low rung on the ladder of humanity I now occupied. I decided this was where I would make my beachhead, establish my turf, so I started mouthing back at Dad.

"I'm old enough to stay out," I argued. I said it wasn't necessary for me to let him and mother know where I was. I could take care of myself. I was feeling pretty frisky. I was a junior in high school, and I was doing well, athletically and academically.

When we got home, he banged me around a little. My mother grabbed him and urged him to stop. "Now, Norman. Don't let your temper get away," she cautioned. He pushed her away and said he would handle this situation.

With that, it was superboy to the rescue. "You're not going to shove my mother!" I announced in my deepest, sternest tones. I made the error of shoving him in the chest.

What followed like a bolt of lightning was The Punch.

It traveled about six inches, and the next thing I knew, I had slid across the floor on my back and my head and shoulders were propped up against the wall. Dad had his knee in my chest and was slapping my face, forehand and backhand, until the inside of my mouth was raw. Mom began beating him over the back with a broom, trying to get him to stop.

He did stop, but only after he had indelibly etched his point on my disrespectful jowls. Then we went through the oft-repeated ritual. He helped me up, took me in the kitchen, got a cold cloth, and washed off my face. He put Mom and me in the car, and we drove into Broad Ripple, a suburb of Indianapolis, for ice cream. Bumping along into town, he told me how much he loved me and why he hated to hit me, but it was something that had to be done because he wasn't going to tolerate that sort of behavior.

We didn't have many bad scenes, and I admit that I was in the wrong each time.

I also admit that still today, I sometimes flinch when I pass an ice cream parlor.

My father was born in the southern part of Indiana and played high school basketball for Cliff Wells, who later coached at Tulane. He attended Anderson College, at first aspiring to be a Church of God minister. He went only one year but completed his degree through correspondence courses. He was mostly interested in math and anything that would help him in tool and die making. The toughest nights I had at home were when he would help me with math homework or in studying for a math test. I enjoyed math, but I got to where I didn't want him to know when I was going to have a math test. I didn't want that kind of pressure.

Dad became a craftsman, a skilled carpenter, electrician, and foundry molder who took great pride in his work. He built many houses from the ground up. One of the fondest memories I have is when I was four or five years old, and he was the foreman of a bridge-building crew. I watched them sink the holes and walked down in the mud with him. I can almost hear the pumps they used to force the water out. It was an exciting and proud thing for me to see my father in charge of a crew building bridges.

Although he was a powerful man, Dad had a marvelously delicate touch when it came to making intricate molds at the foundry. During the Depression, when he was commuting from Anderson to the C&G Foundry in Indianapolis, he molded bug-shaped boot jacks out of scrap metal. You'd put your foot on the back of the bug and pull your boots off. He brought them home, and Mom and I would paint and sell them for a nickel apiece. He also molded a sailing ship that served as a doorstop. We got a dime for them.

Dad wore good clothes. Even in the Depression, he wore Florsheim shoes, which were regarded as the best. He took us to the store to buy school clothes, and he always bought good shoes for us. We got one pair of shoes a year. They became our Sunday shoes. Then the shoes that had been our Sunday shoes became our everyday shoes.

He would buy us expensive shirts, relatively speaking. My uncles and aunts would needle my mother that Norman was showing off, but that's just the way he was. He didn't buy us a lot, but he insisted on quality merchandise. He refused to take us to dime stores and discount houses to buy our chothes. He took us to Block's Department Store.

I was a preschooler when the Great Depression hit, but I can remember us burning corn for fuel. We couldn't sell it for enough to make it worthwhile.

We had a pretty tough time. We ate a lot of navy beans and lot of baked potatoes with bacon grease for flavor, but we ate and my father wouldn't take any charity. He never did, and I've been proud of it.

One Thanksgiving our pastor brought a big basket of food to our house, including a turkey. Dad was busy shaving, so the pastor just set it down inside the front door. When Dad finished and came out of the bathroom, he asked where the food had come from. My mother said, "Pastor Brown brought this basket."

His eyes could have melted the snow outside. He scooped up the basket, burst through the door, and headed through the snow drifts toward the parsonage some six or seven blocks away. I tagged along after him, knowing what was coming but wishfully thinking, *Couldn't we at least keep the turkey and give back the rest?*

Startled by the pounding at his front door, Pastor Brown threw it open, and the basket of food sailed past him. "We don't want any charity," Dad thundered, "and we don't need it!"

The message was clear to the tyke standing at his side: we take care of ourselves, and we don't accept charity.

He couldn't stand to be in debt, and I've been the same way. During my first tenure as coach at Florida, John Jennings, a banker in Gainesville, kept telling me that I should start borrowing some money and invest. Finally, he came to me and pleaded, "Will you please let me loan you some money so you can start making some investments?" But I couldn't bring myself to go into debt. I went into debt for a house, but I assumed everybody did that.

I was the oldest of seven children, all born at home. My dad didn't believe in running to doctors for everything.

Once I stepped on a rusty nail, and Dad took me in the house, got out that straight razor, and sanitized it by holding it over a match. "Dr. Sloan" proceeded to cut a big X in my foot and poured it full of alcohol. If you were in Indiana or any adjoining state that day, you no doubt heard the screams, but the operation was a success. The cut didn't become infected.

One of my sisters, Vivian, was just learning to walk when she toddled in one day and watched my dad shave with his straight razor. When he put it down, she managed to reach it and began trying to imitate what she had seen him doing. She sliced her cheek something terrible. Thankfully, he didn't try to handle this one himself.

At the time, we were living out in the country in Illinois and didn't have a car on the farm. Dad picked her up in a blanket, ran across a plowed field, with my mother behind, me, and one of my brothers strung out across the field. The scars from the doctor's clamps are still faintly noticeable on my sister's cheek today.

We used to raise hogs, and Dad taught me to castrate them. We often had other stock, and he impressed on me how important it was to take good care of the animals. We curried, or groomed, our cows and horses, removing the manure from their coats and keeping clean straw in their stalls. Our pig pens were clean. To this day, when I see someone abuse an animal it disturbs me.

He taught me more about basketball than anyone I ever played for. He built a backboard for me out on the side of the garage and strategically sank nails at each side of the basket. He taught me that if I could bank the ball off the nail heads, the angle was perfect. I'd stay out there until dark, shooting at those nails.

Later on, when I was in clinics listening to a famous coach like John Wooden lecturing on the advantage of bank shots, I couldn't help having flashbacks about my dad and those nail heads. The famous coach would explain that banking the ball created a larger margin for error than you have when trying to shoot straight into the basket. I'd sit up erect in a little surge of pride and say to myself, "Yeah? Well, my dad taught me that years ago." But he taught me things far more important than bank shots and basketball.

He believed in the basics and taught me the value of hard work. He didn't believe in abusing anything or anybody, and he made it clear that lying and stealing were absolutely inexcusable. You didn't lie, and you didn't steal. I never forgot it.

He had one trait that I did not particularly admire. Like most white men of that day in the Midwest, my dad was a racist. A black co-worker once tried to kill him at the foundry, attacking him with a big ladle used to pour molten steel. Years later, after I introduced the first black player to the basketball program at North Carolina State, he warned me that blacks would be my demise. We had such unbending arguments on the issue that we finally agreed not to discuss it. His last comment to me about it was, "They will get you." I didn't know until years later that he then told Mom, "I feel sorry for Norm. He doesn't know what he is dealing with."

My dad was a modest man. I never saw him in a bathing suit, and about as disrobed as we ever ever saw him as kids was when he stripped down to his undershirt—the old-fashioned kind with straps across the shoulders—when he shaved. I saw his bare legs for the first time just a few years ago when he was in a hospital intensive care unit following one of his heart attacks.

The fatal one came early one morning. My mother told me she had gotten up to get breakfast and became curious when he hadn't shown up. She returned to the bedroom, but he wasn't there or in the bathroom. She looked around and found him in the garden, where he was hoeing furiously. She asked him what on earth he was doing. He paused just long enough to say, "I think you'd better call an ambulance," and resumed hoeing.

When she told me that, I recalled something he had said the last time I visited him at home before he died. He took me into a little room we called a parlor, put his hand on my shoulder, and showed me a newspaper photo of some elderly people in a nursing home sitting around in wheel chairs. "Dammit! This isn't going to happen to me," he vowed.

So when Mom told me what had happened that morning, it was obvious to me what he did. He knew he had had another heart attack and that his health was failing, so he was either going to work his way through this one or it was going to be his last. He didn't want to be a bedridden invalid in a nursing home.

When I was allowed in to see him, he lay there wearing an oxygen mask and had all these tubes coming out of him. It was in August 1986. That's in the middle of the slowest time of the year for a college basketball coach, so my hair had grown out. I had always kept my hair neat, but the first thing he said to me was, "Well, looks like you fired your barber, didn't you?"

He was a great family man. He was so proud of his kids that he often bored people bragging about us. He made us have a family reunion every two years. When I say *made* us, I mean that it wasn't voluntary. We complained, but we were happy we had come. We continued until he died at age eighty-two.

I loved him very much. I still do.

You'll understand why I must ask you to indulge me these next few paragraphs so I won't have to stand in a corner if our family reunions are ever resumed.

Marvin, the brother next in age to me, was a tool and die maker like Dad and worked for General Electric. I was always a little envious that Dad and Marvin always had a lot to talk about. When Dad retired, he gave Marvin his tools.

My youngest brother, Chuck, retired from the Army Air Force and works in Raleigh evaluating city vehicles. He played basketball for me at Presbyterian College and once jumped in front of the legendary Frank Selvy to defend against him on a foul shot. Honest.

Vivian now lives in Miami, and my next sister, Twanda, lives in Atlanta. She is married to Joe Negley, a guy Bo Schembechler and I recruited to Presbyterian College. Bo and I did all of the recruiting at that time.

My next sister, Janet, is married to Rich Schrigley, who also went to Presbyterian College. Their son, Rich, played basketball and football at Boston College. I was close to young Rich, who used to come spend some summers with us at Myrtle Beach. I decided not to recruit him because I didn't think it would be a good thing within the family.

Rick Pitino, now the Kentucky coach, was at Boston University at the time. Rick went in to recruit Rich and began selling the kind of relationship he has with his players. He promised Janet and big Rich that he wouldn't be anything at all like that dastardly Norm Sloan, yelling and screaming, tough on players. This, of course, was most interesting to Janet. Pitino went on and on, and big Rich was about to die laughing. He loved every second of it. Finally, he said, "I have to tell you this, Coach. Do you know who her brother is?"

Pitino shrugged.

"Norm Sloan," Rich answered.

They told me Pitino didn't say anything for about three minutes. Then he was up and out of there.

My youngest sister, Mary Jo, the baby of the family, lives in Rock Hill, South Carolina. My mom lives with her.

I started playing organized basketball in the third grade, which is not unusual in Indiana. I played basketball in the cold, shooting baskets in the snow by the hour.

You might say I was a motivated athlete. Through junior high and high school, we lived on a farm just outside Indianapolis, and as long as I was on a school team in season, I didn't have evening chores. At Lawrence Central High School, where my future wife, Joan, was a cheerleader, I made every team we had—baseball, track, football, and basketball.

We once had a track meet on the same day as a baseball game. I caught in baseball and, in between innings, hustled over to the track and ran the high hurdles with my baseball uniform on. Understand, we only had thirty-five kids in our class, so it wasn't too hard to make the teams.

After high school I enlisted in the navy's V–5 program for prospective pilots and was sent to DePauw University in Greencastle, Indiana. I never became a pilot, but I made the football team. In high school I had played six-man football because we didn't have enough kids to play eleven. I played in my first eleven-man football game at DePauw.

An ensign on the staff named DeFrates didn't like me, and I didn't like him. One night I was headed back to the dorm a few minutes late for curfew when he jumped out from behind a bush. "Okay, Sloan. I caught you!" he shouted.

I did the only natural thing the moment called for. I punched him—really dropped him. The next day I was on the bus to the Great Lakes Naval Center. Goodbye, V–5. Hello, boot camp.

I had one more chance at being a navy bigwig after getting assigned to Norman, Oklahoma. The navy was screening all personnel for possible Naval Academy candidates, people who hadn't been to college but who had good grades and athletic ability. When I was approached, I said I was interested; but before we could get around to the formal interview, I was made a platoon leader. At one aircraft identification class, I reported my platoon all present and accounted for when there were about six guys missing. The navy calls this false muster and, apparently, takes a dim view of it: five days on bread and water for Platoon Leader Sloan in the brig. It was tantalizingly located right across from the bakery, which gave off the most appetizing aroma every morning.

While in the brig, the time came for me to meet with the review board about going to the Naval Academy. I thought that was the end of the subject, but when I got out, they contacted me again to ask if I were still interested. However, after my experience in the brig, I didn't want anything more to do with the navy.

When I first visited North Carolina State as a prospect, I rode a bus all the way from Indianapolis to Raleigh, spent two days, and only saw Coach Everett Case—briefly—two times during my recruiting visit. His pitch to me was, "There are three things that you going to have to do in life. One is eat. Second is wear clothes. Third is die. Now you've got a choice of going into a business where you can put the food on the table, put the clothes on people's backs, or you bury them. We have an opportunity here to put the clothes on their backs. I kinda like that the best of the three, don't you?"

So when I enrolled at State, I studied textiles for two years. By then, I decided I wanted to go into coaching and assumed that I would have to start on the high school level. At State they didn't have a physical education degree that would let me go out and get a teaching certificate and coach. But they did have a program with recreation courses that would allow me to be certified to teach.

That was the recruiting pitch Coach Case put on me. I never had the courage to try it on anybody else. It worked on me, but then I didn't have very many options.

Coach Case was a pistol. A small man, he walked with little mincing steps and had worlds of nervous energy. When he talked, he used hand gestures that apparently rubbed off on me. (People tell me that when I talk I look like I'm playing an imaginary piano.) The thing I liked about Coach Case is that he never looked tired or said he was whipped. He always looked like he had just gotten out of bed and was full of life, always going in high gear. In fact, at two o'clock almost every afternoon of his life, he took a short nap. "I've been recharging my batteries," he'd say afterward.

When Cliff Benson, a big supporter of North Carolina State,

started riding Coach Case after games, pointedly asking why he hadn't tried this or that, Coach actually had a red telephone installed at Benson's seat up in the coliseum. "I don't want any more second-guessing after the game," he told Benson. "If you've got an idea that will help us, pick it up and call me down at the bench." I think that taught me to tolerate pushy boosters only to a point.

A service veteran when I enrolled at North Carolina State, I was also a husband and father by the time of graduation. I had a family to feed. I played football my final two years at State because in scouting out the job market I couldn't find people interested in just a basketball coach. Mostly they wanted a combination of basketball and football coach, so I gave up basketball after my third year. I also participated in track, giving me the distinction of being the school's last three-sport letterman.

At first, my plan after graduation was to transfer to North Carolina on a fellowship and get my master's degree in physical education. The head of the physical education department there, Dr. Oliver Cornwell, was very good to me, but I decided I had been in school long enough and had a family to take care of. So I went over to thank him—face-to-face—rather than just calling or writing a letter. When he asked about my plans, I mentioned that I had a feeler to go home to Indiana as a high school coach.

He suggested an alternative. "Because of having played football and basketball," Dr. Cornwell said, "you fit perfectly with what Presbyterian College wants—an assistant football coach and head basketball coach." My football line coach at State, Al Rotella, seconded the motion, reasoning that if I were going to be a coach, I should jump at the chance to start on the college level. It was advice I have often repeated. Some coaches get stereotyped at the high school level and spend their whole careers attempting to make the jump.

I made the drive to Clinton, South Carolina, and Presbyterian College for an interview. Walter Johnson, the athletic director, was a classic. He left Wisconsin for Presbyterian College not long after the turn of the century, never having seen the place. He accepted the job by letter, got off the train for his first depressing look at Clinton, and claimed the only reason he didn't go back was he didn't have enough money for the return ticket.

He stayed and became an institution there. We called him Woof-Woof because when he talked, it always sort of sounded like, "Woof woof, mumphf, frumpf, woofwoof."

Clinton didn't look a lot better nearly a half-century later, and I *did* have a return ticket. My interview consisted of judging the pole vault competition in the state collegiate track meet that afternoon for Walter. We never really talked about the job. He was busy with the meet and the banquet that night, so I told Walter I was going to take the high school offer back home in Indiana.

A few days later, after rethinking what Rotella had told me, I called Walter back and said I had reconsidered. He was a little miffed, I think, because I had turned it down and said he would have to think about it. Soon he wrote me a letter offering the job and outlining the conditions.

I took it. After graduation, my family and I put our belongings in a rented trailer and pulled it with our Studebaker coupe to Clinton. We had borrowed $110 from Joan's daddy to get started, and Walter had promised us a school-owned home to rent for $45 a month. But in the meantime, they had a chance to hire a professor they wanted worse than a basketball coach, so when I showed up they broke the news. I had gone to Walter's house first for two reasons: to get the keys to the rental house and to borrow enough money to go buy some groceries. He hit me with the news that the house was not available but offered me information about an apartment we could rent. I borrowed $150 from Woof-Woof, and he made me sign a note to make sure I realized it was a loan.

Clinton was not to be confused with certain Mediterranean resorts. In 1951 it was a typical small, southern textile town of about three thousand, except that the required square in the middle of town was open. No courthouse, no statue of good, old General Ironhead, or whoever. The main industry was the Joanna & Clinton Cotton Mill. A man named Cy Bailey was the principal owner, and just about everything in town was run by the mill or owned by some member of the Bailey family. What distinguished it from hundreds of other southern textile towns was that it had a Presbyterian orphanage and Presbyterian College. Almost everybody in town lived off the mill in one way or another.

Joan and I met two of the best friends we have today—Marcia and Pete Sloan (no relation)—that first year at Presbyterian College. Now board chairman of Lance Cracker Corporation, Pete was then a student and Marcia was secretary to the school president. Marcia and Pete would come over to the house, along with Bo Schembechler and Barbara Allen, who worked in the school cafeteria. We'd pull the blinds, have a couple of six-packs, and eat steaks Barbara squirrelled out of the cafeteria cooler.

Schembechler was assistant football coach and baseball coach. We worked together and recruited together, traveling many miles and man hours recruiting for football, basketball, baseball, and all the other spring sports.

In the ensuing years, Bo Schembechler has exemplified what I saw in him at Presbyterian College. He was hard-working, demanding, and self-confident. Out of curiosity, he showed up one day and went through a basketball practice with us. We were working on footwork and fundamentals, and when practice was over, he had the funniest look on his face. "I didn't have any idea you guys taught that much stuff," he said. To him, basketball wasn't much of a sport.

He wasn't married at the time and had just come out of military service. He baby-sat for Joan and me a couple of times, tending our son Mike, who was only about two or three years old at the time. One night we came in and Mike was all excited over what "Bo," as he called him, had taught him. Bo had him jumping up and down on the couch and over the coffee table.

I like Bo Schembechler. I liked the way he worked with the players. He was no-nonsense. When I coached football, I helped as much as I could, but I didn't presume to be more than I was. In my mind, I was a basketball coach.

Bo's offensive philosophy in football at Presbyterian was pretty much the conservative blueprint he put to such great success at Michigan. Years later, he wrote in his first book that I was the lousiest end coach he ever had. I wrote him a note and said, "You s.o.b., who *could* be associated with offensive coaching and look good in your philosophy?"

He called, and we had a laugh over it.

After a year as an assistant under Dr. Eugene Lambert at Memphis State in 1955–56, I had a double opportunity to return to the state of South Carolina. Everett Case, my basketball coach at North Carolina State, recommended me for the opening as head basketball coach at Clemson. Frank Howard, the head football coach and athletic director at Clemson, was familiar with me because of my four years of coaching at nearby Presbyterian. He invited me in for an interview. In the meantime, the head job at The Citadel opened up, and I decided to interview at both places on the same trip.

I was to interview with Johnny Sauer, athletic director at The Citadel, stay there a couple of days, then go on to Clemson and meet with Howard. I told my wife I had no intention of taking The Citadel job, because the last time Presbyterian played there, there were so few people in the stands that Joan was pressed into service as the official scorekeeper. I didn't think that would be a move up.

When I met Johnny Sauer and his staff, I became excited about the situation. Johnny offered me the job, and I accepted. When I called Joan and told her that I had taken The Citadel job and was going to cancel my appointment with Frank Howard, she laughed and said, "Get serious. Are you having a good time?"

I said, "Honey, I *accepted* the job here." She had trouble believing me.

Back in Memphis, we loaded up part of our furniture in a rented trailer and made the move to The Citadel. Before I could even get a house and get set up there, I got a call from Sonny Humphries, the athletic director back at Memphis State. Dr. Lambert had just left them to go to Alabama as head coach, and Sonny wanted to know if I was interested in coming back to Memphis State as the head coach.

They were paying me $5,200 a year as the new coach at The Citadel, and the job at Memphis State paid $7,200 with a fine ballclub returning. So I told Sonny I would be tickled to death to come back, but I needed a couple of days to be sure my wife was in agreement and to break the news to The Citadel.

I called Sonny two days later, fully expecting to accept the return ticket to Memphis State. Instead, I heard myself telling him that I had made a commitment to The Citadel and felt it necessary to follow through on that commitment. So for the second time, I went home and shocked my wife.

Somehow I just felt it was the honorable thing to do, that it would have been dishonest for me to leave. I guess it was the way I was raised. I had given my word, and even though there was no contract or anything formal, I had made a commitment and should fulfill it.

It turned out to be one of the best decisions we ever made. The Citadel was a wonderful experience. Those were fun days; life was so basic and so exciting. All we had to do was change jobs, going from Memphis State to The Citadel—not a big deal to a lot of people—with three little kids in the back seat and a trailer hooked onto the back of that old blue and white Buick. It was exciting.

The first place we went when we pulled into Charleston was the field house. Just to go in and walk around seemed like an adventure.

As we went in, we bumped into two guys and spoke to them, Ronnie Spencer and Fred Montsdeoca. They would have a profound effect on the course of our lives. Ronnie was the business manager, and Fred was an assistant football coach and head baseball coach. Fred invited us over to his house that night for a cookout, and we developed two more of the strongest friendships we've ever had.

Years later, after both of them had moved to Florida and had become successful in other fields, they played key roles in our move to the University of Florida.

At The Citadel, I had my best boss ever, General Mark Clark. The commandant, or president of the school, he was one of the most impressive people I've ever met.

The Citadel is a state-supported military school, and they tried to always have at least a three-star general as the commandant. The students were all boys, always in uniform like West Point or the Naval Academy. It was a great school.

Also at The Citadel, I associated with one of the most memorable characters I knew as a coach. I have said many times that I received a great education by sharing an office with an aggressive, smooth-talking young football coach named Al Davis, who later became pro football's wildly successful maverick.

I'd never seen a more intense, more committed person in my life. Smart as a whip and a hard worker, he wore his hair combed straight back and liked to wear short-sleeved shirts, rolled up so you could see his biceps. He used to lift weights religiously with his arms. None of us ever saw him lift weights with his legs or another other part of his body, but he had well-defined arms and obviously liked to impress people with that. Everything he did had a purpose of projecting an image of strength and power.

He had a little mannerism of grimacing like Humphrey Bogart. He walked pigeon-toed, and we speculated whether he was really pigeon-toed or just thought that was the way an athlete was supposed to walk.

Al recruited a lot of kids out of the Northeast. Al was from up East, went to Syracuse University, and changed his name (his real name was Rosenbloom). He was the most effective recruiter I've ever been around. He wouldn't take no for an answer. I heard Al talk to parents on the phone and marveled at his poise. He knew when to be tough, and he never panicked.

He brought in a farm boy from upstate New York, a center, six-feet, five-inches, 220 pounds, a fine-looking kid. About halfway through his first season, the kid burst into the office. Livid, he wagged a finger at Al and snorted, "You lied to me! You lied to me about having dairy farming as a major course here!"

It turned out that Al recruited the kid by leading him to believe we had a dairy science school. Al had befriended some of the people who ran a commercial milk plant in town, West End Dairy. so when this kid came down for his official visit, Al met him at the airport in a borrowed Cadillac—S.O.P. for Al on such occasions—and squired the kid right on out to West End Dairy. There he had his panel set up to say just enough to leave the impression that this was The Citadel's dairy science school.

But I was impressed when the kid figured out the truth. Al was cool under fire; he calmed the kid down and kept him there. "Calm down, sit down. Look, you're halfway through the season. You're making good grades. You've lost a year of eligibility anyway. Stay here through the season, have a great year academically, and I'll help you go anywhere you want to go."

Al kept his word. He helped the kid transfer to Penn State, where he became an outstanding player.

More typically, he'd bring kids out of eastern inner cities and they would make a mockery out of the military discipline. They would refuse to march in garbage cans or submit to other plebe harassment, and they'd wear their uniform caps on the backs of their heads. Things like that.

An example was Angelo Coia, a gifted running back out of Philadelphia. Coia went home to Philadelphia every weekend after the Saturday football games. I don't know how many times I went to the airport at noon on Monday to pick up Angelo at Al's request. Coia did that for a year, then transferred to Southern Cal and later went on to play in the NFL.

I didn't have a clue that Al would one day be the owner of an NFL team and accomplish all that he has, even though he flat predicted it. One day most of the staff was having lunch at the Fork Restaurant, just outside the back gate of The Citadel, and we got into a conversation around the table about career goals. We all enjoyed The Citadel, but we knew it wasn't going to be our ultimate stage. We went around the table declaring our ambitions. I said I'd like to be head basketball coach at a big-time, Division I school. Montsdeoca said he hoped to go back to his home state of Florida and go into business, which he did.

When it came Al's turn, he typically went into some of his mannerisms like the tough guys in the movies. "I," Al Davis emphatically announced, "am going to own a professional football team."

It was all we could do to keep from laughing out loud. Here was Al, making the same $5,200 a year I was making, driving an old beat-up Chevrolet. And he was going to own a pro football team. Yuk, yuk, yuk.

Pete Rozelle and I are no longer laughing.

When Al's wife, Carol, went home to New York one weekend, we invited him for dinner. While Joan was in the kitchen preparing the meal, Al and I were talking in our little living room. He said, "You know, Norm, if I were the head coach and athletic director here, you'd have to go."

I laughed nervously and asked him what he was talking about. He declared The Citadel wasn't big enough to have the kind of football and basketball programs that we both wanted, so one of us would have to go. He was friendly, but he meant it. That was just the way Al was. Brutally frank. He gave me a Ph.D. in the fast lane.

Shortly thererafter, Johnny Sauer resigned as head football coach. Needless to say, I was anxious about what would happen, so I went to General Clark and expressed my concern. General Clark liked Joan and me, so he set up an arrangement whereby I reported directly to him.

I don't know how Al Davis and General Clark got crossed up, but the general finally barred him from the campus. He gave Al an open letter of recommendation for any job in the country, but he wouldn't let him on our campus. Al surfaced the next year at Southern Cal, where he began to lay the foundation for becoming a dominant figure in football on the West Coast.

My stint at The Citadel was the only period in my career, other than my second stint at Florida, that I was one of the top-paid coaches in my school's conference. The general wanted to do that for us.

When I later had the opportunity to leave there and go to Florida, he told me he knew it wasn't the money, but just something I wanted to do. It was simply a matter of me wanting to be at a major school. The Citadel was Division I then, but sort of off-Broadway Division I. It certainly wasn't a big state university, and the military aura made it tough to recruit. A lot of kids in addition to Al Davis's recruits weren't interested in wearing a uniform to class and marching in garbage cans.

One of the best kids I recruited to The Citadel, Art Musselman, stormed into my office one day and said, "I didn't come down here to march in garbage cans. I'm not going to take it."

I had a hard time talking him into staying and toughing it out through the plebe year. We lost a lot of athletes like that, but those who stayed turned out to be great to work with. They never gave us a moment's trouble. We had no disciplinary problems; we had no conditioning problems; and we had no academic problems. No exceptions. I never even discussed exceptions with the general. It was a moot issue.

The only problem was getting people good enough to win with and keeping them through that first year of harassment. Still, we had good years there, and it was a melancholy parting when we left.

The Citadel had never qualified for the Southern Conference tournament until we took them the first year or two after I went there. At the time, if your school colors were red and white, you had at least one ball that was red and white to use during warm-up drills. We got the idea that we'd paint about four of our basketballs in The Citadel school colors, blue and white. Being so excited, we didn't pay enough attention to the kind of paint we used. We bought some oil-based, slow-drying enamel paint. Those suckers still weren't dry by the time we went out on the floor the next night for our opening game. When you bounced them, they left little blue and white splotches on the floor.

Somehow, we made it to the championship game, and the general brought four busloads of cadets from Charleston, South Carolina, to Richmond, Virginia, for the showdown. Alas, we lost by eight to West Virginia, which had a pretty fair young player named Jerry West.

Working for General Clark was a good experience. It was a positive influence on me because the general stood for the kinds of things my daddy stood for: his word, honor. He reinforced a lot of the ideals and personal traits that I thought were important. About six-feet, three-inches, he was always imposing. I never saw him relaxed or slouched. When I walked into his office, I was in awe. He wore his uniform jacket at all times, with the four stars gleaming from his shoulders.

He thought a lot of us, largely, I feel, because of Joan. He liked me, but he was extremely impressed with Joan. She and the general's wife, Renae, became particularly close friends. Renae was from Indiana and a member of the Ball fruit jar family that founded Ball State University.

Joan is a very talented woman and highly trained as a singer. She went to Curtis Institute, a respected and selective music school in Philadelphia. She also studied at Jordan Conservatory in Indianapolis and was in the school of music at Indiana University. So she was well trained and has a beautiful voice. Somehow it was decided that she would sing the national anthem before our games at The Citadel, and the general got wind of those plans. One Friday morning in October, his secretary, Susan, called me and said the general needed to speak to me. I had been there long enough to know that wasn't a common occurrence.

He always got right to the point.

"Norman," he said, "I understand you think your wife is going to sing the national anthem before every home game."

"Y-y-yes sir."

"Well, she isn't. In the first place, the national anthem is not a vocal piece. It's an instrumental."

I was always a little fiery about things that meant a lot to me, and I sort of considered this an insult to Joan. So I guess I startled him by questioning his decision.

"General," I said, "have you ever heard my wife sing?"

"No."

"Well, I wish you would reserve judgment until you do." There was a disconcerting pause.

"Tuesday at one o'clock," he said. "I'll have members of the band at the field house. You have your wife there."

Click.

When I went home that night, I told Joan she had to audition for the general so he could decide whether she would sing the national anthem at our games. To say the least, it was a long weekend. Monday was a long day, and Tuesday morning seemed longer than the whole weekend and Monday put together. Finally, out of my office window I saw the general and his aides coming across the quadrangle in lock step.

He walked in without saying a word, took a seat in the bleachers, and nodded to the band conductor. They played, and Joan sang. When she finished, the general and his aides got up and walked out without ever having said, "Good morning" or "How are you doing?" Nothing.

Joan came over to me and shrugged, and I told her to go on home. I promised to let her know if I received any word.

Arriving home that night, I had to confess I hadn't heard a thing. We went through another night of anxiety. The next morning at nine o'clock, Susan called and said the general wanted to talk to me.

"Norm? General Clark."

"Yes, sir?"

"Your wife *will* sing the national anthem before every home game."

Click.

Then he had the commandant of the cadet corps present her with a dozen roses before the last game, which was typical of him. Plus, he gave her a personal check for three hundred dollars every year for singing the national anthem. I don't know how he picked that figure, but that's what it was, and no questions were asked.

To me, this is a wonderful story that tells a lot about the man. He was a tough, but fair, guy. And when he made up his mind, it was made up.

We had a great relationship with the general. There was only one time when he had to call me on the carpet. I had spoken to the Sertoma Club in Charleston at a time when blacks were just getting into athletics on the big-time level. One of the Sertoma members asked why so many blacks were becoming prominent on the national sports scene. Not thinking anything about it, and certainly not meaning any harm, I went into an honest description of how I thought blacks had the ideal build for basketball: narrow hips, long arms, great jumping ability. To me it was just an honest answer, and I went on to the next question.

Well, what came out of my whole speech to the Sertoma Club was a public controversy over my comments about the excellence of blacks in sports. It became such a big hubbub that I even got a telegram from a guy in Summerville, South Carolina, saying, "We hanged a person in effigy here the other day. I would like to remind you if you continue this support for blacks, your fate might be more realistic."

The local paper even had an editorial about the dangers of my comments.

So General Clark called me in to discuss the situation. I told him how my comments came about and that I couldn't understand why they should have set off such a controversy. I'll never forget what he said to me.

"Well, my advice to you is: forget it. Don't respond, don't talk about it anymore. Remember, Norm, never get into a pissing contest with a skunk."

I later thought of those words many times when I occasionally strayed from his advice.

General Clark was terribly criticized for the Italian campaign of World War II, in which the Allies had high casualties. I was privileged to be at his house one night when some dignitaries were there and revived the debate about the Italian campaign. He said it hadn't been his decision. He said he happened to be commanding officer of that theater, but the decisions were being made by "Ike and Monty," meaning General Dwight Eisenhower and British Field Marshal Bernard Montgomery. "I never agreed, but here I am being held responsible for all the lives that were lost," he said. "It just became my position to command that particular situation."

While the Italian campaign was a terrible thing in his life, he displayed a grim reminder in his back yard. There he had erected an old bullet-ridden city limits sign from an Italian city.

The association with General Clark exposed us to international circles for the first time in our lives. For instance, we met the premier of Nationalist China in the Clarks' home. Such experiences broadened our lives and raised our vision. I really felt the sky was the limit when I left The Citadel, that this old farm boy could accomplish anything because of the people we met there and the way we were accepted by them.

After I had left, one of the local sportswriters asked General Clark how tough it would be to replace me. "We're not going to have any trouble replacing Norm Sloan," he said. "But Joan Sloan is irreplaceable."

CHAPTER 3

Fighting for Respect in the Bigs

My first week or so as a big-time, major-college head basketball coach at the by-gosh University of Florida in spring 1960 was spent trying to find my office.

I was replacing John Mauer, who had been the head basketball coach and an assistant football coach. He stayed on to continue his football duties and had an office that was adjacent to Ray Graves, athletic director and head football coach. It was one of the nicer offices in the athletic complex, and I automatically assumed I had inherited it from Mauer. But when I reported to work, I walked the halls for the first two weeks waiting for John to clear out that office. Finally, Madge Johnson, the secretary for the assistant football coaches, stopped me and said, "Coach, do you know where your office is?"

"Well, I'm waiting for John to move out. I figured that's it."

"Oh, no," she said. "C'mon and I'll show you."

She took me all the way down the hall and swung open the door to what was a football position meeting room, kind of a small classroom. It still had the arm desks and blackboard in it. "This is it," she said.

I can't tell you how upset I was.

Fred Montsdeoca, who had left The Citadel a couple of years earlier, was the first to contact me about the Florida job. He had become sales manager for Dixie Lime and knew a lot of people around the state. Fred is your model Gator. He loves Florida, doesn't have a personal ax to grind, will do anything to help the school, and doesn't want anything in return.

When I showed up two weeks before this for my interview with Graves, the first thing Ray said to me was, "Boy, you know more people in the state of Florida than I do. You must spend a lot of time here." Actually, it was only the second time I had ever set foot in Florida, but Fred had so many people call on my behalf, Graves thought I had contacts and personal friends blanketing the state.

Early on, Ray and I didn't have a good relationship, and it was mostly my fault. A lot of people had a tough time connecting with me at that time. I had trouble arguing. I could fight, but not argue. Most any disagreement with me escalated to nuclear proportions. Ray and I set off a few mushroom clouds because basketball's status at Florida was pitifully low, and I wasn't willing to accept that. The first few megatons went off when I saw what he intended as the office for the grand exalted head coach of his Division I basketball program.

The football team was in the middle of spring practice at the time. Graves was out on the practice field just across from the stadium offices when I was introduced to my Taj Mahal basketball headquarters. I left the stadium practically on a dead run, flew across the street, and went up Ray's coaching tower like a monkey going up a banana tree.

I've laughed about it many times since because I can imagine what Ray must have thought. He was up in his tower concentrating on football practice, and this crazy man suddenly appeared in his face, screaming and yelling and flapping his arms.

"I didn't come here," I bellowed, "to work in any goddam classroom! It's a goddamed embarrassment!"

Pinned against the railing, Ray tried his best to shush me. "Ooooooh, waitaminute, boy. Waitaminute, boy. What're you talkin' about? We'll fix it up. Carpet it, panel it, anything you want."

I climbed down out of his tower, still boiling. Madge helped me set up the transformation of my "classroom" with the right people in the university. They paneled it, found me a nice desk and a couple of pieces of furniture, and put up drapes over one wall to hide the blackboard. We still had a cold, linoleum floor, so I followed Ray's lead and called around to several carpet installers.

Here they came a few days later with the orange carpet, wanting to know where it went and who would get the bill—$107. I thought I had done a good job by getting the whole office carpeted for that amount, but Percy Beard, the business manager and track coach, didn't agree. Percy was a nice man who got excited with me on only two occasions. This was the first.

When he was angry, Percy reminded me of a fish gasping for air. He walked into my office ahead of the carpet man and needed several moments to force out the words. "Who authorized th-this? Y-y-you can't d-d-do this," he stammered, his eyes bugged out like a blowfish. "N-n-none of these other offices have c-c-carpet in them."

I told him Ray Graves' office had carpet in it, and Ray had given me the okay. The bottom line was I had to pay the $107 for the carpet in my office. I later found out Ray had also paid for his carpeting out of his pocket.

The second time Percy got mad at me and couldn't talk was after I had been there a year. I told him we needed to sell season tickets for basketball. Well, his face began to get red, and his lips began forming words that wouldn't come out.

Finally he simply declared that Florida had never sold basketball season tickets, and he made it clear he was opposed to such a foolish notion. A running argument ensued that finally went to Dean Dutch Stanley, chairman of the athletic board. I prevailed.

Dean Stanley pronounced that we could sell season tickets, I think just to get me out of his hair. Percy Beard told me, "You won't sell a single ticket."

He was almost right. A couple, Ben and Grace Franklin, bought four season tickets, and that was it. You can look it up. Florida Gator basketball, 1961–62, season tickets sold: four. I was forever grateful to the Franklins and told Ben as long as I was coaching at Florida, he never had to worry about what seats he wanted. He could just name them.

After that, season-tickets caught on, and we had a better sale each succeeding year as the program began making progress. Florida had been an SEC doormat team, finishing in the second division seven straight years under Mauer. In my first six-year stint, we finished in the top half of the league four times and began to construct the revolutionary notion that Florida might one day soon win its first SEC basketball title after more than thirty years in the league.

Once we got the office problem worked out, the next time Ray Graves and I sent women and children scrambling for the fallout shelters was over the basketball recruiting budget. Basically, there *was* no recruiting budget. Mauer had been quoted as saying that his budget was "five air-mail stamps."

Ray and I had a big discussion, and I came out of it with five thousand dollars for recruiting. Later on, when Ray was angry at me about spending money, he said, "My god, you had a 5,000-dollar recruiting budget and you recruited two players. That's $2,500 per player!"

At the time I still had an old 1951 Buick that I had bought nearly ten years earlier while I was an assistant at Memphis State. The odometer had long since rolled over. After I had been at Florida for a time, I discovered that Ray and his top assistants—Gene Ellenson and Pepper Rodgers—had loaner cars, an arrangement I didn't know existed. A car dealer in Jacksonville, Harry Platt, took pity that I was trying to get around the state in this old, broken-down Buick, and he provided the first loaner car I had.

Not only were my tactics with Graves poor, so was my timing. Once I barged into his office near the end of the 1960 football season to touch off another mushroom cloud about our lack of a basketball trainer. Six megatons, as I recall. It was a terrible time. Ray was in the midst of a tough situation with state and federal authorities after gamblers approached a football player named Jon MacBeth trying to fix a game. He not only turned them down but reported them to the authorities. He came to be known as Honest Jon MacBeth.

It was the day before that very game, and I was in there flapping my arms and breathing fire, unaware Ray was under the pressure of the MacBeth situation. It was stupid and insensitive on my part.

I started harping on the lack of a basketball trainer, saying we were going to have a kid die on us and we'd all be liable. I told Ray these kids deserved to have a trainer. We couldn't get them in the training room because we had to wait until all the football players were taped before we could get our guys taped. I was raising hell at the wrong time.

Ray had a glass top on his desk. I was making my points and he had other things on his mind. All of a sudden, he started screaming at me, "Goddammit, I'm 99 percent the football coach and 1 percent the athletic director!"

"You're telling *me*?" I sneered.

At that point, he hit the desktop with his fist and the glass shattered. The glass top became an instant spider web of cracks, and shards dangled from Ray's hand.

I thought, "Oh, shit! I've gone too far this time." Ray ordered me out.

I went over to Jim Richardson, the trainer, to grumble about the situation. Typical me. I was a crazy ass, but I was still mad and I referred to Ray as that "tin-eared s.o.b." Ray had one ear that had a chunk out of it. Jim related what I said to Ray, who called me in. "I was talking to Jim," Graves said indignantly, "and he told me you called me a tin-eared s.o.b."

So how does Mr. Charm handle this one?

"I knew that bean-bellied bastard was going to do that," snorted Norman L. Sloan, a leading candidate for Dale Carnegie Brand X.

Ray thought I wanted to be athletic director and confronted me with that. I didn't want the job, but he perceived of me and our program as a threat. That was a problem. Basketball was gaining popularity at Florida, but it was not even remotely approaching football, nor would it ever. But an aggressive young basketball coach was something altogether new and represented a change at Florida. I understood and accepted the popularity of football; I didn't want to compete with football. I only wanted to be able to compete with Kentucky and the other basketball programs in our conference.

A friend of Ray's came to me and said, "You're like us," meaning football people. "You've got a lot on the ball. I've talked to Ray. Why don't you get on Ray's staff and help coach football." That was the mind-set. A basketball coach wasn't supposed to be that aggressive.

I faced a lot of that at Florida, more so in my first stint there in the sixties. I'm not so sure Florida isn't headed for the same thing again. Lon Kruger, my successor, is going to go through some of the same agonies I went through in 1960–66 and overcame in 1980–89. I can see it happening. I picked up *The Orlando Sentinel* one day last spring, and on page two of the main news section, where they list birthdays of prominent people, was Steve Spurrier. The infatuation with football is starting all over again at Florida. In the Daytona paper, there was a half-page ad promoting local Gator Day festivities with a huge picture of Spurrier and the words, "Come Talk To The New Coach." Not one word about Lon Kruger, the new basketball coach. Previously, every year both the football and basketball coaches had been included in the Daytona event.

When I was there in the sixties, one of the things that really irritated me was that when Ray Graves, the football coach, went around to speak to the various Gator booster clubs, they never invited me. At my insistence, I went along one time and guess what they expected me to do? Run the film projector showing the football highlights film. I refused and never went again during that stint at Florida. If you have pride and ambition, to be intentionally excluded kills your enthusiasm. You really have to work hard to keep yourself upbeat. When I first came back to Florida in 1980, I explained to Bill Carr, the athletic director, that I thought I should have a place on the program at booster and alumni gatherings. I reasoned that if he was truly making a commitment to have a first-class basketball program, one that could compete for the conference championship, I couldn't be tagging along or left out because it would adversely affect recruiting.

He agreed. The first booster gathering I went to after that was in Vero Beach. Gene Ellenson, a former football assistant who went into alumni fund-raising, was our traveling master of ceremonies. He was a good speaker and did an excellent job. He gave me a nice little introduction, and I said a few words. Then Gene rose again to introduce Charley Pell, the football coach. "And NOW . . . ," he bellowed grandly, "the Bull Gator himself!"

Pissed me off. He didn't mean any harm, but it was clear how he felt. Okay, we've humored the basketball coach a little, and now we can get onto what is *really* important. That was how most of the fans felt, and that's what I had to crack if I was going to be successful at recruiting in Florida.

I went back and explained this to Carr. Being the kind of guy he is, he didn't know how to explain it to Gene. That became my responsibility. It hurt Gene's feelings, and I didn't mean to do that at all. After the end of that year, he didn't go anymore.

But at every recruiting turn, I was having to fight, "Well, you're a *football* school." When we were recruiting Jeff Turner out of Brandon, he said, "All you're ever going to get in basketball is the crumbs that fall off the football table." Those were his words. He went to Vanderbilt where football is not a threat. I got so tired of battling that at Florida, and I wasn't alone in the business.

The basketball job at Michigan should be one of the best in the country, but football has kept it down. Bill Frieder did a super job there, and it was obvious that Bo Schembechler wasn't terribly unhappy to get rid of him. I talked to Frieder about it, and he said, "Norm, it's a killer." Jimmy Orr, the basketball coach at Michigan earlier, told me he got tired of it. That's why he left to take the job at Iowa State. He wasn't against football. None of us are. But you don't want to be smothered by football.

Yet, a base of emotional support for Florida basketball had begun to build, although I wasn't really aware of that until after I was pushed out. I began to bump into it in restaurants and on the beach. Boosters used to just wave to me, but now they come up and put an arm around my shoulder. Some even get tears in their eyes, expressing sorrow for what their school did to us. They really did have an attachment to the basketball program at Florida that I hadn't noticed. There wasn't that much reason for them to be that emotional while I was still there. Now it's like the guy who stopped me in a drug store recently in Daytona Beach. He came running over two or three aisles to say, "Coach, I'm so glad I ran into you. I may not see you again, and I just want to tell you you were the best thing that ever happened over there in that athletic program." Whether that is true or not, he was talking about basketball.

I think my staff can take credit for a lot of that. We went out and broke down some barriers. When I talked to the Miami group on our combined football/basketball summer booster club circuit, I let them know I would welcome the chance to go back down there in September for a separate basketball gathering. They set it up, and it became an annual affair. We did the same thing in Tampa and Tallahassee, and eventually we had crowds almost as large as the football gatherings.

When I went back to North Carolina State as coach in 1966, Earle Edwards was the football coach. Earle was not a very powerful speaker. He was a nice guy, but not very charismatic. I was there in one of those wonderful honeymoon periods when everybody was on fire about basketball, with the transition out of the Everett Case era. Earle got to resenting me. Warren Carroll, head of the Wolfpack Club, came to me and said, "Norm, I don't know whether you can do anything about this, but maybe you can talk to Earle. You're young, you're a better speaker than Earle, you're more entertaining. He's feeling overwhelmed."

I spoke to Earle, telling him Warren had sent me and why. He denied it was true.

Then Lou Holtz came in as football coach in 1972. Here's a guy who is a magician, who can tell jokes left and right. You talk about the roles being reversed. I didn't want to be on the same program with this guy. He was too good. So what happened, a little selfishness and a little common sense was put into place. I went to Warren and to Willis Casey, the athletic director, and suggested it didn't make sense for Holtz and me to go to the same clubs all the time. The evening gets too long, I reasoned. Why couldn't we split this up so each of us took half the schedule in the summer and then flip-flopped in the fall, so each club got two programs, one with the football coach and one with the basketball coach? We did that, and it worked out fine.

Galen Hall, who succeeded Charley Pell as football coach during my second stint at Florida, was marvelously sensitive to the relationship between football and basketball. The school plane was at the football coach's disposal—in his budget—for booster club trips. Typically, the basketball coach drove to the booster clubs, but Galen started inviting Joan and me to fly with him. In fact, he went so far on the first trip, he almost embarrassed me. As we were deplaning, he grabbed my suit bag and carried it off for me. Having been an assistant coach for so many years, he understood what being left out felt like. And he went out of his way to be sure Joan and I didn't feel that way.

Many of these clubs wanted us to bring an autographed football to auction off. To appease me, there would be both a football *and* a basketball. But one night in Ocala, Galen, bless his heart, jumped in on the bidding and bought the basketball himself because nobody was bidding much of anything for it. He sensed the frustrations I was feeling.

But I can tell you, having been through it for so many years, if you're a Frieder at Michigan or a Fred Taylor at Ohio State or a George Raveling at Southern Cal, it's an absolute killer.

Another guy who wouldn't sit still for that is Dale Brown at LSU. He and Bill Arnsparger didn't get along when Bill was the LSU football coach. There's a clear resentment toward basketball by people like Arnsparger who are consumed with a football mentality. Another is Roy Kramer, commissioner of the SEC. Roy is a product of the good ole boy system, and he's willing to go along and rub the humps of the football powers. It was no surprise to me that under the leadership of Roy Kramer the SEC failed to get Florida

State in its expansion efforts. When you put Kramer up against Gene Corrigan of the ACC, it's a foregone conclusion who will win that battle.

There was a saying in the South back then that they didn't care how close the blacks came, as long as they didn't rise too high. Well, I had the feeling the same thing applied, in many cases, to basketball. Guys like Arnsparger just didn't want to see us become too successful.

Indiana and Duke have the opposite situation. When Steve Spurrier was at Duke, he says it was tough to accept that basketball was the most popular sport there. When I left Florida in 1966 to go to North Carolina State, ironically, the two schools met in football that fall at Raleigh just about the time basketball practice was about to begin. A lot of our friends and Gator supporters from Florida came up for the game, so I had a pig-picking for them at my house. All they could talk about was that the front sports pages of the Carolina papers that morning was covered with basketball practice stories.

Later, when I went back to Florida for the second time, we opened the 1980 season at Ohio State. It was my first game back, and my wife didn't make the trip. I got a phone call the morning of the game from Joan. She was hysterical. "What in the world is wrong?" I asked. I thought maybe something awful had happened to someone in the family.

"You won't believe this!" she wailed. "There wasn't one word in this morning's *Gainesville Sun*! I've called [sports editor] Jack Hairston! I've called [Florida publicist] Norm Carlson!"

She went on and on.

Well, that was wrong, but it was strong evidence of basketball's low esteem in Florida as late as 1980. It was only the opening game of the season: SEC vs. the Big Ten.

Joan went along on all the booster club trips and became angered at picking up the fliers promoting the meetings only to see that my name wasn't listed. "Other members of the athletic department will be there," it would typically say. Through her prompting, I said something about it and it improved.

The second year back at Florida, Joan and I drove to Pensacola for a booster meeting that was being held at a Methodist church. We arrived early and one other car had just driven in about the same time we had. Obviously from his orange garb, he was a Gator there for the same reason we were. He walked up and said, "What year did you graduate?"

"I didn't graduate from Florida," I answered.

"Oh? What you doin' here, then?"

"I'm the basketball coach," I replied. Keep in mind, this is my second year.

"Yeah? What's your name?" he said.

I thought Joan was going to get in the car and leave. I said, "My name is Norman Sloan, and I'm going into my second year at Florida."

You see, that hurts. It's a depressing experience to go through, particularly since we were just coming from North Carolina State where the basketball program commanded respect and a high profile.

We used to go to the Florida–Georgia football game in Jacksonville every year. They always have a booster barbecue at the Coliseum, just across the parking lot from the Gator Bowl. They would ask me to get up and say something, and I kept saying this wasn't the time or place for me to be saying anything. I appreciated what they were trying to do, and it may sound a bit as if they couldn't make Sloan happy no matter which way they turned. If you don't introduce him and let him speak he gets mad, and if you do he gets mad. But this just wasn't the time or place. The people are rowdy and yelling and had only football on their minds.

This one year, I went to the men's room at halftime of the Georgia–Florida game. I was standing in there at one of those long troughs like everybody else and some guy started yelling. "Hey, Coach! Coach Sloan! Hey, everybody know who this is? Boy, Coach, you wouldn't be able to do this at North Carolina State, would you? Everybody'd be pulling on your sleeve!"

There I was standing at the urinal, and this guy was pointing out to me that if I had gone to the men's room at halftime at North Carolina State, I couldn't have taken care of business because of all the people wanting to shake my hand or ask me questions. He was intoning that at Florida I was practically anonymous among the fans of my own school, and he was right. I was standing there just like anyone else, which is fine with me. Don't misunderstand. But it points up what Steve Spurrier must have gone through when he first went back to Duke as head football coach. It was the same thing I was going through when I first went back to Florida as the basketball coach.

Spurrier had a parallel experience at Duke. After his first season there, he played in a charity golf tournament in Durham. At the par-3 holes, volunteers were stationed at tables inviting players to pay extra to enter a contest. Hit it in the circle, and win a sleeve of golf balls, or whatever. Steve peeled off the money to enter, and the first young lady asked him for his name. Ditto at the second and third par-3. When the fourth and final volunteer also failed to recognize him, his pride was wounded enough that he lost his composure and was somewhat less than gracious to the young lady. I don't want to sound like I'm picking on Steve, because I'm not. More than others, I can relate to the disappointment he felt.

Football barriers were not the only ones I challenged during my first stint at Florida. Another, made of plywood and orange paint, was the focal point of the pregame staging at Tennessee. The dressing rooms in Tennessee's old Stokely Coliseum were down one level below the playing floor, and both teams would ascend the same set of stairs just before tip-off.

This was 1963 and Ray Mears was the Tennessee coach. Ray was a guy who had a lot of gimmicks at the games. Just before the Vols left the dressing room, he would have them yelling and kicking the metal lockers. We heard them doing that and figured they would come out in a frenzy. I wanted our team on the floor before the Vols arrived.

We started up the stairs a few minutes early but had to stop because the national anthem had begun. They had a big wooden *T* with swinging doors on it near the stairwell. As the Tennessee team entered the floor, they would burst right through the base of the *T*. The main lights were down, and spotlights cut through the darkness to rivet attention on the home team breaking onto the floor. The band played; the place went berserk.

But unbeknown to the crowd on this particular night, we—the hated enemy—were trapped at the top of the stairs waiting for the national anthem to finish. Behind us, the Tennessee players had rumbled out of their locker room and had bumped into the back of our team in the stairwell. Some jostling and profanity were exchanged because we had unwittingly disrupted their routine.

The more I listened to all the yapping back down the stairwell, the madder I got. So I just instructed my players to follow me when the anthem ended. The spotlight shifted to the *T*, and something just came over me. I burst through their *T* with my team giggling along behind. There was a reflexive cheer that gave way to a groan when the crowd realized the coach and team coming through the *T* were not their heroic Vols.

We had to have police protection. Fans were coming down out of the stands after us, and it got scary. To make them madder, we won the basketball game by eleven points. We were lucky to get out of there with all our appendages attached.

The next year, they still had the *T* for the Vols to run through. When we reached the top of the stairs this time, the situation was comical. They had stationed a cop by the *T*, and he was glaring right at me, his arms folded defiantly. I put on my best menacing look, and as we passed close to the *T*, I gave a head fake as if I were going to run through it again. The poor cop nearly fell down trying to get in position to protect its sacred honor.

My first year at Florida, I inherited a pretty good club. It was the second-best team I ever inherited. The best was at Presbyterian College, my first job. But in my first year at Florida—1960—we started off by winning our first seven conference games. Later, we were 9–3 and still in first place in the league when we went to play at Vandy, which was coached by Skip Skinner, a former player of mine at Presbyterian.

We had some problems with some of our players when I first went to Florida. I was very strict at that time, and they were used to going on the road and having a big party. Early that season, I laid down the law that the next player violating curfew on the road would be sent home.

We got kicked by Vandy pretty good, 77–60, and I was despondent. Joan was on the trip, one of the few times she went along during that era because we had young children at home. At about 2:30 in the morning, I was miserable. So I got up and started walking around the hotel. As I rounded a corner, there was one of our best players, Paul Mosney. He explained that, like me, he couldn't sleep.

For some reason, I decided to make a room check and discovered that Robert Shiver, our captain and leading scorer, and Clifford Luyk, our leading rebounder, and the manager were nowhere to be found. I went down to the bus station and picked up three tickets to Gainesville. On the way back, I saw a fruit stand open and stopped in and picked up a bag of apples.

So when they walked in the lobby about 4:00 A.M., I handed them their bus tickets and the bag of apples and sent them home.

We went from there to Georgia Tech and lost, 52–50. Any hope of winning the SEC vanished.

Hope was about all we could cling to just hours after winning the 1963 Gator Bowl tournament one frightful December night in Jacksonville. Sometimes things like championships and office carpeting are relegated to their proper perspective.

We beat Air Force in the championship game. Afterward, Joan and I and two of our three children, Michael and Leslie, who were staying over with us, went out for a snack. We had a two-bedroom suite with a parlor on the top floor of the Roosevelt Hotel.

In the middle of the night, we were awakened by the piercing wail of sirens. I dashed to the window and discovered a thick layer of black smoke just inches above our window. "My God, Joan," I shouted, "this place is on fire!" Like a fool, I started getting dressed, but Joan streaked into the other room to check on the kids. When I entered the parlor, she was standing in the door—I'll never forget this—with black streaks below her nostrils where she was breathing. The children were gone. We panicked, of course, and bolted down the hall, fighting the heat and smoke. In a moment or two we ran into the kids coming from the other direction.

The situations that tug on your heartstrings most are those that involve your children when they're in pain, or sick, or scared. We went back in the room and discovered that the first truck ladders reached only to the seventh floor and we were on twelve. My first instinct was to tie together everything we could get our hands on—blankets, sheets, clothes, anything. I threw it out the window, but, alas, it reached down only about two or three floors.

Outside the windows were little false balconies with decorative railings. One floor below us and one room over, a man had run into the hall, apparently saw all the smoke, and ran back and threw open his window without closing the door to the hall. The smoke rushed through and overtook him. He died outside of his room, clinging to that railing.

Finally, there was a banging on our door; it was a fireman in a mask. He instructed us to clasp hands, and he led us down the interior fire escape—Joan in front, me in the rear, and the two children in between.

Most of our players had stayed over also. One of them, Tom Baxley, had left his room and was almost overcome by the heat and smoke. He banged on doors until a couple let him in. It was deadly serious at the time, naturally, but what happened in that room became funny as Baxley retold it later. The three of them took turns going to the window for fresh air. When the man and his wife weren't at the window, they were back in the room smoking.

Once we all made it out, we went on home to Gainesville, about seventy miles away. I was in shock, was nauseated, and had a roaring headache. Michael, seven years old at the time, was having a hard time with the trauma of the fire. We could tell he was very upset, deeply affected by what had happened.

We were to fly to New Orleans the next weekend to play Tulane, then continue on to Baton Rouge on Sunday for a Monday night game against LSU. I thought it might help to get Mike out of town, so I took him along on the trip.

We were chartering a DC-3 at that time from an independent flight service and had great misgivings about the personnel. The pilot, a guy I remember only as Robbie, was a heavy drinker.

We beat Tulane and took off the next day for Baton Rouge on a gorgeous Sunday for flying. Hubert Mizell, a sportswriter now in St. Petersburg, was on the flight. It was supposed to be a forty-minute flight to Baton Rouge, and he recalled checking his watch to discover we had been in the air more than an hour.

Concerned, I stuck my head in the cockpit to discover the co-pilot down in the well, grease up to his elbows. I jumped in and closed the door behind me. They explained that either the landing gear was not locking in the down position, or the panel light indicator was faulty. I told them to keep me informed but urged them to keep in mind this group had undergone a bad experience just a week earlier.

I went back into the cabin and explained there was a small problem, trying my best to assure everyone.

But after a moment or two, the cockpit door swung open and out burst the co-pilot, who came walking down the aisle—still covered in grease—shaking his head in frustration. That had a wonderfully calming effect on the team. He explained that we might have to belly-land in Baton Rouge, and we were circling to burn off as much fuel as possible.

The stewardess, Marilyn Legg, pulled out her manual and began reading the crash-landing safety procedures. Take all the hard objects out of your pockets. Put a pillow on your lap. Put your head between your knees. Lock your arms under your knees.

So we all followed instructions. Little Mike was in the seat next to me, and I began thinking what a brilliant father I'd been. We had just pulled him out of a hotel fire a week earlier, and now I had thrust him into this terrifying situation.

Everybody was down and we were flying and flying and flying. Every now and then a head would pop up, but the silence was eerie. Mike peeked up and nudged me with his elbow. "Daddy," he said, "is it all right if I don't make any more of these trips for a while?"

Thankfully, it turned out to be only a malfunction of the panel light, and we landed without incident.

An odd footnote: several years later, after I left Florida and went back to North Carolina State, I happened to sit next to a Raleigh auto dealer and Wolfpack booster named John Amburn on a flight to Atlanta. He had been at the Gator Bowl the year of the fire—North Carolina was one of the teams in the Gator Bowl football game that year—and also was a guest at the Roosevelt that night. He asked what floor, and I told him the twelfth.

"Us, too," he said. "Did you happened to have any children with you?"

"Yes, two of them."

"Boy and a girl?" he asked.

"Yes."

John shook his head in amazement and recounted that when the fire broke out, he and his wife went into the hallway. A little boy and girl were at the elevator door, but the elevators weren't working, and he asked them if they were with their parents. They said yes, and he advised them to go find them.

"Those two children left and disappeared into the smoke down the hall. I often wondered whatever happened to them." Obviously, it was Mike and Leslie. I shudder to think about what might have happened to them if John Amburn hadn't sent them back down the hallway.

One of the more interesting players we had during my first turn at Florida was a highly recruited center-forward out of St. Petersburg Dixie Hollins High School. Gary Keller was arguably the top prep player in Florida in his senior year in 1963. He was six feet, nine inches, a good student, a good kid, and, mandatory at that time at Florida, white. Ohio State and Duke were among the national powers hot after Gary, and it became a long, tough recruiting battle. For us, it was a comedy of errors.

We sprang for dinner for his family, girlfriend, and coach at a fancy restaurant in St. Pete—legal at the time under NCAA rules—that was right out of a "Three Stooges" script. For starters, a glass of water was knocked over, and assorted silverware went clinking onto the floor. Then Gary plucked a radish with a carrot curl on a toothpick off the Lazy Susan in the middle of the table and had trouble freeing his delicacy from the toothpick. He tried, bless his heart, to work it off in a slow, suave manner, but the little devil broke loose and shot across table right into my cup of coffee.

I was still calm. "Good shot," I said brightly.

But things kept deteriorating. The service was slow; the food was cold; one of his younger brothers dropped food on the floor. Finally, the climax. Mrs. Keller was a rather large lady and as she started to get up, she somehow hooked a thigh under the edge of the table. The whole table went over on the floor.

Somehow, despite all the awkward moments, we landed Gary. His mother was a great lady and became a good friend. Her son, however, was a kid I had to pressure to work on the weights and practice with intensity. He had all the tools except toughness. We've talked about this since then, and he still doesn't agree.

Gary had every reason in the world not to like me, because I drove him hard. I was still young enough to think I could make kids work who didn't want to work. Later I came to realize it doesn't happen that way.

Gary would cut class, and I'd run him at five in the morning. He kept cutting class, and I kept running him. It would still be dark, and I'd have him running the football stadium steps. All ninety rows. To make sure he ran the steps, I would sit in the car with the interior light on, reading the morning paper.

One morning it started raining, and he disappeared. I ran up the stadium and discovered him sprawled between two rows, clutching his shin. The seats had become slick, and he had fallen. "I'm not going to do this anymore," he said. So I moved him to a little cinder track beyond the end zone bleachers. He started around the track, but at maybe half the speed of the world's slowest catsup. So I got in behind him with the car and made sure he kept up a decent pace.

Now I was mad, and he was resisting. If anybody had seen us, they would have thought old Sloan had snapped and was trying to run down Keller in his car. Keller probably wondered about it himself. Finally, he began to stagger and went down in a rain puddle. Now I was scared and jumped out to check on him.

It was a wonderful scene. I was trying to be nice and make up, and he was heaving. I told him, "Tell you what. You go in and have a shower, and we'll go have breakfast."

"I don't *want* any breakfast," he whined.

Now I got stubborn again. "You're gonna have breakfast with me," I ordered.

He took a shower, and we went out to the old Holiday Inn. After we finished eating, he threw up again on the way out to the car.

Since I came back to Florida, Gary and I have discussed those times. He was one of the first of my former players I saw when I returned in 1980. I had a sense that despite the way I drove him, Gary liked me. I would always sit down with him and say, "Gary, this is why we're doing these things. You can be a great player. But you're going to have to toughen up and learn to work." I like him, too.

Years later, he said, "You know, Coach, we've both grown a lot since then." I've never forgotten that. It was easy to say this kid or that kid had some growing to do. Well, old Norm had to do some growing, too. It's difficult to accept that.

The year after I had left, Gary hurt me. The Gators had a great team and went 21–4. They almost won the SEC. Gary was a senior in Tommy Barlett's first year there. *Sports Illustrated* interviewed him, and Gary did what most all players do: rap the coach that left and say how much better it is with the new guy. This was a kid who had gone through three tough years under me, and those years had helped him. He was a great player his senior year, and a lot of it was because of the hard work I forced him to do.

It hurt me to read where he said he was glad Sloan was gone and he could now play in a relaxed manner. I didn't have to be there at 5:00 A.M. making him run. But I did it because I wanted a good team and because I thought it would help him become better.

As our program improved and gained support in the mid-sixties, I started talking up the need to build a coliseum to get us out of Alligator Alley, Florida's cramped little relic that seated 5,200. Georgia had a coliseum, and Auburn and Ole Miss had coliseums under construction. We couldn't compete. It was difficult to recruit with that old building.

Percy Beard was the first to tell me I was out of line in talking about a basketball building. I wasn't going to pay any attention to

Percy. He was the business manager, and I didn't think he had a right to tell me what I could and couldn't do.

Shortly thereafter, the man who did have the right buttoned my lips. Dr. Wayne Reitz, the school president, called me into his office and was very emphatic. "You will not bring up a coliseum to anybody at this university. This isn't the time for that," he said. End of conversation.

So that, coupled with Ray's later reaction to my first official overtures from North Carolina State, convinced me that if I had any chance at all to get the job in Raleigh, I should jump on it.

In fact I went so aggressively after the job that I didn't know how much money I was making until I received my first paycheck. It turned out I was making a thousand dollars less at North Carolina State than I had been making at Florida. Shed no tears, though. I also had a basketball camp, which at North Carolina State paid me about ten thousand dollars, more than my salary.

Two years earlier, when Everett Case realized he couldn't coach any longer because of the ravages of bone-marrow cancer, he came down to Gainesville and visited me during the 1964–65 season. We were preparing to play North Carolina, and Coach Case was there watching practice each day. After about two days, he says, "Now, you know that I can't tell you anything about North Carolina. They're in my league, and it just wouldn't be right."

"I understand, Coach, that's why I haven't asked you anything."

I had hardly got the words out when he blurted, "Well, by God, they can't play against a zone."

We zoned them, and beat them, 73–54.

Coach Case was big on loyalty, but he decided his loyalty to one of his former players was greater than it was to the league. Coach Case and I had a great relationship, and keep in mind that I was a tough player to coach. One time right after I began coaching, he said to me,"Ooooh, I'd love to be a little mouse and just see you coaching and working with a little s.o.b. like you were."

He had no heirs and intended to leave all of his money to the North Carolina State athletic department, but in the last couple of years, he got into a squabble with them about salary. He was a bachelor and had accumulated an estate worth about a half-million dollars. The story was that he had very deep pockets and rarely paid for anything.

When they made him mad at the end, he changed his will. Instead of leaving his money to the athletic department, he left it to former players. Darnedest thing that ever happened. He divided up the players into categories of one share, two shares, and three shares. This all broke in the Raleigh newspaper when I was up there for his funeral and was being interviewed for that job. I was one of the ones chosen for the three-share list. You talk about prestige and pride. I was thrilled that the old man thought that much of me. There had been some All-Americans who played for him that were left just one share. That told me that even though I was a difficult person to coach, he appreciated me from a standpoint of loyalty and effort.

I don't even remember how much money it came to, but that wasn't important. All that was important was finding out what he thought of me.

During the last two years of Coach Case's life, Press Maravich, one of his assistant coaches, took over running the team. However, at the time of Coach Case's death, Press had just announced he was going to LSU because his son, Pete Maravich, had not been accepted, academically, at North Carolina State. Pete could be admitted at LSU, so they went to Baton Rouge, and the job at North Carolina State was open. This was May 1966.

When I was approached, I indicated that I was interested, but I had to call Ray Graves for permission to interview. Ray's response was, "Yeah, boy, you can't turn that down. You've got to take that job. That's too good to pass up, boy."

I called my wife, laughing, and said, "I *better* take the North Carolina State job because Ray has practically moved me out."

The minute I left Florida, Ray Graves and I got along fine. When I went back to Florida in 1980 he was one of the biggest supporters I had.

CHAPTER 4

Wolfpack Wonders

Vic Bubas and I were teammates competing for the same position at North Carolina State. He played ahead of me, most likely because he was better. But at the time, I never thought he was, and it was a very personal thing with me.

We used to have a lot of arguments about it. Correction: I used to argue about it. Vic didn't say much. Bubas was always a poised individual, an organized guy, and it was very frustrating to him for someone bombastic like me to argue with him. I wanted to get down to it and go head-to-head, but Victor would sort of tangle you up in parliamentary procedure. I liked Victor, but we were intense competitors, perhaps more from my point of view than from his. He'd say, "Well, I'm starting, and I'm playing." And he'd walk away. End of argument.

When I came back to North Carolina State as head coach, Vic was head coach at Duke, where he had built an excellent team. In my second year back, 1967–68, we lost both of our regular season games to Duke, decisively. They had a center named Mike Lewis, a big strong six-foot, nine-inch kid from out West that we just couldn't handle. Our center, Bill Kretzer, was six feet, six inches, with small hands and eyesight so bad he couldn't read the scoreboard. But he was the best big man we had.

In the opening round of the ACC tournament that year, we beat Maryland. That in itself was a stunner, and it put us into a second-round matchup with Duke in what was to become the most unusual game of my career.

Before the tournament, we were sitting around the office and somebody said, "If we had a chance to play Duke again, what would be the best strategy?" Willis Casey, our athletic director, was always coming up with outlandish strategies. He and Bubas were good friends. "You ever give any thought to this?" he said. "You run into Vic in the tournament, let him get up two, and you start holding the ball. The silly s.o.b. would let you do it, just thinking it would make you look bad."

But we never really seriously talked about it. We certainly never practiced a prolonged stall. We were just talking personalities.

So here we were in the semifinals, facing Duke, a team ranked number six in the country with a glorious 21–4 record. In the opening moments, Lewis rejected our first couple of shot attempts. They rumbled back down to the other end, and Lewis powered over Kretzer for a bucket. We're down, 2–0, and I say to myself, "We aren't going to play with that big guy under the basket any longer." That was *my* thought process. It wasn't a flashback to our fantasy strategy session back in the office.

So we held the ball.

At that time, the NCAA had just put in the hash-mark rule. Hash marks were put on the floor just beyond the free-throw circles, and if the offensive team was holding the ball outside them, there was no required count to force an offensive penetration.

We took a time out, and I told Kretzer, "When we get the ball, I want you to come out and stand at midcourt. We aren't going to try to play with Lewis under the basket. That would be suicide."

So we came down the court, and Kretzer stopped just over the midcourt line. Duke was in a man-to-man, and Lewis didn't come out to guard Kretzer. So there was this pregnant pause, and my kids started looking over at me, wanting to know what to do. Eddie Biedenbach, a marvelous, hustling player who later became an assistant coach for me, was running the club on the floor, and I told him just to hold the ball. I motioned for Kretzer to come over close to the sideline where I was standing and told Eddie to get Kretzer the ball.

Eddie blinked, bewildered. Normally, we had a hard and fast rule that you don't throw the ball to Kretzer when he was moving or when you were moving. He couldn't see the ball and couldn't catch it. Other than that, he was a terrific player.

Eddie shrugged and gingerly handed the ball to Kretzer. Well, that didn't bring Lewis out from under the basket, either. The other Duke players were sticking with their men, so nobody was making any moves toward Kretzer, who was just standing there with a silly smirk on his face. With nothing else to do, he bounced the ball.

"Dammit! Don't dribble the ball!" I yelled and instructed Eddie Biedenbach to go over, take the ball, and give it back to Kretzer so his dribble would be alive in case he needed it. This was the way the rest of the first half went, Kretzer standing there and me giving him instructions, such as reminding him which was his pivot foot. I was afraid he'd stand there so long he might forget which was his pivot foot and move the wrong one for a walking violation.

Kretzer would get antsy now and then and put the ball on the floor. Then Eddie would have to go get it and go through the process all over again.

It became such a bizarre situation we were starting to have fun with it. The game was being played in the old Charlotte Coliseum, and the crowd hadn't really become rebellious yet. The Duke people were taunting us, and our people were dumbfounded, not knowing what to think. As the first half wound down, we took the last shot, to no avail. So we went in at the half still down, 4–2.

At that time, I didn't think Joan knew I was still smoking. I used to sneak a smoke at halftime, and I was standing outside our dressing room with a cigarette. I talked things over with my staff, and we decided things were going pretty good if we could trail by only two points at halftime. We hadn't been nearly that close at the half in the previous two games with Duke, so we decided to continue the same philosophy in the second half.

One of my coaches asked what to do if Duke got the tip and scored to start the second half. "So we're down by four," I said. "That's still pretty good, so we'll just keep holding the ball."

Sure enough, Duke got the tip, and we swapped baskets to open the second half. Duke went up, 6–4, then 8–6 with possession. But they missed a shot, and I got nervous again. I ordered Kretzer the Ice Man back to his statue duties.

This time, our own people got mad. My wife sent my eight-year-old son all the way around the coliseum to tap me on the back. With nothing much happening, we had plenty of time to talk. "Mama wants to know what's going on," he said.

Next came some Wolfpack boosters. A prominent supporter named Willie York wanted to know what on earth had happened to me. Had I snapped? He sent word he would rather lose than go through this kind of embarrassment. Here we were well into the second half, just two points behind heavily favored Duke, and my own people were putting pressure on me.

I held my ground, and we rocked along deeper into the second half. With all the inactivity, some unprecedented things took place. Television broke for a commercial with the clock running and Kretzer holding the ball. When they came back, Kretzer was still holding the ball. One of the game officials sat on the scorer's table while the game was in progress, so to speak.

I was constantly talking to Biedenbach, who was being guarded by a little five-foot, six-inch, Duke player named Tony Barone. When I'd call Eddie over, Tony would stick his head in to listen and ham it up with the crowd.

We had decided we would take a crack at it with about 2:30 left in the game. With three minutes to go, I summoned Eddie. Barone was right with him, mimicking our every move.

"With 2:30 to go," I told Eddie, "go ahead and take the ball and make something happen."

"Do you want me to call time out?" he asked, with Barone taking it all in.

"No," I said, "because if you do, they'll take out this midget and put a normal-sized player in the game."

Sure enough, Eddie took the ball and went right over Barone on the baseline and tied the game, 8–8. Duke scored easily to go back on top, and we tied it again, 10–10.

With only a few seconds to go, we were fouled and went to the line. We had a kid on our team named Dick Braucher, from Kutztown, Pennsylvania. He was a high school All-American who never really blossomed in college. We missed the free throw, but Braucher slipped inside, got the rebound, and put it back. We won, 12–10.

Seven ACC tournament records were set, including lowest score by one team and two teams. All seven still stand.

Bubas did exactly what Willis Casey said he would do. He let his ego take over and thought he'd let me make a fool of myself. All he had to do was come out after us, and they would have blown us out of the building.

Just like that, we were in the ACC championship game against North Carolina. We had no business being in the final, which Carolina would prove the next night, 87–50.

But after beating Duke, I went to the post-game press conference—nervous and happy—and lit up a cigarette. The next morning I was awakened by a thump. It was the morning edition of the *Charlotte Observer* that Joan had slam-dunked on my chest. There on the front was a huge photo of me, the nonsmoker, gleefully puffing up a storm.

Two footnotes to this. First, a few days later, I received a memorable four-page letter from a Duke law student. He made point after point about the game in the most eloquent of terms. He wrote that he understood the pressure I was under, that we were outmanned, and that he admired my sticking to my game plan.

I was thinking this was a classy guy. It hurt, but he took it right. Then I reached his closing paragraph. "What I really want to say," he concluded, "is that you are the rottenest, lowest, son-of-a-bitch on the face of the earth."

Second, when we went to Duke the next season, they jumped out in front of us by a dozen or so and Bubas went into what he called The Mongoose. It was his version of the stall. They spread it out and forced us to chase the ball. He was going to punish us for that 12–10 game the year before. But, lo and behold, our kids fought back and we upset them again, 77–74.

I've always felt that was Vic's ego getting to him again.

By the time Joan and I got home that night, fans had already been by our house to leave signs and notes of celebration, like "The Mongoose Is Dead!" Things like that.

My first years back at State were happy times. While we had some successes and some heartbreaks, it seemed we were inching the program forward in small strides, not really aware a lifetime high for all of us was waiting around the next curve.

After we put the 1974 North Carolina State team together, I was often asked if we realized that a championship squad was being assembled. We were simply recruiting players, filling needs, just like you do any other time. Once we made the 1970 breakthrough of signing seven-foot, four-inch, Tom Burleson, the first great in-state prospect we landed, he became our main sales pitch. It wasn't hard to get other top players interested in hooking up with big Tommy.

Joan was very much a part of the recruiting of the Burlesons. We recruited them as a family. Joan made just about every trip up into the mountains to Newland to see Tommy—for games and in his home. At that time, visits were unlimited. You took them to dinner, to lunch, whatever. I remember taking Tom's entire family over to Blowing Rock to a restaurant called The Farmhouse. We had a great evening.

Tommy's mother, Billie, became pregnant while we were recruiting him. We became so close to them that they named the baby after Joan—Martha Joan Burleson.

Tom Burleson was the biggest recruiting success we ever had, including David Thompson. Billie Burleson worked in a drug store owned by a North Carolina graduate. Tommy and his older sister, Connie, worked at Grandfather Mountain resort for Hugh Morton, who is arguably the biggest Tar Heel of them all. Carolina thought they couldn't have been in better shape with Tommy, and under those circumstances, I would have thought the same thing.

But Tommy liked the idea of being the first big guy to bring State back, and his daddy, Loren, was crazy about us. In November of Tommy's senior year in high school, Loren called me at home one night about ten. At first I didn't recognize his voice. "I just got through talking with Tommy," he said, "and I've got to tell you what he just told me. Norm, he just told me that's he's going to North Carolina State." He started crying. That's why I didn't recognize the voice at first. He was so emotional over this and so happy that Tommy had decided to play for us, he was overcome.

I said, "Loren, I can get in the car and be up there by 2:00 A.M. to do whatever I need to do."

"No, no, Norm. It's no problem. That's not necessary. He'll sign with you at the end of the year."

"Well, how am I supposed to act the rest of the year?" I asked.

"Just like you didn't know this," he answered.

So the rest of that year, every game that Burleson played that didn't conflict with one of ours, Joan and I got in the car and drove up into the mountains to see Tommy play. But I couldn't say a word about it.

Tommy didn't want to make his intentions public because he had some teachers that were Carolina grads. Come signing time, Tommy made the big announcement he would be signing with State the next week. Dean Smith jumped in his car and raced to Newland. He got Tommy in his big Cadillac and cried and asked where he had gone wrong. When he found out that Tommy had committed to us way back in November, he went into a rage. That really shook Dean. He felt we had pulled an underhanded trick and even accused me, privately and publicly, of keeping this a secret to pull his chain. I told him I had only followed the wishes of the

Burleson family. I would have loved to have announced that Tommy was going to sign with us. It would have helped our recruiting.

The same year, Dean had gotten an early commitment from Tom McMillen. McMillen actively recruited Tommy the whole season. "You and me and Carolina," he kept telling Tommy.

At the end, Lefty Driesell convinced McMillen to switch to Maryland.

Bill Curry was a guy who did play-by-play for the Tar Heels, but on the side he wrote pornographic books under a pen name. Some really raunchy stuff. Lefty found out about it, bought copies of all the books Curry had written, and delivered them to the McMillen family. He asked if they wanted their son to be going on all these trips and spending all this time with this kind of guy. Hello, Maryland. McMillen tried to stick with Carolina, but in the end his parents won out. They absolutely refused to sign a grant-in-aid to Carolina.

All's fair in love and war and recruiting.

Tommy Burleson is back in Newland now, where he operates his own electrical supply store. He not only survived success at North Carolina State, but he survived a personal misadventure that only made him stronger. As a student, he found the keys to several pinball machines on campus and began pilfering a few dollars at a time for spending money. He had accumulated $117 when he was caught and had to stand trial.

In an interview for this book, Tommy gave this touching account: "When I was caught, I felt genuine remorse and wrote a letter of apology to the fans and team. But it didn't really hit me what I had done until I got into court. There was the man who owned the pinball machines, his wife and his two children, ages nine and twelve. Those kids looked up to me. In fact, they even asked me for my autograph. For the first time, I realized that wasn't just quarters I had taken, but food right out of those kids' mouths. I felt so low, I'd have had to reach up to tie the shoe strings on my sneakers."

When asked about coping with Norm Sloan's toughness, he said something else that day that I cherish.

"He had to be. Athletes are like pretty girls. People cater to them. You get a lot of privileges and favors. Coach Sloan tried to teach you reality. He was tough on me, but he needed to be."

Point guard Monte Towe wasn't a difficult catch. He had Indiana Central as his only other scholarship opportunity, and the biggest problem in recruiting Monte was me. I didn't think we should take him. He listed himself as five feet, seven inches, but NBA scout Marty Blake always kidded him, "You better shape up, or I'll tell everybody exactly how short you really are." Sam Esposito, our assistant from Indiana, was high on Monte.

Dick Dickey, a former teammate of mine at North Carolina State, lived in Bluffton, Indiana, not too far from Monte's home in Converse. Richard watched young players in that area and was always recommending top ones to me. When I told him we needed a really quality point guard, he called to suggest Monte. He said Monte was good enough, a big-timer. I had serious reservations about his height, but I sent Espo, a fine judge of talent, to check him out. Espo came back and said, "Skip, you've got to take him. He's a winner. He can do the job."

I resisted. "Who in the heck is a kid this size going to defend?" I challenged. Same thing you hear NBA guys say about Muggsy Bogues and Boo Harvey. Espo told me not to worry about it, noting that having the big guy—Burleson—back there would take up any slack on defense.

Dickey kept persisting, sending clippings. He even got my dad involved. The two of them went together to see Monte play, and my dad started bugging me about taking this kid. I became irritated and even made the comment to them, "You know, it's Florida State that has the circus, not North Carolina State. We don't need midgets."

I sent Sam again, and he came back saying, "I'm telling you, the kid can play."

So I went to see Monte in a game at Bloomington. I sat there with Dick Dickey and my father and had to admit that Monte could do everything. But again, I didn't get to see him being posted up because high school people weren't going to post him up. They had small point guards, too. So I came back still skeptical that a guy that size could do enough offensively to offset how he would hurt us defensively.

Finally, Espo talked me into it, but I warned that we would keep stats on Monte and see if what I was saying didn't bear out. I don't remember the specific numbers, but it turned out to be this: when teams did attempt to post up Monte, they not only were unsuccessful scoring, but we caused turnovers more times than they scored. We'd gain possession repeatedly, and other teams eventually stopped doing that. My gravest concern about Monte turned out to be a plus. That freshman team, with Monte, David Thompson, and Tim Stoddard, was 15–1. When they became sophomores and moved up to join Burleson for his junior year on the varsity, they went 27–0, but they couldn't go to the NCAAs because of probation—the so-called David Thompson sanctions. The next year, when Morris Rivers, a Bronx guard, transferred in from Gulf Coast (Florida) Junior College, they went 30–1 and won the 1974 national championship.

It was easy to put that team together once we had Burleson. They all liked the prospect of playing with the big guy.

Stoddard, a six-foot, eight-inch, kid who went on to become a big-league pitcher, was from Washington East High near Chicago. After his own major league career ended, Esposito had been the assistant coach at the school under legendary Coach John Barato. Stoddard had several major college prospects on the same team with him, including a guy named Pete Trgovich, who went to UCLA. The team was undefeated and state champs.

We couldn't get in on Pete, but we thought we had Stoddard and another player off that team, Junior Bridgeman, who went on to become a great player at Louisville and with the Milwaukee Bucks. By this time, the coach there was John Molodet, whose brother, Vic, had been an All-American at North Carolina State. Also, we had two or three former North Carolina State players who were living back in that area helping us. With Esposito and all the other connections at work, we thought we were going to get two or three players off that team.

At signing time, we went up there confident we were about to fill our dance card. The first thing Molodet hit us with was that Bridgeman had signed in the parking lot the day before with Denny Crum of Louisville. We went to Stoddard's house that night to sign him. We sat there in his house, with his mother and father. An hour went by and Timmy hadn't signed. Two hours, still no signature.

"Have you changed your mind about coming to North Carolina State?"

"No," he answered. "I'm just not ready to sign."

"Do you still plan on coming to North Carolina State?"

"Yes."

"Well, why won't you sign?"

We were there three hours going through this routine. Finally, there was nothing else to do but leave. As we drove away, Sam just shook his head and said he didn't have a clue what was going on. We didn't like the looks of it at all.

The next morning we told Molodet we were having trouble with Stoddard.

"No, you're not," he said.

"We're not? We sat there three hours last night and couldn't get him to sign!"

Molodet explained that after what Bridgeman had done, he made the rest of the team promise they wouldn't sign without first coming in and getting his approval. "And I just hadn't had a chance to tell Timmy it's okay," Molodet told us.

The other kid on that team we thought we might get was Darnell Adell, a bullet of a point guard, but he chose to go to Murray State. He later became unhappy there, and we had him at North Carolina State for one year of eligibility. If he had signed with us, we probably wouldn't have taken Monte Towe. That was one case where fate was on our side.

The recruitment of David Thompson was a long, hard situation. He was a genuine talent and everybody knew about him. David had decided to stay in the state, and, one by one, schools were eliminated. The smaller schools were eliminated quickly, except for Gardner-Webb right there in his hometown. They hung in there until near the end, thinking he didn't want to leave home. In truth, I think David just didn't want to tell them no and hurt their feelings.

It came down to North Carolina and us. Carolina really thought they had him.

Recalls David: "One of the things I was concerned about if I had gone to Carolina was being compared to Charlie Scott. He was a big player during that time. I wanted to go to a place where I could have my own identity. Dean Smith spoke at my high school sports banquet at the end of my senior year in April."

I remember Dean speaking to his high school banquet better than David does, because it made me sick. That wasn't a good sign at all. I thought Ed Peeler, David's high school coach, was leaning the other way if he was having Dean speak to his banquet.

Our whole pitch with David was that Carolina had had a ton of great players and that he would be just another great player that went there and not be given credit for turning a program around like he could do at State. We told him he wouldn't be remembered and immortalized at Carolina like he would at State, if he came with Burleson and Stoddard and won a national championship. See? Truth in advertising.

David and Tommy already knew each other. Both played in the Western North Carolina Athletic Association, which was a separate league of mountain schools. Tommy played at Avery County High in Newland, and David was not far away at Crest High in Shelby. I don't think they really had a pact to go to the same college, as Burleson has intimated, but David liked the idea of playing with Tommy.

Eddie Biedenbach, by then an assistant coach, was assigned only to the recruitment of David. From the time the high school season ended until David signed about two months later, Eddie probably lived at a motel in Shelby more than he lived at home. Eddie took David to breakfast just about every day, and one morning, as they were coming out of a restaurant, David turned to Eddie and said, "You got one of those pieces of paper?"

Startled, Eddie asked—stammering—if David meant a grant-in-aid form. "Yes," said David. "I'm ready to sign."

Eddie didn't have one, but David had plenty at his house, sent to him by assorted other schools. So they used one of them to sign, marking through the name of the other school and filling in North Carolina State.

During those weeks, the basketball world in North Carolina was naturally consumed with the question of where David Thompson would sign. We were having a Wolfpack golf outing at Southern Pines, North Carolina, that day, and the foursome I was in was coming in on the ninth hole when Eddie Biedenbach came running down the fairway waving a piece of paper. It was the grant-in-aid form with David's signature on it. When David suddenly and unexpectedly told Eddie he was ready to sign, Eddie became so excited that, rather than call, he jumped in his car and drove the three hours to Southern Pines to personally deliver the spectacular news.

The golf tournament abruptly stopped. Everybody broke up and started celebrating. As people on the golf course heard what had happened, they left the course and joined the celebration. It was unbelievable.

Getting Mo Rivers out of junior college completed what would be our championship starting five. I've never known a team that complemented one another as much as that one did. They were the perfect fit. Stoddard didn't care whether he scored or not. He was a fine passer and rebounder. Monte was the point guard, Rivers the off guard in perfect tandem. David Thompson was the small forward, Stoddard the power forward, and Burleson the center. It was a heck of a ball club, one of the best ever.

Phil Spence was our number six man, a six-foot, eight-inch, forward from Raleigh. And he was a good one, on the floor. Off the floor, he had a problem. When Martin Luther King was killed, Phil went downtown and participated in a protest rally. When he came back he told me, "I got me some white guys with an ax handle." Phil was a festering racial militant, and he hated David Thompson because David wasn't.

Phil used to write beautiful poetry, but the eloquent verse was tinged with hatred, often ripping David for being an Uncle Tom. He would bring it in and proudly show it to me. Phil was the only real problem we had on that ball club.

Before the 1973–74 season, one of the major networks arranged a game between us and UCLA, more or less to settle the big unanswered question of the prior year. UCLA had won its seventh consecutive title, but we were undefeated and unable to challenge the Bruins because of our probation. Could State have beaten UCLA? We met in St. Louis in December on national television, and they won by eighteen. It would be our only loss over two seasons. We were 57–1 over those two years, winning 32 consecutive conference games, a record that may never be broken.

The loss to UCLA was devastating to Towe and Thompson. On the plane ride back home, Monte lay down across two seats and stuck his face back against the cushions the whole way and wouldn't speak to anyone. The next day, he came to my office and said we needed some strict training rules.

Vic Bubas called me prior to that season. He had retired from coaching and had gone into administration as an assistant to the school president at Duke. He said, "Norm, just a word of advice. Sit back and relax and enjoy these guys because they are so good that nobody is going to be able to beat them in the big games." So I used that as a theme that year. I went around telling our supporters the same thing. Relax and enjoy.

So when Monte came to me, I argued that stringent rules

weren't necessary with this team. They were so good and focused, I was into other motivational tactics. I required them all to read *Psychocybernetics* and *The Power of Positive Thinking*. Those books made a big impression on me. Recently, I was pleasantly surprised to hear David Thompson recite our slogan for that 1974 team: "Constancy of Purpose by Individuals Results in a Team of Champions." It was a little ditty I invented.

But at the moment, Monte Towe was only into inventing team rules. "Yep. Gotta have them," he said adamantly.

I tried to reason that we simply had an off game, UCLA had a great game, and our team was doing a good job of taking care of itself. "Nope. We gotta have tighter rules," he said.

Finally, I told him to get the players together and come up with the set of rules they thought necessary. But I warned if anybody violated those rules, it would be an automatic suspension of at least one game. We were not going to have training rules without penalties. He agreed.

I guess more than anything else, they felt they needed to punish themselves. They put in things like an eleven o'clock curfew, and so forth. The very next month, I got a phone call at midnight from Morris Rivers to tell me he missed curfew.

"Why?" I asked.

"I got arrested," he said, explaining he was calling from the police station.

Mo's story was that he picked up a thirty-nine-cent box of aspirin in a convenience store, put it in his pocket, and forgot about it when he checked out. The storekeeper had him arrested.

Now Morris not only had a problem with the storekeeper and the police, but also with me and with Monte's training rules. The question of whether he had intentionally shoplifted was one issue, but there was no doubt that he had missed curfew. I announced that Morris would miss our next game, which was at Virginia.

All hell broke loose. Monte came to see me, emotionally charging that I was being unfair. "Whoa, wait a minute," I responded. I reminded him that it was *their* rules *they* wanted, and now they had to live with them. The shoplifting charges were dropped, but Morris missed the Virginia game, which we won, 90–70.

A few games later, we played at Duke, where the students are among the most ingenious in the country at taking an issue and using it to taunt the visiting players. When Morris was introduced, you would have thought we were in a snow storm. Aspirin cascaded out of those stands in waves. It looked to me like they were an inch deep on the floor. Workers needed about fifteen minutes to sweep all the aspirin off the floor. I got enough aspirin in the mail to keep us supplied for years.

Nothing much bothered this team, though. We won, 92–78, and Rivers gave Duke a headache. He scored eighteen.

We finished the regular season undefeated in league play, but that meant little—a first-round bye—as we headed into the conference tournament. At that time, only one winner would advance to the NCAA tournament, and that team was always the winner of the tournament, not the regular season champion. There were seven teams in the ACC at that time, and the strongest team other than us was Maryland. Lefty Driesell had Tom McMillen, John Lucas, and Moe Howard, an awesome club. We had super games with them, close and exciting.

Our first game with Maryland that year, January 13, 1974, was the first college basketball television game ever played on Super Bowl Sunday. That has become a big thing now, but it was a radical experiment for the networks back then. With sixteen seconds to go, we had a tie game, with us taking the ball inbounds.

I called for a pass to Burleson and told him to look to dish off to David. Really intricate, clever stuff on inbounds play, right? We threw the ball in to Tommy, who turned and looked for David. Maryland had everybody in Cole Field House covering David, so Tommy held the ball and the five-second count for a jump ball was mounting. He had enough presence of mind to bounce the ball to break the count and give him another look. In desperation, Tommy looped a long shot at the basket. It hit the rim, bounded off to David—unguarded because all the Maryland players had been fronting him. David put it back in, and we won, 87–85. That's the kind of game we typically had with Maryland during that era.

As we left the floor, Bones McKinney, who was doing color commentary on the telecast, ran up and told me to "be smart enough to take credit for that. Tell 'em you work on that sort of thing day after day."

With the big victory, I was full of myself, so when somebody indeed asked me if we worked on that inbounds play, I said, "Religiously. Every day. David's part is real easy. He just goes up and grabs it about three feet above the rim and drops it in on his way back down. But Tommy really had to work on hitting the rim at the right angle with that long shot for the ball to go straight up in the air."

You'd be surprised how many reporters wrote that the next day as if I were really serious.

With the first-round bye in the ACC tournament earned by our perfect conference record that season, I had the luxury of sitting there the first day in Greensboro Coliseum and watching the first three games. Maryland was awesome, romping through the first round, then killing Carolina in the semifinals. We played Virginia in the semifinals and blew them away by twenty-one behind a thirty-seven-point David Thompson masterpiece.

Now came the final, North Carolina State and Maryland, both ranked in the top three in the country. Only one would advance to the NCAA tournament. The pressure was awesome.

We especially had boxed ourselves in, because we couldn't even go to New York and the NIT, normally the consolation tournament. We were scheduled to host one of the NCAA regionals that year, and there was a rule that if you did that, you couldn't accept an NIT berth. The thinking, naturally, was that if you played in the NIT and hosted an NCAA regional in your own building, it would detract from the regional and perhaps even hurt the local gate. So we had put ourselves in a position where if we didn't win the ACC title game against Maryland, the rocket ride would suddenly end, leaving us sitting at home, despite a 25–2 record.

Many have called this the greatest college game ever played. Maryland came out and took a twelve-point lead. We battled back. At the end, we had a tie game when Maryland's John Lucas missed a tough shot at the buzzer. We went into overtime and won, 103–100. Maryland shot 62 percent and had one turnover. They scored 100 points and went home.

Lefty was so devastated, he rented a car and drove all the way home to Maryland that night rather than wait for the team flight the next morning.

In a game against Maryland earlier that year, Tommy Burleson had an awful night, shooting something like five-for-twenty-four. Afterward, Maryland's six-foot, ten-inch, center, Len Elmore, told the media, "You go tell that dude over there than I am *the* center in the ACC."

Those words burned in Tommy's head the rest of the season.

When they met in the championship game, he destroyed Elmore, getting thirty-eight points and thirteen rebounds.

Next we moved to the NCAA regional in our own building. First up for us was Providence, a great team with Kevin Stacoum and Marvin ("Bad News") Barnes, coached by Dave Gavitt, who later went on to become commissioner of the Big East and then an executive with the Celtics. We had a surprisingly easy game, winning by fourteen, in large part because Burleson, still on a roll, had his own bad news for Barnes: twenty-four rebounds.

An aside: Marvin liked his nickname "Bad News" so much he always wore a T-shirt with that name on it. At one point in his life he held up a bus while wearing one of those shirts, and was arrested within forty-five minutes. "How'd you know it was me?" he asked.

In the regional championship game against Pittsburgh the next week back in our Reynolds Coliseum—with the winner advancing to the Final Four—David kept getting bumped on the arm as he shot. Untypical of him, he became visibly upset at the refs for not calling a foul, and he very nearly drew a technical. Finally, he became so frustrated after having his elbow bumped on a shot, he flew down the floor on the transition, determined to snuff out the shot by the guy who had been bumping him. David took off from just inside the free throw line in an effort to block a Pittsburgh shot. He went so high, his foot hit a player's shoulder, and he flipped upside down. David went to the floor headfirst, like a spear.

He was out instantly.

He lay still for a long, long time, unconscious, his scalp split open and gushing blood. Worse, he had no movement and urinated, suggesting serious nervous-system impairment.

Recalls assistant athletic director Frank Weedon: "I thought he was dead. Blood came out of one ear. There was a total silence, like you had suddenly turned off a blaring radio."

I thought about something David's mother had said. She was always worried about him taking a bad fall. "He jumps too high," she said, shaking her head with concern.

A moment later, Dr. P. G. Fox, one of our team physicians, grabbed my hand and excitedly said, "I just saw him move a toe. I think he's going to be all right." I'll never forget how much pressure Dr. Fox used when he squeezed my hand.

David was rushed to old Rex Hospital, which was flooded by

calls from all over the nation, including one from Walter Cronkite on behalf of the "CBS Evening News."

Dr. Jim Manley, another of our team doctors, followed the ambulance in a state trooper's car and had just entered the emergency room when he was handed a telephone. "It was Cronkite, wanting to know about David," Manley recounts. "I told him it was too early to tell and suggested he call back. He said it was too important, with fifty million people wanting to know about Thompson's welfare, and asked if he could just hold on. So I kept giving him little updates after each step of the examination process. 'He's hurt, but he's coming around.' Then after X-rays, 'He has a wound on his scalp.' I shaved around the cut and put in sutures and told Cronkite that David was coming around, not seeing double. We moved him to a private room, got somebody to watch him, and I went back to give a final report to Cronkite. David had a concussion but appeared to be okay."

Unfortunately, this medical play-by-play was not immediately available back at Reynolds Coliseum, where the atmosphere became funereal. The stands were quiet. Monte told me the team didn't want to continue the game. Rumors were running wild: David was dead. David was a vegetable.

We made it through to the half and trudged downstairs to the locker room. The players wanted a report on David's condition, but we didn't have one from anyone in authority. "We don't want to play, Coach," said Monte, who had played out the end of the first half literally wiping away tears. I gave all the usual arguments. We couldn't help David by not playing, and he would want you to play. That's all we talked about at half. There was no discussion of strategy or how the game was going. I don't even know what the score was.

We came out for the second half still in a state of shock. It was surrealistic. Was this really happening? All I know is that at one point in the second half, Tom Burleson went to the free throw line when, suddenly, our entire team left the floor. I could only assume they'd had it and had decided to quit. There was a tremendous roar from the crowd. What I couldn't see was that David Thompson had returned.

Because there had been so many calls and so many false reports about David's condition, the doctors decided to bring David back to the Coliseum—just forty-eight minutes after he had been admitted—so the crowd and the national television audience could see that he was okay. Dazed and bloodied, but okay.

He was heavily sedated and had a white bandage around his head. When they brought him in a side door, our team spotted him coming up the tunnel before he came into view of me or most others in the building. They rushed off the floor and surrounded him. It was an extremely emotional scene. I don't know how long the game was stopped, but I don't think there was any thought of giving our kids a technical for delay. Like everyone else, the refs were happy to see David in a vertical position.

Finally, our team was back on the court, overjoyed. David was escorted to our bench and took a seat beside me. David leaned over to me and at 33⅓ speed said, "How . . . they . . . doin' . . . Coach?"

"David, all they've cared about is you," I said. "They don't care about the game. They're doing fine."

He looked up in time to see Monte, who had become a maniac of joy on the floor, make another steal. David cupped his hands around his mouth and shouted as best as he could to his roommate, "'Atta . . . way . . . to . . . go . . . Midget!"

Our kids were so pumped, the Detroit Pistons couldn't have touched them the rest of that game. We won, going away, 100–72. Afterward, the Pitt coach, Charles Ridl, accused us of bringing David back from the hospital to give the team a lift. I thought that was in incredibly bad taste. I didn't have anything to do with David coming back and was just as surprised as everyone else to see him standing there, looking like a combat survivor.

Jim Manley accompanied David back to Rex Hospital, where he remained overnight for observation. The best sign of his rapid recovery came in the form of David's first words upon his return to the hospital. "I'm hungry," he announced. By then, the hospital kitchen had closed, so Manley called his golf club—Carolina Country Club—and had a steak dinner prepared and delivered to David's hospital room.

Manley put fifteen stitches in Thompson's head, and they remained there through the games of the Final Four the next week. When Manley took them out, he said prominent boosters offered one hundred dollars a stitch as keepsakes. Instead, he kept them and gave them out one at a time to young boys as a reward for being good patients.

With Pitt dispatched, we were off to the Final Four, right up the road at Greensboro Coliseum, with Marquette, UCLA, and Kansas. We were paired against UCLA in the first round, a rematch of our decisive loss early in the season. The pressing question was whether David Thompson would be ready to play.

There was so much interest in David, the hospital had to have security guards outside his room over the weekend. We decided not to have practice on Monday, partially because we didn't know what David's status would be and partially because my philosophy always had been not to have heavy practices before big games. I believed in having my players fresh and not risk a freak injury. Tuesday, David was going to join us for our first workout heading into the Final Four.

We were on pins and needles. The doctors hovered about, watching David very closely as we began, typically, with a team meeting down in our locker room. David was in the front row. Like everyone else, as I spoke I watched him out of the corner of my eye. We were going to take it easy that day, I decreed, just lollipop around, do a few simple drills and go in.

Suddenly, David's head dropped, then jerked first to one side, then to the other. His eyes widened and rolled back, and his body stiffened and began shaking in spasms.

I just about had a heart attack. The doctors began banging into one another trying to get to David. As they did, he started laughing at his little joke.

David later said, "At that time, the movie *The Exorcist* was out. So when the coach was up talking, I started rolling my eyes and spinning my head sort of like the little girl in *The Exorcist.* I think it scared Coach to death. I started laughing, and everybody else did. It sort of loosened everybody up."

That was David. He had a feel for the situation and was going to relax everyone and break the tension. And he did. In the process, he nearly caused about four fatal coronaries, including one by me.

We hit the floor and had a nice workout. As usual during most of my career, our practice was open. We really didn't know what to expect, given the general state of our fans at that moment and the intense interest in David's condition. More than eight thousand showed up, yelling and screaming, all eyes glued on David. At the end of our session, as David jogged from the far end of the court, he tossed up a playful shot from half-court. It hit nothing but net.

"When that shot went in," David remembers, "I knew something good was destined to happen."

You talk about magic moments. The place went berserk.

It was like an omen of what was to come that weekend. Those people hooted and hollered and had to be urged to leave the building. Once in the parking lot, they still didn't want to leave. Security police had to herd them off the campus. They were ready to celebrate.

Sam Esposito, my top assistant, was a true competitor, and he was wound tight like the rest of us as we approached the Final Four. Unfortunately, he also had his coaching duties with the North Carolina State baseball team, which by now was already into its schedule as our basketball season stretched into late March. He had a baseball game scheduled on the same day as our game with UCLA.

Espo figured that if he left after five innings, he could make the tip-off, so he hatched a plan. He told the plate ump he might do something unusual about the fifth inning and asked him not to hold it against him. Sure enough, Espo burst out of the dugout in the top of the fifth, flapping his arms and disputing a routine call. The ump shrugged it off, but Espo persisted, turning up his language another shade of purple. Finally, the ump tossed him. Espo smiled and thanked him, and raced to the back of the stands where Noreen, his wife, had the car packed and idling.

As they drove to Greensboro, a car passed, and Sam thought the driver shot him the finger as they went by. When Sam took out after the guy, Noreen thought he had gone crazy. Sam floorboarded the car, caught up to the "bird" man, and forced him off the side of the road. Sam leaped out ready to fight the guy. It turned out to be one of our supporters who had recognized Sam and now had to calm him down. "Sam, Sam," he explained, holding up an index finger, "I was saying, 'We're No. 1!'"

I certainly don't want to take anything away from the fine squads from Kansas and Marquette, but the consensus was that the true championship game was our first-round match with UCLA. The game measured up to all expectations. We jumped out front, they countered. They'd spurt ahead, we'd catch them. At the end of regulation, it was 65–65. After a cautious first overtime, it was 67–all. Then in the second overtime, with 2:07 to go, the Bruins accumulated a seven-point lead that would have been fatal to any group not blessed with the drive and determination of this very special Wolfpack team.

UCLA had the ball, and, for some reason or another, John Wooden called timeout. In clinics, I've always emphasized a need to keep things simple in sideline huddles. I looked up and said, "Fellas, there's 2:07 to go and we're down by seven." They looked up and determined from the scoreboard that I was right.

"*Somebody,*" I said, slowly for emphasis, "better make something good happen quickly." That's all I told them.

Back on the floor, Bill Walton inbounded the pass, and Monte jumped in front of him like a pint-size wooden Indian. Walton lumbered onto the floor, running over the top of this unexpected, hip-high obstacle, and Monte drew the charging foul. For years after that, Walton told me it was a lousy call, one that cost them the championship.

Monte went to the line and knocked in two. Still upset, Walton threw the ball in and had it picked off by David, who scored. Now we were down by just three and had only used about ten seconds. We fouled; they missed. We shot; we scored. As happens so often in big games, the momentum had turned a neat 180 degrees.

We won, 80–77, and the celebration that erupted throughout the state suggested we already had won the national title. But there was still Al McGuire and Marquette to dispatch in the championship game on Monday.

On Sunday we had a press conference, and all four teams worked out. The big question—more than whether State or Marquette would win—was whether Walton would show up to play in the third-place consolation game against Kansas. He did, but Wooden later related to me that he was not sure whether or not Walton would play.

At the practice session that afternoon, we had the final time segment. We were there waiting and watching the end of Marquette's workout. They had three scuffles on the floor, and McGuire was in two of them. They were yelling and knocking one another around, and finally an NCAA official had to shoo them off the floor. Al, still combative as he walked by me, stopped and shook his finger and snapped. "You know, you only get an hour! Just because you're the last ones here, you can't stretch it out."

I laughed and said, "Hey, Al, you can have fifteen minutes of *my* time. I'm enjoying this."

So we went out there with a totally opposite philosophy. We

were lollipopping around, trying to drop-kick field goals, football-fashion, posing for pictures, yukking it up. We were out there for about fifteen minutes, and then we frolicked off to the lockers.

That Marquette club might have been Al's finest. All five starters that year became NBA draft picks, two of them—Maurice Lucas and Bo Ellis—in the first round. He kept saying that Lucas was his "Secretariat."

We got a nine-point lead just seconds before the half. For all of his four years at State, Tom Burleson wanted to take the ball on the dribble, baseline to baseline, and make a layup. So with us up by nine and things going our way, he got a rebound and started down the floor dribbling. I saw what was coming. "He's not going to pass the ball!" I shouted in disbelief. "He's going to try to take it all the way!"

He made it to about the free throw line before Marquette stole the ball from him. Fortunately, there wasn't enough time for them to score, but we could have been up eleven at the half. Psychologically, a double-digit lead can be important.

For the first time all year long, I lost my composure in the locker room at halftime. I was so upset at Burleson for the stupid play he attempted, and I was in front of him letting him have it. David tugged at my sleeve and in pleading tones said, "Coach, we're up by nine."

That made me realize that I was making a fool of myself. I stepped back, went out in the hall, got myself together, and went back inside to discuss the second half. Marquette made one nice run at us, but Al McGuire lost his cool and was called for two technicals. One came when David was fouled for a one-and-one. Taking on the technical, David made all three shots, and we scored with the subsequent possession for a five-point spurt. The game was never in doubt again. We won, 76–64.

In our dressing room after the game, it was deathly quiet. I expected bedlam, people going crazy like after our ACC championship game against Maryland and after the UCLA game two nights earlier.

I, too, felt washed out, but I hoped that by the time we got to the motel, we would be in more of a mood for celebration. As usual, anytime we were in Greensboro we stayed at the Albert Pick Motel. Art Flynn was the manager, and his place became known as Flynn's Inn to Wolfpackers. We always stayed there for the early-season Big Four tournaments, the ACC tournaments, and, in this case, for the Final Four. It was "our" hotel in Greensboro.

From the coliseum, we filed onto the team bus. It was as quiet as could be—eerie. All of a sudden, through the front door of the bus burst Lefty Driesell in classic Lefty form. Flapping his arms, yelling, and screaming, he shouted, "You guys are the greatest! God you're an inspiration! I'm going back and go to work tomorrow. My team's gonna *win* one of these!"

Years earlier, in my second coaching job as an assistant at Memphis State, Ken Loeffler, who won a national championship with Tom Gola at LaSalle, had just taken the job at Texas A&M. Bear Bryant had hired him there to crank up the basketball program. We were playing them at Memphis State, and it became my duty to drive him around town one day to help promote our game. As a young coach still dreaming, I couldn't resist asking him what it was like to win the national championship. I've never forgotten his response.

"It was the most disillusioning moment I've ever had," he answered. "Norm, the minute the game ended and we had won a national championship, one of our alums ran out and said, 'Coach, how's recruiting going? You know, we can do this again next year.' We hadn't even left the floor, Norm."

In my mind, I shrugged that off, figuring that could never happen.

But twenty years later, I was winding down at Flynn's Inn hours after winning the national championship. All was quiet, and I was kind of letting things soak in when here came two of our young turks, State graduates in business in Greensboro. They rushed in and dropped down on one knee beside me. "Norm, got your eye on a big guy?" one of them asked. "You know, if you get you a good big man out of junior college to replace Burleson, we can do this again next year."

I smiled and shook my head, flashing back to what Ken Loeffler had told me that day in Memphis. These guys couldn't enjoy what we had accomplished. They couldn't even wait for the sun to come up, read the papers, and enjoy the moment. They were already painting the 1975 Final Four Wolfpack red and white.

The next day, we bussed back to Raleigh. More than ten thousand fans were in Reynolds Coliseum to greet us, and each player went out on the stage to give a response to them. Greg Hawkins stole the show, walking up to the microphone on his hands. When it came time for Tom Burleson to speak, he said into the microphone: "When I was a freshman here, I couldn't even walk across here on my feet, let alone on my hands!"

He brought the house down.

CHAPTER 5

From Dominant to Downer

The year after the championship season was an unforgettable experience. It taught me a lot about why so few teams—college or pro—ever repeat as champions, even if they ran away with their season. They just don't function like they did the previous year.

Keep in mind that we had an undefeated season, 27–0, then a 30–1 season with the national title, 57–1 over a two-year period. We didn't have the opportunity to be champions in 1973 because we were on probation, but we nevertheless were the champions of everything we played in that year.

Winning the national title the next year was a tremendous high. It even changed our office routine. We had to hire a couple of extra women to help my secretary, and we lapsed into a circus of ceremonies and functions, like Monte Towe Day in his hometown back in Indiana. People wanted to honor the team, and rightfully so.

I really didn't give much thought to the season that was approaching. We had lost only one starter, seven-foot, four-inch center Tom Burleson. Our recruiting was basically centered around replacing him. We had a commitment from a junior college transfer, Tommy Barker, who at the last minute decided to go elsewhere.

Rival recruiters plied Barker with the idea that he would be under tremendous pressure at State. "They won the whole thing with Burleson," went the warning, "so now if you go in there and they don't win it again and you're the only change, it's all your fault."

Barker's main advisor and legal guardian was an attorney named Lewis Schafel, now the general manager of the NBA Miami Heat.

Even after I found out that Barker wasn't coming with us, I wasn't all that concerned. We still had plenty of size, depth, and experience to be a viable contender again. Except now the goals had changed. Now you weren't thinking about merely the conference championship as a target. There was that big banana as the new standard—the national championship.

Soon after the fall semester began, I sensed some problems. I was receiving feedback that this player was at a bar, that another was living it up at a campus party, that our guys were conducting themselves differently than they had in the past. I never had any objection to my players having a good time. I know they're human beings. Hearing on occasion that one of them was out having a beer never really bothered me. I might call him in and caution him, but that was about it.

But this had the scent of excess. I was getting too many reports.

When time came to get into our preseason program—weightlifting and conditioning—we weren't getting the attendance or effort we needed. There was resistance even to going through the normal preseason program.

The old hunger just wasn't there. In previous years, the players were getting ready to prove themselves and win something. Now, it was, "Why are we having to go through this drill?"

I didn't expect that from this team. To this day, I regard them as a unique collection of human beings. They all are special people, a cut above.

First thing I did was to tell them they were not getting after it and they would be the number one target wherever they played that year. "That means, instead of having a few breathers where you can take it easy, you are going to have twenty-seven knock-down, drag-out ball games. We'll have to be in shape for that. I think you need to get yourselves together, change your whole approach to this, and get excited about being the defending champs," I said. "I don't think you're excited about that. You're just going through the motions."

The meeting was in our locker room in Reynolds Coliseum. We had lined the walls with oversized pictures from the championship season, and one particularly striking photo in which we had just gotten a rebound and all five guys were turned, digging in on a fast break, impressed me. I thought it was an inspiring environment in which to talk about the previous year and the coming challenge.

We went through another week or two of conditioning, and I didn't see any improvement. So I elected to call in Monte, the unofficial spokesman for the team, to discuss the situation. We began by going through the same things I had mentioned to the team. "Monte, we're not getting ready properly. Last year was super. But the fall—now—can be a harder fall than you've ever taken once you've been up on that mountain top."

Monte was defensive, suggesting I was overreacting. I reminded him that during the previous season, after we had lost to UCLA, that he and the players were the ones demanding team rules and curfews that I didn't see as necessary. That reflected the team's determination and ambition. "Now I am saying the same things, and you're being defensive and trying to tell me things are okay when they aren't. I don't understand this. You guys are looked up to—idolized already—and you have the opportunity to play together for another year with that great talent."

He became quiet. Tears came to his eyes. Monte is an emotional person, and as he began to talk, his voice broke. "Y-you know, Coach. We can't live up to what they expect."

He was more aware of what was expected of the team than I had imagined. I thought they weren't aware of the expectations, but they were and it frightened them. Realizing that, I had to take a whole different approach. "Monte, you guys will be fine," I began to assure him.

I told him he had built this up in his mind, that he had made it larger than it was. I told him they needed to pull together and go to work. There would probably be more sacrifices than in the past, I told him, because they were more in demand. I was talking about giving up the increased social opportunities, going to bed earlier than the typical students.

"Coach," he said, tears still running down his cheeks, "that's not the way we see it. We've talked about this a lot, and we've come to this conclusion: let's say that we sacrifice and do everything we did last year and we don't win it. That could happen, couldn't it?"

"Well, certainly. Just because you're the best prepared and the best team doesn't mean you always win. That's true."

"Okay," he said. "Let's say we make all these sacrifices and still don't win. Then we don't have anything. Our attitude is this: we're going to party and have the good times. We might win it anyway, right, Coach?"

I kinda laughed and had to agree. "Yeah, there's that chance, but it's not likely. If you do all that and still win it, then we coaches have been teaching and preaching the wrong things for a long time. I think, Monte, you would agree that proper preparation is very important."

"Yeah, Coach, but what we've decided is that we're going to have these good times. If we don't win it, then at least we will have had these good times."

I never thought I'd hear that out of a player, particularly one like Monte. To begin with, if I had thought that when I was a player, I don't think I would have expressed it to my coach. But that's the courage of Monte Towe, one of the many things that I respect and admire about him. He had the courage to sit there and be candid with me.

Time and again that fall, I'd stop practice and preach to them, bring players in for individual talks about this. But they continued to lope along and did not have the type of preparation they had the previous year. Not even close. Still, we had a pretty good year, 20–5, and were ranked seventh in the nation as we went into the ACC tournament.

Right or wrong, my approach with them at the tournament was, "Okay, fellas. This is what you've decided to do, and now you're at crunch time. You've told me you can have all this fun and make this kind of lesser preparation and still do it when it counts. Now the burden is on you. Show me. I hope you can."

By the time we took the floor for that first-round game against Virginia, they were so psyched, dedicated, committed, I thought in the early part of the game it might be a shutout. They ran off a big opening streak on Virginia, and we won the game comfortably. But in the course of the game, David Thompson's legs locked up in severe leg cramps.

This is what I had kept saying to them about getting ready for the games. "If you don't get those legs in shape, your heart may be there, your mind can be there, and you can call on it and say, 'I want it.' But those legs won't be able to respond." Well, David called, but his legs didn't hear the phone. My trainers and doctors told me they had never seen a set of leg cramps like that in their lives. It was so severe that it left him temporarily handicapped. The muscles completely locked up.

We had two games left, but we didn't know how effective our star player would be. We were lucky to win the next game against Maryland. On sheer guts and talent, David Thompson limped to a thirty-point night. With the game tied in the closing seconds, Morris Rivers lost control of the ball. It bounded around off an elbow and a knee and somehow ended up in Kenny Carr's hands under the basket. He put in the gift at the buzzer, and we won, 87–85.

Now we were in the championship game against Carolina, and we couldn't answer the bell. We stayed within striking distance, but we were playing a fine team that had won the regular-season championship. Phil Ford was just coming into his own for Carolina and they won, 70–66, to advance to the NCAAs.

Retreating to the locker room with a 22–6 record, we were handed a telegram from the National Invitation Tournament extending us an invitation to play in that tournament. Without thinking, I asked for silence, said a few consoling things about what a great career they had had, and how they would be remembered as one of the outstanding teams in college history. "Now we have here an invitation to go to the NIT. That's a great tournament and used to be *the* tournament," I said.

Obviously, the timing was wrong, and they were in the wrong emotional state to be given that kind of choice. They unanimously voted not to go. That's the last time I ever gave a team that opportunity. Two days later—Monday—Monte and a couple of other players came to me saying they had changed their minds. Well, the NIT hadn't changed *their* minds. They already had filled the field.

In the weeks and months after we had won the national title in 1974 there was some question as to whether David Thompson would return for his senior year or jump to the NBA one year early. David and I talked about it right after the tournament, and I made it clear that I would support his decision as long as he and his family decided what was best for him. "I'm coming back, Coach," he insisted. "I promised my mother I would get my degree."

David had that kind of respect for her, and she had that kind of influence on him. However, as the NBA draft approached that summer, the Philadelphia 76ers wouldn't leave him alone. I had been invited to coach that year in the old Liberty Bell Classic, an all-star affair held in Philadelphia right after the college season ended. At a cocktail partly in conjunction with the classic, I was approached by Irv Kosloff, then the owner of the 76ers. We began by talking about the pro potential of Tom Burleson, who had just completed his senior year.

I spoke highly of Tom as an NBA prospect, and Kosloff casually asked me about "this David Thompson fella." I explained that David was an underclassman.

"Yeah? But what about him?"

"He's indicated he isn't interested in turning pro early," I answered. "But he can't miss. Can't miss."

The next thing I knew, they had Vellie Thompson, David's father, in Philadelphia, wining and dining him. They had convinced Vellie that David wanted him to fly to Philadelphia and talk about this situation. So Vellie agreed, and up he went.

David called the office one day and asked me what was going on. I told him I didn't have a clue, except I was reading in the paper where his father was in Philadelphia. David said he knew that and had even talked to his father.

"Well, what do you think?" I asked nervously.

"Let him stay," David said. "He's having the time of his life. They're buying him clothes. They're taking him to the best restaurants. Let him stay as long as he wants to."

They were trying to use David's father to help lure David to Philadelphia, but David didn't want any part of it.

As the draft approached early that summer, the 76ers couldn't find David because he decided to disappear. He and Biff Nichols, our manager at North Carolina State, took a trip to Biff's home in New York just to get away from all the pressure.

Undaunted, the 76ers sent a telegram to David in care of me, offering a five-year, no-cut contract for two million dollars. It was signed by Richie Phillips, an attorney for the club who later represented the NBA officials and now heads the baseball umpires union. Phillips told me it was in David's best interest to go pro, and I shouldn't try to keep him at North Carolina State just for selfish reasons. I never exerted the least pressure on David in either direction; it was going to be his decision all the way.

The Sixers, who had the second pick in the draft, eventually took Marvin Barnes, but they wanted David. When David returned from New York a few days later, I called him in and handed him the telegram. He read it, crumpled it up, and dropped it in a wastebasket.

"I'm tired of this, Coach. I have decided what I am going to do."

I said, "David, two million dollars is a lot of money. Would you please call your father and discuss it with him?"

We got Mr. Thompson on the phone, and I explained the telegram offer. He spoke very deliberately. "Well, whatever David wants to do." David explained to his father that he fully understood the offer but was not interested.

After David left, I collected the telegram out of the waste basket, smoothed it out as best I could, and had it laminated as a keepsake.

He had decided to come back on his own with no guarantees of any kind. He had turned down a two-million-dollar offer. What if he got hurt?

We consulted Fred Joseph, an insurance man in Greensboro, who worked out an arrangement whereby some company in America put up half of the one-million-dollar policy and Lloyd's of London put up the other half. The policy insured him against any eventuality that would cause him not to play as a pro: injury, disease, accident in the street, anything related to his health and well-being. The premium was one thousand dollars a month, and we checked with the NCAA and determined there was nothing wrong with Northwestern Bank loaning David the money to pay for the policy. The NCAA hesitated for a long time, but finally approved.

The bank loaned him twenty-five thousand dollars, enough to pay the insurance premiums for a year, with enough left over that David bought himself a car.

The very next year, the NCAA passed a rule to prevent that. It came to be known as the David Thompson Rule. Years later, they rescinded it and once again permitted kids to borrow money for that type of insurance policy, but not above and beyond the premiums.

After his senior year, David went to Denver of the ABA to be with Monte, rejecting the Atlanta Hawks who had picked him in the first round of the NBA draft. The struggling Virginia franchise had picked David in the first round of the ABA draft but traded his rights to Denver for three players and cash.

Larry Brown literally recruited him to Denver by offering to sign both David and Monte. David was basically insecure about going somewhere with a group of people he didn't know. I couldn't get him to go out for the Olympic team at the end of his freshman year for that very reason. I called Hank Iba, the U.S. Olympic coach that year, and said, "I've got a kid you don't know much about because he just played freshman ball this year. But he would make our team and start. I don't know that he wouldn't be one of the stars of the whole Olympics." Hank said he had six personal picks for the tryouts roster and promised he would use one to assure David a spot. I shared that with David, but he indicated he wasn't interested. They sent the official invitation, and I gave the papers to David.

Some time later, the Olympic people called and said David hadn't responded. I brought David back in, and he said he didn't want to go. He didn't know anyone on the team.

Understanding this about David, Larry Brown used a late-round draft pick to select Monte. Then he started recruiting David. Part of the deal was they gave Monte a three-year contract. In fact, David got Monte a raise right there in the office. As David was getting ready to sign his deal with Denver in Larry Fleisher's office in New York, he looked over at Carl Scheer, the Nuggets' general manager, and said, "Can't you give Monte a little more money?" They did, and David signed. The two of them went off to Denver and the ABA together.

Cotton Fitzsimmons, who was coaching in Atlanta at the time, thought the Hawks wouldn't have any trouble getting David. After all, they were the NBA, and they were the closest team to David's home. I had told Cotton this kid had a strong desire to be around friends.

That didn't sink in until David was in Fleisher's office about to sign. Cotton called me, frantically, saying the Hawks would raise their offer to David by another $150,000. I told him I didn't think it would make any difference but agreed to relay the message. I called Fleisher's office, and they put David on the phone. "Coach, I'm not interested," he said. "I've got a chance to go to Denver with Monte."

In recounting the sequence recently, David said, "I went to Denver because of Monte and because they had a good team. Atlanta was struggling. I didn't want to go there like Pete Maravich did and have the pressure on me to turn the franchise around."

Although David Thompson was easily the most remarkable player we had during my stint as coach at North Carolina State, another young black man ranks high on my list of sweet memories with the

Wolfpack. This one was not a player, booster, or fellow staff member. He was an inmate.

A few years after I went back to State, I was invited to make a talk at the state prison in Raleigh, just a short distance from the campus. I was hesitant until I was told the inmates there were mostly "youthful offenders."

I imagined wayward teenagers in a minimum-security place with, perhaps, barbed-wire fences. It was unsettling, to say the least, to discover after the steel gates clanked behind me that I was inside solid walls with rapists and murderers.

But I enjoyed it. I seemed to have a good rapport with this, well, captive audience. The officer who had invited me could tell I was into it and asked if I was familiar with their sponsor program. I wasn't.

Before I knew it, I had agreed to sponsor one Charles Monroe. He was a good-looking young black man in his early twenties. They told me I could come visit him whenever I wanted and could even take him out of the prison and home to dinner on occasion. I came home and told Joan I had decided to do that. She looked at me a little apprehensively, but agreed.

"What do I feed him?" she said.

"Shoot, they probably don't eat very good in prison, so anything you fix will be fine." Joan prepared a feast of fresh vegetables—squash, green beans, and so forth—figuring they didn't often have that in prison.

When I went to pick up Charles, he was terribly nervous. When I shook hands with him, his perspiring hand just squirted out of mine. We walked out through the gate, and when it shut behind us, he said something that got me thinking for the first time that old Norman might be in over his head. "You know," he said, "that's the first time in seven years I've walked through that gate without being handcuffed."

We slid into my Chevrolet Caprice, a beige four-door, and started home. I said, "Charles, I'd like to know more about you. What are you in for, anyway?"

Without flinching, he said, "Murder and armed robbery."

I almost ran off the road. It turned out that he had driven the car in a robbery, and when they were stopped, one of his accomplices killed a deputy sheriff. I'm thinking to myself, *I'm taking this guy home to Joan and little Leslie, Robbie, and Michael. I've gotta be nuts.*

Joan prepared a wonderful meal, and the one thing she had

worked hardest on was a fresh squash casserole. Charles looked it over and said, "The one thing we get every day, three times a day, is squash." They grew squash right there on the prison farm and fed it to the inmates. You've heard of "summer squash"? Well, at the Raleigh prison they had "breakfast, lunch, and dinner squash." So we were off on the wrong foot. It was kind of a tough evening, but everyone in the family developed a fondness for Charles.

Before long, we'd get Charles and let him baby-sit Leslie and Michael for us. We would take him on team trips, and he'd go in and sleep on the floor in David Thompson's hotel room. I could get special permission to take him on our basketball trips as long as it was to a school within the state.

Wolfpack people got to know Charles and became fond of him. I explained to Charles that it was his responsibility to advise them who he was and what he was doing, and he handled it well. He would tell them he was an inmate at the state prison, and Coach and Mrs. Sloan were his sponsors. Our players gave him Wolfpack shirts, sweats, and sneakers. He'd sit on our bench and was in the dressing room with us before and after games and at the half.

A lot of people thought he was a prospect.

The only problem we ever had was one night when we came home and Charles and one of our cars was gone. It was not long before he came driving in, explaining that he just had an urge to drive around. I told him I understood that and trusted him, but as long as I was sticking my neck out for him, we couldn't have any more of that. He apologized and gave his word it wouldn't happen again. And it didn't.

Finally, I went to Governor Bob Scott to see what we could do for Charles. They put him on service at the governor's mansion. Typically, a trustee could work about a year in a job like that, and if he kept his nose clean would be given a pardon. The release papers were on the governor's desk when Charles had a fling with one of the workers there from the women's prison. So that shot that down.

Charles went back to prison, and we worked him back up to a return to the mansion after Jim Hunt became governor. Things went along smoothly, and the release papers were prepared for Hunt's signature. This time, Charles stole a can of peanuts. He did it in such a way that it was obvious he wanted to be caught.

Back in prison, we talked about that. He admitted he was scared of the outside. "Do you understand, Coach, that inside these walls it's a whole different society. Prison is the only society I've known."

This happened about the time we left North Carolina State and returned to Florida. We corresponded with Charles for a while, then lost track of him.

When we were playing Syracuse in the Meadowlands in the East Regional of the 1987 NCAA tournament, Charles showed up in front of our hotel just as we were about to board the team bus for the arena. He was out of prison, living in upstate New York. He looked great.

He had driven all the way to East Rutherford, New Jersey, to see us play, but he didn't have a ticket. "I just never told you people how much I love you and how much you meant to me," he said.

To this day, I feel horrible that I didn't have the presence of mind to pull him on the bus and somehow squirrel him into the arena. Instead, with the game on my mind and a school official yelling that it was time to go, I could only think to tell him I was sorry, but I didn't have any tickets. I just wasn't functioning. We pulled away and left him standing in the motel parking lot.

My conscience started bothering me, and I tried to track him down in the town where he told me he was living. But I've never seen nor heard from him again. Charles, if you read this, I hope you'll contact us and let us make amends.

On January 23, 1980, the Wolfpack had a game at Maryland, and we flew a day before the game to stay just outside Washington, D.C. Fred Montsdeoca, our longtime friend and former Citadel staffmate from Ocala, Florida, had become president of the National Limestone Association, which was having its meeting in Washington. He noticed in the paper that we were playing and gave us a call out at the Crystal City Marriott, just across the Potomac. Joan and I arranged to join him for dinner that night at the Washington Hilton.

He gushed about the new O'Connell Center, a twelve-thousand-seat basketball arena, being built at Florida and asked what kind of basketball program the Gators could have and what kind of coach they could attract. I told him I thought Florida could have one of the finest programs in the country and ought to be able to lure one of the top people in the business.

I went on to tell him about the talent in the state, the resources at Florida, and so on. A little grin spread across his face, and he playfully warned, "You better be careful. You're talking to a member of the selection committee. You sound like you might be interested in coming back."

I told him it had always been on my mind that Florida could be one of the finest jobs in the country, and I always felt like I had left there in 1966 without completing the job I had set out to do. We hadn't won the conference championship.

Fred obviously had started the conversation just to pick my brain, not thinking that I would be interested, and I had no idea he was involved in the process of selecting a new coach. But when Fred realized I was serious, he resigned from the committee to avoid the appearance of a conflict.

It all came about accidentally. There were no plans to meet with Fred, and it had never crossed my mind that I'd like to go back to Florida. As I talked to him about it, I could feel my interest growing. There aren't many schools that are *the* school in the state, as in The University of. I always wanted to be associated with *the* state university.

I wasn't having any problems at North Carolina State, but I couldn't take the program any higher. We had won a national championship, and we were hanging in there, finishing second. We were going to the NCAA or the NIT most years, but I couldn't see us becoming a consistently dominant factor. Everywhere I've been, I've built programs, and I was ready for a change. Without knowing it, I was ready to move on.

There were a few people who didn't like me, but that's going to happen anywhere. Heck, right after we had gone 57–1 over a two-year period, a booster named Larry Tyree wrote me a letter telling me he was convinced I couldn't coach major college basketball.

When Fred and I parted at Washington, he told me to think about it for a few days and give him a call. I thought about it and called. I wanted to look into it. He said, "Do you know how bad the situation is here?"

I said I did. He said, "No, Norm, I don't think you have any idea how bad it is."

He didn't want me to think there was some pot of gold there.

Florida had just fired John Lotz and had elevated his assistant, Ed Visscher, to become the interim. They were in the process of taking applications. I never wrote a letter of application, but I applied by having a confidential conversation with Bill Carr, then the athletic director at Florida, telling him I was seriously interested.

I went to my own athletic director, Willis Casey, and told him I would appreciate knowing how he saw my future at North Carolina State and what he foresaw as my financial potential at State. He said he didn't see much change. I was unhappy with my salary. At thirty-five thousand dollars a year, I was the lowest paid coach in the ACC although I had won a national championship. The perks included about twenty thousand dollars from a television show I had to sell myself and another fifteen thousand a year from our summer camps, but I wasn't getting a nickel from a shoe contract.

I found out later that Dean Smith was getting one hundred thousand a year from Converse. We had won the national title wearing Converse, and they didn't even give us our shoes, much less a fee. We bought our own shoes.

Joan got mad and finally got us something out of Converse. At our house one night, she cornered Joe Dean, the LSU athletic director who was working for Converse back then, and told him, "You've never done anything for Norm, and he's been loyal to Converse." Nailed him to the wall. So he set us up to do a clinic in London. They sent us there, first-class, and put us up for a week in Paris after the clinic. That trip led to a curious little side adventure in our lives, coaching the British Olympic team that summer. But back to that in a minute.

At the time of my chance meeting with Montsdeoca, I had been working to improve the salary situation for myself and my assistants. (Monte Towe, my top aide, was paid just fifteen thousand dollars in our final year at State.) I waged my campaign with Willis Casey and members of the board of trustees. The trustees were stunned to learn we were bringing up the rear in the ACC. Willis knew it.

I don't know why Willis chose to be so frugal with salaries. First, he said he wasn't worried about the assistant coaches anytime, anyplace. I argued that wasn't wise, not if you wanted to make certain you got people who belonged at State, meshed well with my personality, and fit the program. I always tried to hire people who had played for me or for the university. If an assistant is out recruiting for North Carolina State but had gone to Minnesota, it makes it a little tougher to sell North Carolina State as the school with the greatest opportunity for a kid's future. The kid says, "Hey, you went to Minnesota." It's just another edge if your recruiter has gone to that school and truly has his heart in it when selling his school or his head coach.

Soon I could tell I was running into a stone wall with Willis on salary reform. As I look back on it, I probably mishandled the whole affair by allowing it to become an issue for the athletic board. In my frustration with Willis one day, I told him I didn't think the athletic board understood how our salary structure compared to others. When it escalated to a campus-wide issue and a public issue, that upset Willis. He bowed up and became defiant. We got to the point where I couldn't talk to him about it. He'd say it was a dead issue, and I'd argue that we couldn't afford to let it become a dead issue. It just wasn't right.

He opened the door to the athletic board and, like a fool, I walked right in.

He said, "Go talk to the board. If you think you can get a better salary for you and your staff and think that I'm the one standing in the way, go talk to the board."

The matter actually became one of the agenda items at a board meeting. So here was Willis Casey sitting there, the school president, Dr. Joab Thomas, and the full board. I showed them the salary figures from around the ACC and made my case that we deserved more.

This was before the fateful meeting with Montsdeoca, and I truly wasn't thinking about another job. I wasn't threatening to leave if they didn't cough up a big raise. I wasn't that dumb. I was just trying to fight for my turf.

When I was finished, Willis stood up before the board and said I hadn't been to him with any of this and he didn't realize that I was unhappy. That was untrue, so, typical of me, I stood up in the back of the room and shouted, "That's a lie!"

Dale Carnegie I'm not.

I mishandled the whole thing. The board chairman, Dick Mockrie, was on my side, and after the meeting, he told me, "Norm, I think basically the board agrees with you, but you've challenged Willis, and Dr. Thomas is likely to back him up. I don't think you can win." He explained that the board had only advisory powers, and unless I could change Willis's mind or somehow convince Dr. Thomas to go against the recommendation of his athletic director, the Wolfpack would continue its firm grip on last place in the ACC salary standings.

Any chance that Dr. Thomas would overrule his athletic director had been eliminated by his frustrations over hiring a football coach. Earlier that year, he wanted to hire Pat Dye, who was then at East Carolina; but he was shot down by the board. On a Sunday,

Thomas and Dye shook hands, and Pat went back to East Carolina and resigned. His appointment at State was supposed to be announced at midweek; but Pat came out and blasted East Carolina and its school president in the press, and the North Carolina State board was upset that he would do that. So they vetoed his appointment before the planned announcement, which is how Dye ended up out in the frozen tundra of Wyoming for one season. So Dr. Thomas was disenchanted that he had tried to take an active role in the athletic department and had been unsuccessful. When I went to talk to him about my salary situation, he more or less let me know that he had had it with athletic decisions.

So when I ran into Montsdeoca, I was a wounded man, and I started getting excited about going back to Florida. My wife was never excited about it, nor were my children. Michael was in dental school at Chapel Hill, and Leslie and Debbie were married and living in the Raleigh area. They reminded me that when we left Florida in 1966, I had promised I would never change jobs again. Coming from them, it was strong and it hurt. I reasoned that I hadn't foreseen the situation that would develop and had to start thinking about retirement. What was happening at State, financially, just wasn't right, I argued.

Bill Carr flew up and visited informally in our home. I laid out some basics that would have to be met for me to consider jumping to Florida, and he indicated that they were within reason. He said he needed to know if I would take the job if it was offered, and I said I couldn't make that decision at the moment.

The next day, I went to Willis Casey and told him I had an opportunity to talk to the people at Florida on an official basis. I told him I didn't really want to go that far with it, but I felt I had to if there was no hope for what I saw as shortcomings in my situation at State. "I'm not threatening you," I underscored again, "but now I have an option."

Without hesitation, he said, "Oh, you have my permission to look into it."

Well, that angered me. He acted almost as if he thought I was bluffing with some power play or he was perfectly happy to see me move on. So I looked into it and met—officially—with Carr and Dr. Robert Marston, the University of Florida president, in a motel in Richmond, Virginia, on the Sunday before the 1980 ACC tournament. Marston, whose family had some land in that area, simply said to me, "You need to come on home." He wasn't interviewing me. He was doing a selling job, and that tickled my vanity because I had just been through a situation where I had been hurt by the reaction of the administration at State.

The way I left it with Carr and Marston was that I was very interested and it was my inclination to take the job. But I said I was duty-bound to go back and talk to Willis Casey about it. The next day, I told Willis what Florida had offered: fifty-thousand dollars base salary, plus a guarantee of thirty-thousand in radio-television, plus the rights to a basketball camp. The fifty-thousand dollars had been the figure that I had in mind at State. When that got around, a prominent booster told Willis, "Well, if Sloan thinks he's worth that kind of money, he ought to leave." This from a guy I thought was a friend. I was hurt by that kind of comment. My pride was wounded.

Well, when I told him about the Florida offer, Willis said, "We'll match it."

That really made me mad. If he was willing to pay me that—or anything even approaching it—we could have avoided the whole Florida issue, the weeks of anguish, and the board meetings and frustrations.

"Willis, it's too late. My decision is made," I said, defiantly, somewhat surprised by the words coming out of my own mouth. That was the first time that I realized I had made a decision. When I went home and told Joan what had transpired, she immediately broke into tears. It was devastating to her to leave Raleigh. But not half as devastating as what we would ultimately encounter after returning to Florida.

Back to our British Olympic adventure. The London clinic was during the summer of 1979, prior to my last year at North Carolina State. As I lectured on the motion offense, a gent poked his hand in the air and said, "That was fine for your lads, but our lads aren't that accomplished."

"Quite the opposite," I said. "This is offense where you can always get somebody open to receive the ball. Great athletes don't need this to get open. If you're saying you don't have great basketball players, then this is the type of offense you need because you always have an open receiver."

I did such a great job of selling this concept that after I had finished, a guy came up and introduced himself as England's minister of sports. He said they were looking for someone to coach Great

Britain's team that next summer in the 1980 Olympics. The United Kingdom: a traditional Olympic basketball power.

That's a joke, gang.

Anyway, he said he wanted to talk to me. I said I'd be interested and gave him my address. I didn't think much more about it, but after we returned home, he called and invited me back to London to talk more in depth. He sent a plane ticket, and I flew back.

I said that having an American coach might erode the nationalism connected with the team. They said they weren't worried about that: nationalism hadn't gotten them very far before. In fact, they had never won a game in an Olympic competition. Now they wanted to try a foreigner who knew what he was talking about.

I signed a contract to coach the U.K. Olympic team. We were going to bring them to North Carolina State to train and then take them to Europe for a series of exhibitions, but in the interim, I took the job at Florida. So we brought that team to Gainesville and trained them on campus. We were basically looking for dual nationals—people with passports from two countries. You only have to have a passport from a country to play for that country in the Olympics. Some of our players were born to American servicemen while they were stationed in the U.K.

When they asked me what I wanted for a fee, I told them I only wanted them to let me take my wife along and let her have a great trip. Just our expenses.

That was the Moscow Olympics, which the U.S. boycotted because of the Soviet/Afghanistan situation. I was asked what I would do if this British team qualified. How could I justify participating in the Olympics that my own country was boycotting? I said I didn't think we had a problem. They had to get out of the European zone qualifying and into the actual Olympics first, something they hadn't been very successful at doing.

But we began having success on the exhibition tour. The British minister of sports was so excited he almost had tears. We beat Finland. "We've *never* beaten Finland," he said. We beat Belgium. "We've *never* beaten Belgium," he gushed.

So we were playing pretty well when the qualifying tournament started in Lucerne. In our group were Spain, Finland, and Poland. We started off with the big, strong Polish team. We beat them and moved on to the next round to play Finland. We already had split a pair of exhibition games with them, and we beat them again. Now we were 2–0 and ready to play Spain for the championship of the tournament. The winner would go on to Geneva to compete for two spots in the Moscow Olympics.

Joan and I had plane tickets the next day out of Zurich for our return to the U.S. Joan asked what we were going to do if we beat Spain. I told her not to worry about it. Spain had a hell of a team, and we weren't about to beat them.

At halftime, we were up by four points, and as I walked past Joan on the way to the dressing room, I just smiled and shrugged. "What am I gonna tell you?" I said.

We lost by three points in a heck of a game. That took care of the dilemma of whether we would go to Moscow when our country was boycotting the games. Thankfully, I didn't have to make that decision. I don't know what I would have done. I had just about made up my mind not to go, although I didn't agree with the boycott. I thought it was silly.

To boycott on the field of sport for political reasons didn't make sense to me. I had told the assistant coach, a Brit, that he would probably be in charge of the team if they made it to Moscow. But if we had won the tournament, amid all the excitement and euphoria it would have been pretty hard to climb down off those kids' shoulders and turn them down.

CHAPTER 6

Don't Call Me "Boy"

Of all the forces of change that have affected college basketball during the past half-century, easily the most dramatic and far-reaching has been the advent of racial integration. The wonderful skills the black player brought to the college game have produced a wholesale shift in the style of play and a sometimes reluctant adjustment on the part of many coaches, administrators, and fans.

On the floor, integration introduced a fast-paced, ad lib playground style into what had been highly disciplined, patterned, methodical offenses. That's why, later on, there was such a shocked reaction when at North Carolina State we had a 12–10 victory over Duke and when North Carolina held the ball and stood around to offset Virginia's Ralph Sampson. By then, the game had moved to another level.

Not long ago, I was given some old films of Indiana high school state tournament games. It was something of a shock to me. I had always thought of Indiana as the benchmark of high school basketball. Absolutely the best. Wide-open, exciting. I looked at those films and could hardly believe how bad the basketball was. There was no defense to speak of because they didn't have to play defense; no one came at them on offense. They would handle the ball and handle the ball, and finally one of a couple of players would take the shot and the others defended against those players. But after integration, it was not uncommon to have five guys on the court who could score.

The successful coaches learned to change their philosophy of substitutions. With the quickened pace, you could no longer go with five players virtually the whole game. You had to have eight or nine decent players to play an up-tempo game. Some coaches had trouble accepting the change because they felt they were losing control of the game. A lot of coaches simply couldn't adapt to the change.

But the more significant and meaningful effects of intercollegiate athletic integration happened off the court. Though the melding of blacks and whites in the intimate, emotional confines of basketball arenas was at first an uneasy, even stormy, marriage, I am hard-pressed to think of an American institution that has been more at the forefront of producing understanding and acceptance across racial lines than sports in general and college basketball in particular.

This chapter must begin with the ironic role played by one Samuel Esposito, an Italian-American sports star, devoted assistant coach, and still the beloved father confessor of the North Carolina State athletic department. In short, Sam is a hell of a guy.

Espo played a key role in the integration of athletics at State, despite taking the job there, in part, to escape the growing problems in dealing with blacks in the rugged East Chicago school district where he was a high school teacher and coach. He expressed that motivation in the earthiest of terms during his job interview with Dr. John Caldwell, North Carolina State's president. Caldwell, charter member of the All-Liberal team, turned ashen, changed the subject, and dismissed us within two minutes.

Walking back to my office, I shook my head and said, "Sam, why in the hell did you do that?"

"Well, I just told him the truth."

"Well, I think you just blew the job right there."

But, surprisingly, they hired him as assistant basketball coach and head baseball coach. He was eminently qualified with his ten years of big-league baseball background, mostly with the Chicago White Sox, and his basketball coaching experience under East Chicago legend John Barato. Sam was one of the great schoolboy athletes in Chicago. He went back to the days of Johnny Lujack, the Notre Dame great.

The year was 1967. The previous spring, I had made the jump from Florida to North Carolina State at a time when both athletic programs, like those at virtually all major southern universities, were just about pure WASP. If there were some blacks among the general student body, there weren't many. There were none among the athletes.

The next September, a skinny little black kid walked into my office a couple of weeks before the start of preseason practice. Even before he spoke, I had a flash that he was going to say he was from a small town, played forward, had enrolled in school, and wanted to come out for the team.

"My name's Al Heartley. I'm from Clayton," he said. "I played forward in high school, and I'd like to come out for the freshman team."

I smiled and nodded, proud of myself.

I gave him the usual stuff about making an announcement in the school paper about when freshman practice starts and that he was certainly welcome to give it a try. I forgot about it.

We started practice a month later. As usual, the practice courts in Carmichael Center were partitioned off with a high curtain. I was on one side with the varsity; on the other, conducting tryouts, was North Carolina State's brand-new freshman basketball coach, Sam Esposito. About the second day of trials, Sam came over to me and said, "Skip, I've got something I want you to see."

At that time, we could have twenty-five people on scholarship in basketball and we had already recruited seven freshmen. Well, the little black kid from Clayton was kicking everybody's butt in sight, *including* our prized scholarship recruits. It was unbelievable.

Al Heartley made the team and became the very first black athlete in North Carolina State history to play on any level. He became a freshman starter before the season opened, meaning he put three scholarship guys on the bench. The next year, we put him on scholarship and he was a starter—off and on—for the varsity. He became a full-time starter in his junior year, a captain as a senior, and won the Alumni Award, which at North Carolina State is a very prestigious award for the most outstanding student-athlete.

Al's brother, Harvey Heartley, was then, and still is, the basketball coach at St. Augustine's College, a predominantly black school in Raleigh. He does an outstanding job. When Al first came in, he never mentioned his brother. That's the kind of kid he was. He just came in, went out for the team, and made it on his own. Halfway through that first season, Harvey called to ask how his kid brother was doing. That was the first time I realized the connection.

As a result of the Sam Esposito/Al Heartley infiltration of North Carolina State athletics, some of the boosters experienced more than a little discomfort. One of them, a man from Little Washington, North Carolina, even dropped out of the Wolfpack Club and wrote me a letter saying I had "only been here one year and already you have introduced dagos and niggers to the program." He vowed he would no longer send any of his money to support that kind of program.

That was the beginning of athletic integration for my career and for North Carolina State, although it hardly touched off a gusher of black athletes. We signed black guards in 1968 and 1970, but neither of them, Ed Leftwich from New Jersey or Carl Lile from Indianapolis, stayed with the program beyond their sophomore years. When we scored the great coup by landing David Thompson in 1971, he was the only black signee. Al Heartley was a senior.

I called David into my office three or four times to make sure he understood that I wasn't intentionally refraining from recruiting black players. Rival coaches and black militants were trying to use that against us. Bowing to that pressure, we brought in a couple of blacks the next year, frankly, just to have some other black kids on the team. They were the Hunt brothers, Joe and Jerry, David's buddies from his high school. In David's junior year, we brought in Mo Rivers and Phil Spence out of junior colleges.

David kept saying, "Coach, it's not a problem." He used to wear a lapel button with a white hand and a black hand clasped in a handshake.

It was ironic that here I was explaining to David Thompson why we had a scarcity of black players when later on, I would be explaining to boosters why we had a scarcity of white players. I felt compelled to do that because people make ridiculous charges and allegations. I probably shouldn't have responded, but I did anyway.

I also hired the first black coach at State, Wilbert Johnson, in 1972. He was not in coaching when I hired him, but was working in a social services program on campus that helped minorities get into school. Wilbert was a personable guy with a slight weight problem. In the summer he would roll up the windows in his loaner car and try to sweat off the pounds. This didn't do a lot for the fragrance of the car; soon Bob Murray, the dealer who loaned Wilbert a car, discontinued the practice.

By then I had experienced some communication problems with our first few black players, and I thought Wilbert could help. Wilbert's father was a professor at St. Augustine's, a Ph.D. His mother had her master's degree and worked for the local school board. I figured here was a black family in which education had been prominent, and it would be a good thing to have a man like that on the staff.

We had some problems.

First, Wilbert couldn't recruit anyone. That went on for about two years. He just couldn't come up with a recruit. Finally, I had a few complaints from black high school coaches who said they didn't want him coming around their school anymore. That, coupled with the fact he wasn't recruiting anybody, led me to sit down with Wilbert and talk about it.

My office in the Everett Case Athletic Center was every bit as big and impressive as the football coach's. That was important to the State people because the building was named for the school's legendary basketball coach. I had huge windows overlooking the campus. The walls were richly paneled, the furniture top-shelf.

Wilbert sat in the chair to the left of my desk, and I could look out at the campus over his shoulder. I asked him point blank about the coaches' complaints, explaining that it seemed to me that he should attract black kids to our program that I couldn't. He asked me if I had ever heard of the crabs-in-a-basket theory. It was the first time I'd ever heard the expression. He asked if I had ever done any crabbing. I had, but I still didn't get the connection.

"You ever see a crab try to get out?" Wilbert asked.

I nodded, still confused.

"Did you notice what the other crabs do?"

"Yeah," I said, "the rest of them hold on to him."

"That's right. They aren't going to let him get out," he said. "And that's what's happening to me. These black high school coaches resent me being at the college level. They don't feel I paid my dues, and they're not going to help me. They don't want me to succeed."

Another incident with Wilbert stands out to me, mainly because he was from such a highly educated family. This incident involved Morris Rivers, who was from the Bronx in New York and had gone to Gulf Coast Junior College in Panama City, Florida. He was a great athlete, particularly tough on defense, but he was hard to coach and sensitive. He liked to fall back on the excuse, "You don't understand where I'm from. You don't know my background."

Well, after a short time, I knew his background very well. One day I was lecturing him in my office about the dangers of using his background as a crutch. I told him he needed to do the best he could in college to prepare himself for the outside world. That afternoon in practice, he became insolent, going out of his way to show anger with body language and refusing to answer any question I directed his way. The best acknowledgment I could get was a sneer and a "Yeah."

After three or four responses, I said, "I'm tired of that 'yeah' business. It's, 'Yes, sir,' or, 'No, sir.'"

We had a tough, head-to-head confrontation about respect right there in front of the team. Finally, I pulled a reluctant "sir" out of him.

Afterward, downstairs in the dressing room, I could tell Wilbert was disturbed.

"Coach, I've got to bring up something I need to talk to you about," he finally said. "I'm very upset about what happened up on the floor."

I told him I was, too.

"No, it's a little different. My mother and father taught me never to say 'sir' or 'ma'am' to anyone. Their attitude was, 'You're not subservient to anyone, and you don't have to 'sir' or 'ma'am' them.'"

Now, I hadn't even come close to seeing that as a problem. From my point of view, it was a matter of respect. I didn't really care about myself. I wanted Mo to start showing a little more respect to anyone who was a little older and in a position of authority; he was going to need that out in life. But Wilbert was adamant. We talked for some time. I won't say that my relationship with Mo Rivers improved greatly, but we didn't have *that* problem again.

Mo went on and got his degree, even though he professed no interest in one when he first arrived at State. He taught and coached high school ball in Charlotte for awhile, and eventually I lost contact with him. Years later, when we celebrated our six hundredth victory in Florida and the starting five from our 1974 North Carolina State championship was brought in for a surprise banquet, Mo was there. He had gone to work for a stock brokerage firm in New York.

So here was a kid that we—and I mean everyone connected with the North Carolina State program—had influenced in a positive way. When he came there, he just wanted to play basketball and take a shot at pro ball. He had no intention of graduating, but he left there with a degree and went on to a successful life.

Morris Rivers was just one of the many triumphs of integration that heartened me during my career. Two, in particular, were most gratifying: Monte Towe Day in Converse, Indiana, and what I call the break down of the Great Chatman Barrier.

Converse, Indiana, is a small, all-white, one-stoplight town that is typical of many small towns in Indiana. After we won the national championship at North Carolina State in 1974, the residents of Converse wanted to have a special day that summer to honor a native son, Monte Towe, the sawed-off point guard who was the heart of our team.

Doc Towe, Monte's father, called to ask me about it, and I was delighted to give my blessing and support. I said we'd get up a small plane load of coaches and players, and we would come to Converse. Northwestern Bank in Wilkesboro had a company plane, an old DC-3, which they provided for the junket. We took Wilbert Johnson, his brother, Dwight, David Thompson, our black superstar, Monte, and a few other teammates. We flew into Marion, Indiana, which is where my parents were living at the time, only a few miles from Converse.

The plan was to go by motorcade to Monte's house for a big spread of food outside on tables. Typical of midwestern villages, any big event took place at the fairgrounds where the biggest building was always the hog barn, an exposition-type pavilion for hog shows and other agricultural events. Converse had its hog barn all decked out in red and white and had assembled several members of the high school band for the occasion. It being summer, the band hadn't been practicing, and its performance was sincere but, as they say, out of stroke. It's the thought that counts.

The place was packed with about five hundred people. The emcee was a little guy named George Smith, a local athletic booster who adored Monte. Mr. Smith had a handful of notes and was terribly nervous. The band played the national anthem. We assumed it was, anyway, and dutifully stood at attention.

George Smith opened the program by saying, "We are here today to honor the greatest college basketball player in America."

Now David Thompson was sitting there in the audience, and I was squirming a little at that one, but it was fine. It was Monte Towe Day, not David Thompson Day.

My mind flashed back to a year earlier, at the end of Monte's sophomore year. We were in Greensboro at the Albert Pick Motel basking in the glow of an undefeated season topped off by our victory hours earlier in the championship game of the Atlantic Coast Conference tournament.

We were all happy, I thought, until Doc Towe threw a sour note into the celebration. Like Monte, Doc was an aggressive stump of a man. He was an electrician, not a doctor. Doc was just a nickname. He said he had to see me and pulled one aside. I fully expected him to say some nice things, like, "I'm happy my son is in your program. You're doing a good job." Something like that.

"I'm unhappy about some things," he began. It stunned me.

"What are you unhappy about, Doc?"

"Well, I sent my boy to you two years ago, and you and I talked about hair and dress and things like that. You were very much in favor of short hair. And then you let Monte grow his hair way down over his ears last summer, and I didn't appreciate that at all."

"Doc," I argued. "It was out of season."

"Out of season is no reason," he said in rhyme. "But the thing I'm really upset about is you know where Monte was raised and what community he was raised in. Then the first thing you do is make him room with one of those coloreds."

Monte and David Thompson were roommates.

I said, "Doc, David is a fine young man, and he and Monte are best of friends."

"I don't care," Doc replied. "I just didn't expect that to happen when I sent my boy to you. When we sat down and had long, tough discussions about where Monte should go to school—"

I interrupted him right there. "Wait a minute, Doc," I said. "I hear what you're saying, but Monte Towe had one other scholarship offer out of high school, and that was Indiana Central. You didn't have a tough time making a decision on that."

I insert this incident to paint a picture of the racial mind-set in Converse. Doc's attitude was typical of others in Converse and, for that matter, just about every other rural Indiana town at the time. To bring in David Thompson and a couple of other blacks to Monte Towe Day caused more than a few of the old homesteaders to swallow hard.

So George Smith, emcee, began by extolling the virtues of Monte, who in addition to his basketball exploits had quarterbacked an undefeated football team in high school and was an outstanding baseball player. When Monte got up for his response, he mainly talked about David. He talked about what a fine person David was and how close they were. He called David to the podium, and they embraced. You could sense Converse's tough outer shell peeling away, its heart beginning to melt.

David took the microphone and started talking about Monte and Converse. He said, "Monte talks about Converse and you people all the time—what wonderful people you are. I've been looking forward to this chance to come here and meet you. You're better than he said you were. I can now see why Monte has so much affection for people."

The hog barn became deathly silent. Tear ducts were straining at their "hinges." Even ole Hard Ass here was beginning to water up. David concluded with a few more touching salutes to Monte and Converse, and the two of them embraced again, tears streaking down Monte's face.

George Smith was a mess. He began to cry, and his notes were getting all out of order, which wasn't what he had in mind at all.

It was one of the most emotional scenes I can recall. My father was in the audience. Be advised that he was George Wallace North. It disturbed him greatly that his son coached the first black athlete in North Carolina State history and hired the first black assistant coach. We got into such heated arguments about integrated athletics that we finally agreed not to discuss it.

But when the presentation was over, my father was so moved and so impressed that he approached David Thompson with the intention of expressing his feelings. I happened to be standing next to David when my dad walked up. I didn't know what to expect. It used to make me nervous just to see him around David or any of my other black players.

He extended his hand to David and said, "What a fine moment that was. It moved everybody."

David was a very perceptive young man. He could smell a racist, but he wasn't too tough with my father. David clasped my dad's hand in a two-handed soul shake and wouldn't let go. He was "sawing wood," and my dad's head was spinning around to see if anybody was looking.

We wound up at my parents' house for the evening meal to conclude what was a warm, emotional, landmark day in rural Indiana. It was so full of love that even the animals seemed to sense what had happened. My father had a large German police dog named Drex, who would not allow a black person on our property. And yet we were going to have the evening meal at my folks' house. I was concerned that Drex was going to be the only one eating and that his main course might be David Thompson and the other blacks in our group.

When we arrived, Drex was loose, but he never left the back porch. There's no other explanation than Drex sensed these were good people. He acted like nobody else was on the property. I had never seen anything like it.

Years later, David Thompson commented on the day. "I had talked to Monte about his high school team and knew there were no black players on his team and not many in the town. So I knew what to expect. Some of us were pretty skeptical at first, but they treated us very nice. They were a little standoffish at first, but after they met us and saw how close we were on the team and how much we cared for one another, we had no problems at all."

The first time I met Livingston Chatman, I could tell that he was intelligent and that education was important to him. He not only let you know it, the people advising him let you know it. An insurance man named Archie Smith was an adviser for Livingston in his hometown of Lakeland, Florida. The black community there was very proud of Livingston, and during the recruiting process, Smith confided that he wanted him to go with us at the University of Florida. "I think he's the kind of kid who could be student body president his senior year," he said.

So that was Livingston. He arrived as a Florida freshman in 1987 carrying impressive credentials, but I had a difficult time with him on the basketball floor from day one. He was filled with a resentment of some kind. I couldn't say things in the right way for him. I couldn't give him advice, couldn't critique him. Everything I said ended up twisted and misconstrued to where I was being unfair to him. I had phone call after phone call from his mother, chewing me out. Though she wouldn't admit it, I could tell from the things she'd say that she had just talked to Livingston about some incident in practice, the previous day.

She once said, "Your offense doesn't have any continuity and doesn't have enough options." Well, I knew *that* wasn't her talking. I'd go back to Livingston, and he would act surprised that she had called. That went on for a year.

At the outset of his sophomore season, we moved him to the small forward spot, something he had wanted badly. When we recruited him, I told him he would have to play inside at power forward for us as a freshman, but then could probably move out on the wing position, which would probably be his best shot at realizing his dream of playing in the NBA. At his height, just a little over six feet, six inches, he wasn't going to be a power forward in the NBA. So as a sophomore we moved him outside, where he could shoot from the perimeter and learn to put the ball on the floor.

But again, we had the same problems. At the new position I was having to coach him a little more because he was on the perimeter looking in, instead of being inside with his back to the basket. More constructive criticism, more advice. He resented it, and the Great Chatman Barrier grew steadily higher.

One November day not long before our first game that season, I kept him there in the middle of the practice court in the O'Connell Center after his teammates had gone to the showers. "I'm tired of this. I don't want to go through any more of it. We've been through more than a year of it now," I began.

"What do you mean?" he asked.

"Your resentment of me," I said. "You won't let me help you. You won't let me advise you. I don't dare criticize you because if I do, you fall apart."

He was very aloof. "That's not true," he said, defiance in his voice.

"It *is* true, and you know it is," I insisted and went for the jugular of this problem. "I think the trouble is you don't like me because I'm white. You haven't given me a chance because I'm white. I'm surprised at that because we try to conduct a program here that is colorless. I don't think color has ever been a factor here from the coaches' point of view."

A look of shock spread across Livingston's face, and he vehemently refuted what he was hearing.

I told him it was showing up on trips with comments like, "Well, y'all don't understand because you're not black."

I told him what Archie Smith said about student-body president. "You're that kind of leader. You can stop this," I said. "I'm not saying you're responsible for it, but you can stop it."

Whatever the explanation, we struck a nerve and it *was* black-and-white. Until it was confronted and put behind us, we were going nowhere. We were there at least a half-hour, going at it pretty good. He started to walk away a couple of times, but I'd say, "No, just stay here while nobody else is around, and let's deal with this."

Finally, his arms fell by his side, and he softened. I could see him changing right before my eyes. From that instant on, he and I developed a wonderful working relationship.

I don't want to be too hard on him. Livingston had an arrogant tinge to his personality, but he started answering me and contributing, instead of making me force him to answer. We started having real conversations about things that were problems for us.

If you were ever going to have a falling apart with a kid, the conditions were perfect for it that season. We lost seven of our first twelve games, but instead of falling apart, we became closer. By the end of the year, when we won the regular season SEC title for the first time in Florida's basketball history, we had a wonderful relationship. I liked Livingston. I knew I would.

Livingston had what Dr. Pete Indelicato, Florida's team orthopedic, said were "the knees of a hundred-year-old man. I really don't know if he'll make it through a college career or not."

We had to work this out. We would have been fooling ourselves if we thought Livingston Chatman was going to be able to go through what we considered a normal practice and still have something left for games, but we weren't able to work it out until we started communicating. He knew how much he could do in practice and would protect himself when he felt pain. He might not go full speed on a sprint, or he would take himself out of a scrimmage. But I didn't realize why, and I'd get upset that he seemed to be dogging it in practice, even giving the appearance that I had created a double standard for him.

After we connected, he understood why this was creating a problem between me and the other players. And I came to understand his problems—that he wasn't goofing off or taking advantage of us. The plan we worked out was that I wouldn't overwork him, but he would have to go all-out while he was on the floor and in every way possible let his teammates know he wasn't getting special treatment. I would find reasons to play him shorter periods and hold him out of sprints.

Proof to me that Livingston and I had developed a productive bond came through his mother. She is a short, stocky woman. When she talks, she communicates. When she was upset, I always knew how upset she was and what she was upset about. We were getting ready to go into his junior year and Livingston and I had come to our agreement about how to get the most out of him so he could get in the best shape possible and still protect his knees. We had an understanding that if he had a knee problem, we weren't going to make a public issue of it. He didn't want that. He wanted to keep the pro doors open and not have people think he had knees that wouldn't allow him to play beyond college.

Right after Livingston and I had come to our agreement, had had one of his knees scoped to be sure it would stand up through the season. His mother was on campus at the time, and I took her up to Livingston's room on the third floor of Yon Hall, the athletic dorm. For some reason, I remember she wore gray slacks that day and looked especially nice.

Livingston was lying in bed, and we all chatted a few minutes. When Mrs. Chatman and I stepped out into the hall, she said to me, "You know, Coach, you and I have had our differences. But I believe you care about Livingston. I believe you *do* want to do what's best for him and that you *will* do what's best for him."

I knew then that Livingston and I had turned the corner. Livingston shared everything with his mother.

In the beginning, she resented Dwyane Schintzius, Livingston's seven-foot, two-inch teammate. When we played Stanford in Orlando Arena during Livingston's sophomore season, she stopped by the press table and laid into David Steele, our radio play-by-play man. Poor David was in the middle of his postgame wrap-up when she grabbed his arm and started blasting him. "All you do is talk about that big white guy. You never talk about my son," she railed. David frantically made hand signs to show her he was on the air, but she didn't slow up.

Sometimes she would call me at home, and when I couldn't reason with her, I'd finally just say, "I don't need this," and hang up. Then, quite unexpectedly, she called me at home one evening just before Livingston's junior year and said, "Coach, you and I haven't always agreed, but I just wanted to tell you I really appreciate you and I know you like my son and want what's best for him." It made me feel so good for her to say that.

When the barrier between us fell, it fell completely, but such things take time to work out. I think a lot of Livingston's problems during the disastrous 1989-90 season under interim Coach Don DeVoe was that he never got over having the coaching staff he trusted jerked out from under him.

Most great athletes are difficult to coach. They don't want to be told they're doing something wrong, that there is a better way to do something than the way they're doing it. Most of them have large egos, and when you get all the problems worked out with a David

Thompson, Livingston Chatman, Dwayne Schintzius, or Tom Burleson, then you have a wonderful relationship, better than you can imagine. In the process, if you build another little bridge between the races, that makes it all the sweeter.

For those of us in coaching who made the transition from basically all-white programs, the education stretched far beyond the mere abolition of Arthur Murray offensive schemes: one step here, dribble, two steps there, pirouette, shoot. There were language adjustments, personal grooming discoveries, and even exciting recruiting forays into parts of town we never had visited.

Everett Case, my coach at North Carolina State, routinely referred to his team as "my boys." In high school I devoured the comments of one of Indiana's fairly well-known coaches, a guy named Knute Rockne, who regularly said, "my boys" this and "my boys" that. Obviously, I was in for a terminology transplant after our program integrated.

I can't recall exactly which player it was, but after a certain press conference one of the first black kids I coached at State came in and said, "Coach, I've got to tell you something. Calling us 'boys' is going to cause some trouble. Black players will resent that." I was a little defensive and debated it with him a moment, but I could see it was a genuine concern.

The irony of that term came to light at our dinner table one night when my son Michael, then about twelve years old, listened intently as I told about referring to players as "my boys." Michael looked up with the saddest eyes and said, "Daddy, I thought *I* was your boy."

I also had a habit of underscoring a point by adding, "And that's in spades." David Thompson pulled me aside on that one, chuckling to keep his admonishment friendly but pointed enough to let me know he meant it, uh, in spades.

I suppose my course in becoming racially bilingual wasn't completed, however, until a session with the parents of Ronnie Montgomery, a black guard on our Florida team near the end of my career. We had a problem with Ronnie in his sophomore year. Usually, freshmen are so overwhelmed with the whole new situation and with being where they are, they don't get into too much trouble in terms of socializing. But in their sophomore year, they start feeling their oats, spreading their wings.

Ronnie had a thing while he was at Florida: he wanted to do

everything that Vernon Maxwell did. If Vernon cut class, Ronnie was going to cut class. If Vernon lived with a girl for a week or two, sneaking out after hours, ditto for Ronnie. When he was caught, his defense always was, "Well, I'm just doing what Vernon did."

With the campus located in his hometown, Vernon had a lot of social opportunities even in his first year. He already knew the girls around town. Being from Jacksonville, Ronnie didn't have that advantage as a freshman, but he did all he could to make up for lost time as a sophomore. He hooked up with a young lady and was practically living with her. His academics began to suffer. So did his basketball.

Unable to get through to him, I called his parents and asked them to drive over on a Sunday to meet with Ronnie and me. Mr. Mongtomery was a mechanic who worked at a Ford plant, and at the time there was talk about the possibility of the plant closing or relocating.

We sat down, and I laid out the problem: Ronnie was simply spending too much time and energy on his relationship with the girl. I said I wasn't objecting to his being intimate with a girl, acknowledging that was his personal life. "But when it starts interfering with his academic life and interfering with his basketball," I said, "then I feel I have an obligation to step in."

Ronnie kept jumping in to say, "Vernon this" and "Vernon that." I said we weren't talking about Vernon. We were talking about Ronnie Montgomery.

Mr. Montgomery observed the heated discussion very quietly and intently. I had told him I couldn't get Ronnie to understand my concerns, and once he grasped the situation, he broke in.

"Ronnie, listen to me," he said evenly. "Coach don't care what you do with your Jonathan. He don't care if you stick your Jonathan in a mule! Do you understand, son?"

I almost fell off my chair.

"He wants you to go to class and play the kind of basketball that you can," Mr. Montgomery continued, deadly serious. All I could think about was "Jonathan." I was shaking with laughter.

"Son, you're gonna wind up doing just what I'm doing," he railed on. "You're gonna wind up working for somebody. They're gonna talk about movin' the plant, and you're gonna be out of a job!"

Counselors with a wall full of degrees couldn't have put it in more understandable terms. That meeting was one of my most meaningful experiences in working with parents and a son who was going through the throes of spreading his wings a little too much.

I retooled my tongue, but I have been a little slower on certain other concessions. I would discover that to the black student-athlete, head dress is very important. There is nothing wrong with that. But to me, there are some places that you don't wear a hat: on an airplane, in a restaurant, in an office. Maybe I was wrong on this, but when players came into our office, I asked them to remove their hats. I have been accused of clinging to some old-fashioned philosophies, but I just thought this was a sign of respect that would reflect positively on the player.

We played in Salt Lake City in the 1988 NCAA tournament, and former Celtics great Bill Russell, then the Sacramento general manager, was staying in the same hotel. My team came down for a pregame meal in an area set aside in the main dining room. While my guys were eating, in walked Russell, touching off a rash of rubbernecking. He was by himself, and he was wearing a cap, one of those floppy, Ben Hogan-type caps. He sat down, ordered his food, and ate without ever taking his cap off.

I'm not picking on Bill Russell, but suddenly I had a problem. I thought I had pretty well gotten through to our kids, but now it was, "Why can't I wear my hat in the restaurant when Bill Russell wears his?" Here was a national figure and role model bent over his plate of food with a cap still on his head.

That bothered me. I think these are things these young people—black or white—can do that will make the public receive them more positively. I think how they act and carry themselves in public places is very important in reflecting favorably on them, their families, their schools, and college basketball in general.

When Phil Ford was on campus on his official recruiting visit, my daughter, Leslie, then a student at North Carolina State, and Biff, her boyfriend and now husband, went along for the ride as I showed Phil the campus. I don't think I've ever been as surprised in my life as when Phil asked, "How would you feel if I dated a white girl?"

I blinked and said that was his personal choice, but I warned that it would be creating problems at that time and place. I related that I had had black players who did date white girls. David Thompson had.

Then he said, "Well, what would you say if I dated your daughter?"

Fortunately, I didn't hit a parked car. I stammered something about that being up to Phil and my daughter. "But she would certainly have to discuss it with me," I added. "I can't sit here and tell you what would happen. We're talking about personal and intimate things that you don't make casual and quick decisions about. We'd have to talk about it."

That was one of the few times I was totally unprepared to give a prospect an answer to a question. Ford wound up at North Carolina and became an All-American.

Many of our fans and prominent boosters had a more difficult time with all of this than I did. I had calls from boosters saying they wanted State to "be known as a predominantly white basketball program." Early on, some urged me to adopt what they called the "Dean Smith system," which suggested that Dean had an unspoken policy of never having more blacks than whites on the floor at the same time. I never saw any evidence that Dean had such a policy, but that was the kind of undercurrent that went on during the early stages of integrating the team.

Even something like a knee operation would draw out racial overtones. David Thompson sustained a knee injury as a sophomore and was to undergo surgery right after the season. This was before arthroscopic surgery; back then, they did the big cut, a genuine operation with oak leaf clusters.

I gave no thought to who would do the operation. It didn't enter my mind that there would be a problem with who did it, but our team's orthopedic surgeon was an elderly guy named Gus Harer. Harer believed to be a racist of the first order. Well, all of a sudden we started getting phone calls—from the black leaders in the community, from a group of nurses, from lots of people all saying we should not allow Gus Harer to perform this operation.

A classy black doctor in town named George Debnam led the protest, saying the operation shouldn't be performed by Gus Harer and maybe not at all. "You're going to commit on him the same kind of genocide they committed on Gayle Sayers," he warned darkly. "They're going to take him in there and ruin another great young black athlete under the knife."

When the time for the operation came around, it had become one of the most celebrated surgical procedures this side of Christine Jorgenson. I was in the waiting room at Wake Memorial Hospital. My wife was there; the rest of the staff was there. Throughout all of this, I felt I should talk to David about the questions being raised, but he wasn't concerned at all. David was an unusual young man. He had confidence and faith in everybody. The surgery had to be done, and he didn't question the qualifications of the people who were responsible.

Gus Harer did the honors, but four or five other doctors were with him. Everybody was checking everybody. Eventually, George Edwards, another orthopedic surgeon, came out holding a little glass jar containing David's torn cartilage. "We struck oil," he said.

The operation was in May, and by August we were in practice for the World University Games. David played, and I was an assistant coach on the team. He never had any swelling throughout the practices and games, which were played in Moscow. We made the long flight home, and I went directly to the office to catch up on a few things. When a friend dropped by and asked how David's knee had held up, I joked that I was thinking about having the whole team operated on if this was the way it would affect them. I recounted that David didn't miss a practice and usually stayed late, working on his own.

"I know what you mean," my friend said. "I just left the gym, and David is over there shooting baskets."

My biggest mistake in the transition to integration came long before it even began. In the early sixties Joan and I attended a cocktail party where the guest of honor was Jesse Helms. I didn't know Jesse Helms from Adam's house cat. He was a local television celebrity in Raleigh who made a name for himself, as I later found out, for his racist editorials for WRAL-TV, Channel 5. At this party, the talk was of him running for the Senate, which seemed a little far-fetched to me. I didn't think he was that impressive. But I was not paying attention to what was happening outside of basketball, and I was in the house when they made the decision for Jesse to run. He ran and won.

When it came time for him to run for reelection, I was in Chicago early one morning boarding a plane to Raleigh. On the same plane, up in first class, was Jesse Helms. He came back in the coach section and sat down with me, and we talked all the way to Raleigh. I was flattered that a senator came back to talk to me. We talked a little basketball, and then we got into what he was doing in Congress.

Shortly thereafter, a young man came to me and asked if I would be willing to sign a fund-raising letter on behalf of Jesse Helms. He said the letter would go to the residents of McGregor Downs Country Club, a rather upscale residential area on the outskirts of Raleigh. I was a member, but I was not a resident of McGregor Downs.

I didn't think a thing about it. "Well, sure. I'd be glad to do that," I said.

All hell broke loose after I signed that letter. Blacks, liberals, and other civil rights advocates couldn't understand how a David Thompson could play for Norman Sloan when he was supporting a racist like Jesse Helms.

A great black prospect named Buck Williams was graduating from Rocky Mount High School at the time. His coach called me and said that if I had any inclination of trying to recruit Buck Williams, I could forget it. I wouldn't even get an interview, he vowed. The coach, a black man himself, explained that he always made it a point to listen to Jesse Helms's editorials on Channel 5 just so he could hate the man all the more.

For awhile Claude Sitton, editor of the Raleigh *News and Observer,* carried an editorial at least once a week criticizing me for supporting Jesse Helms. How could I be in the business I was—recruiting young black men—when I supported a man whose racism is known to the world?

It was one of those things I hadn't even thought about.

But from that day on I would think about it every time I recruited against someone like Georgetown's John Thompson. John was faithful in bringing it up. I don't know how much it hurt us, but I do know I didn't get a chance to talk to Buck Williams, who ended up going to Maryland.

We had better luck fending off John Thompson's Helms–Sloan ticket in the 1979 recruitment of Thurl Bailey and two other Washington, D. C., All-Metro prep stars who became the nucleus for Jimmy Valvano's 1983 national championship team at State. Thurl, who now plays with the Utah Jazz, was a tremendous young man whose family was originally from North Carolina.

Thompson made up his mind that he wanted Thurl, and when John Thompson recruits, he puts everything on a racial level. He makes it clear what he does to help blacks as opposed to what that white coach over there is doing to help blacks. He dredged up the Jesse Helms thing ten years after the fact and accused me of being a racist. When that didn't work, he vowed that if Thurl didn't sign with Georgetown, John would see to it that he would never play on any of our national teams. I can't really say if John followed up on that, but it struck me as curious that an outstanding player like Thurl never was selected to play on any national teams.

Early in Thurl's freshman year, there was a distasteful incident involving a few of our own yokels. They would lean over the front of the upper deck and dump popcorn on Thurl's parents, while yelling racial taunts. We had to threaten to move the offenders to remote seats to get them to stop.

In Thurl's sophomore year in a game at Wake Forest, another group of "fine Americans" was leaning over a railing, taunting Thurl's parents. His parents managed to ignore the racial epithets until one of the jerks actually reached down and began poking Mr. Bailey. He put the guy in a headlock and yanked him down over the railing. The game had to be stopped.

That was a terrible embarrassment for all of us. We were busy telling parents not to pay any attention to what John Thompson was saying, that their sons were going to be in a fine, healthy situation even in Raleigh, North Carolina. But all the while, the Baileys were having to fend off the rednecks.

Charles ("Hawkeye") Whitney used to get up and catch a bus at 5:30 in the morning to make his way across Washington, D. C., to DeMatha High School. The first time Hawkeye and I drove down Martin Luther King Drive toward his home, I realized we were getting deeper and deeper into the projects. A sweet kid and fine young player, Hawkeye sensed my discomfort and said, "You're all right, Coach. You're with me."

"Hawkeye, what would the situation be if I were by myself?" I asked.

"Coach, I wouldn't recommend that you come back here by yourself."

Finally, we pulled up in front of Hawkeye's apartment building. I never lock my car; my wife has to remind me to do so all the time. Stealing is something that is foreign to me, so I never expect anybody to steal from me. As we started inside, Hawkeye said, "Wait a minute, Coach. Better lock your car."

Several children of all ages were outside playing and milling around. Hawkeye patted some of them on the head and said, "This is Coach Sloan from North Carolina State." He introduced me to several of them, and each was anxious to show he had a special relationship with Hawkeye. "I'm Hawkeye's cousin." Or "I'm Hawkeye's friend." And so forth.

Just as we reached the front door of his apartment, we met a teen-age girl who looked to be about seven or eight months pregnant. Hawkeye didn't say anything about her, but she said, "Hey, Coach, I'm Hawkeye's girlfriend—ain't I, Hawkeye?"

Inside, the walls were crawling with cockroaches, but Hawkeye and his family were so used to it, they hardly seemed to notice. I sat there terribly uncomfortable. I had been in David Thompson's house, which was a converted barn or animal shelter out from Shelby, North Carolina. Its walls were unfinished, leaving the studs exposed, but it was clean. The Thompsons were clean, proud people.

But in Hawk's house in D. C., my skin crawled. I wondered how those people kept coming back to that day after day. Hawk must have been relieved to get on the bus and go across town to school.

In spring 1980, my first visit to Liberty City, the area of Miami infamous for the race riots and other disturbances, was to recruit a player named Vernon Delancy. I had just returned to Florida, and Vernon was the first player we tried to recruit. The best unsigned talent in the state, Vernon visited the campus but wanted me to come to his home and meet his mother before he signed.

So I flew to Miami and, for some reason, had the impression we were going to where Vernon's mother worked. The riots were over with, but evidence of the aftermath was strong. Smoke rose from smoldering, burned-out buildings, and people stood around in groups watching police patrols rumble by. As we drove to Vernon's house, I realized we were in the heart of Liberty City. We were in a big, two-toned Mercury Grand Marquis that I had rented at Miami Airport. I remember it because the farther we went, the more I wanted it to be a smaller, unpretentious car. Maybe something rusting with a shattered window. I began to sweat profusely.

The building next to Vernon's apartment house had burned down, and across the street a group of about fifteen people glared at me. It occurred to me that they probably thought I was a cop who had arrested him. I figured I could be in deep trouble.

"Vernon, are we going to be all right?" I asked.

He repeated basically the same thing Hawkeye had said a few years earlier in the D.C. ghetto. As long as I was with him, I was okay. But when we stopped the car, he jumped out, saying he would be right back. He ran into an apartment house, leaving me in the car by myself with those people standing across the street, all looking larger and angrier. All kinds of thoughts ran through my mind about what they might do and who they might think I was. I started reflecting on the absurd lengths coaches go through to recruit outstanding prospects. I knew it was crazy for me to be there like that. People were being killed in Liberty City. It was a mess down there at the time.

Vernon soon came to the front door and told me to come in. It must have been only thirty or forty feet from the car to the door, but I was scared. I had the craziest thought: if I just had a television set to put on my shoulder, they might think I had stolen it out of a store and might accept me. I went in, nervous and upset, but had a wonderful conversation with Vernon's mother. She basically said that whatever he wanted was fine, and she just wanted to be sure that he would be taken care of wherever he went to school.

A short time later, there was another riot in Liberty City, and some poor guy was jerked out of his car and killed. Two days later, Joan was with me on a trip to see Shakey Rodriguez, the coach at Miami Senior High. We were driving on I–95, not quite sure where we were; so I cruised down an off-ramp to call Shakey from a pay phone in a fast-food restaurant. The clientele was all black and ominously silent.

"Coach, where are you?" he asked when I called.

"Just off I–95," I said, "on 79th Avenue at a Wendy's."

In very strong and deliberate tones, he said, "Get the hell out of there as quickly as you can!"

He told me where to go, then call him again. I realized what I had done. I had pulled into a very tense situation and had left my wife sitting in the car by herself. I tried my best to look nonchalant, but the steering wheel kept slipping in my hands.

The racial trouble spots are not always so apparent. Not long after our 1974 championship, I recruited a pair of brothers out of Lebanon, Indiana, Brian and Steve Walker. Lebanon was virtually an all-white town.

Their parents, Bob and Nancy Walker, had dedicated their lives to their two sons. They held them back a year in high school so they could have the advantage of maturity in sports. Because the school system in Lebanon wouldn't allow them to hold their sons back, they sent Brian and Steve to school for one year in Indianapolis, twenty-five miles away, to circumvent the rules. Both made the Indiana high school all-star team that plays the Kentucky all-stars. Brian, a year younger that Steve, was considered the better player, scoring a lot of points in high school, mostly off of steals and fast breaks.

When we were recruiting him, I remember thinking that he had a weak outside shot. When he came into our level of play at NCAA Division I, his shot became a factor. When he was trying to score from the outside, he shot a low percentage. The one thing you don't want is players attempting shots they can't make.

I had to put a damper on his shooting.

Without my knowledge, Bob and Nancy Walker had moved to Raleigh. When I found out about it, I sensed it would be a problem—this intense involvement with their sons' careers. Sure enough, Bob Walker started keeping stats to show me how well his kids did when there was basically a white team on the floor as opposed to how they did when there was a predominantly black lineup in the game. Philosophically, Bob and I had difficulty from day one. When I tried to bring high-percentage efficiency to Brian's game by cutting down on his outside shooting and concentrating more on playmaking, his dad interpreted it as showing partiality to the black players. He intoned that they had a free hand to do the one-on-one things anytime they wanted. Well, they were given a freer hand at that than Brian, but they were better one-on-one players.

Soon the Walkers began having meetings with the white kids on the team, questioning my coaching tactics and substitution patterns. At the end of the year, the Walkers moved Steve and Brian back to Indiana. They went to Purdue, where Brian averaged two points per game. We had to rebuild the team because two other white players confused by the Walkers also transferred.

When I returned for my second coaching stint in Florida, a state that considers itself more liberal and contemporary in matters of race relations, I ran into an unexpected kind of racial problem. Black parents could attend games with little concern about fending off popcorn or insults, and no one seemed to be counting the number of black players on the floor. But out on the recruiting trail, coaches of formerly all-white southern universities were starting to pay for the years of inattention to homegrown black talent.

The Big Ten had developed a strong connection in South Florida. Minnesota, Illinois, and Michigan, in particular, had pipelines into that area because of all the years that they had recruited blacks in football and basketball before the University of Florida and other prominent Dixie schools joined the twentieth century. The Big Ten schools had picked off great Florida players with little or no effort, and now many of those players had finished their pro careers and had returned home to start businesses. They became black role models in many of the Florida cities and towns. So when a gifted youngster came along in, say, West Palm Beach or Fort Lauderdale, and looked for guidance, his local hero told him the only place to go was Minnesota or Illinois or Michigan. It was a powerful force to combat in recruiting.

A lot of the veterans were still angry that Florida and other schools had dragged their feet so long in even making an attempt to integrate. The mother of Renaldo Garcia, a Tampa guard we signed in 1987, was a stickler on that point. Her older son had gone to Tuskegee, a black college in Alabama, and she wanted me to explain to her why I thought it would be better for Renaldo to go to Florida than to some well-known black institution. Frankly, I didn't have a very good answer. What could I say without insulting her pride in black schools? I couldn't dare say anything about the quality of education at one school over the other. I had to rely on the importance of Renaldo's friends and family being close to him and being able to give him support.

I know we lost Derek Harper to Illinois and Richard Rellford to Michigan because of those sentiments. We didn't have a chance with them. Anthony Carter, the great football wideout from Riviera Beach, also went to Michigan.

In one area of South Florida, there was a group called the Black Coalition that included a black police chief and some successful white people, and I made it a point to meet with some of them. The Black Coalition was formed to advise these kids on where to go to school, and they made it abundantly clear that the white schools had snubbed the black community for years and that black students had been denied the opportunity to go to law school or medical school in the state. The resentment was strong, and it still is in some places.

CHAPTER 7

Drugs and Dunks

Drugs are a nightmare.

It took some time for that cold and simple truth to infiltrate this thick noggin, and it took a couple of tragic situations to awaken me to the stark reality of what chemical abuse can do to athletes and their relationships with coaches, teammates, and family.

If someone had told me early in my career how serious a problem drugs would become in college athletics, I would have said they were hallucinating. I never would have believed it could have gotten to such a heartbreaking state that so many programs would have to cope with drug nightmares similar to what we encountered at Florida during my second tenure there.

We now have drug testing in high school. An Olympic sprint champ is disqualified. The drug disaster has exploded beyond the point of understanding. I never could have anticipated what has happened in society in general and in athletics in particular.

Does anyone honestly believe that a coach doesn't care if his players are on drugs? Once a coach fully appreciates the implications, he fights it every day, as much as if the kids were his own flesh and blood. I might have reached that point earlier if I had only listened to Willis Casey.

Willis was the swimming coach and assistant athletic director at North Carolina State when I ended my first coaching stint at Florida to return as basketball coach at my alma mater. Casey had outstanding swimmers and traveled to meets all over the country, indeed, all over the world. In a casual office discussion one day, he brought up the problem drugs were becoming in athletics on the

West Coast. My reaction was that we didn't have that problem at North Carolina State and never would.

In 1969, three years after I became coach at State, Roy Clogston resigned as athletic director and the hunt was on for his successor. I was on a speaking tour with the Wolfpack Club early that summer when I was given a message to return to the campus immediately and get in touch with the school chancellor, Dr. John Caldwell. He wanted to offer me the athletic director's job. I accepted it. We never discussed whether I could continue to coach or not, but soon it became obvious that he didn't intend for me to have the dual role. He wanted me to be just the athletic director. It was Friday, and they were planning a press conference on the following Tuesday.

Over the weekend, Joan and I were absolutely miserable. We both determined we didn't want to do this; we wanted to stay in coaching. So I went to Dr. Caldwell's house that Sunday morning to tell him I didn't want to be the athletic director and to give him the reasons why. He said he understood and appreciated me coming to him ahead of time. I asked who he planned to name. They had been considering Doug Weaver from Georgia Tech. He was a fine candidate, but I wanted to see Willis Casey in the position.

Roy Clogston and Casey didn't get along, and Clogston had shot him out of the saddle. I said, "Dr. Caldwell, what's wrong with Willis Casey?" He mentioned a couple of things—Willis was having family problems and had gone through a divorce not long before this. I said, "Everybody knows Willis can do the job. Is it possible that Roy has poisoned your mind against Willis?"

John Caldwell was a Christian Scientist, so that kind of statement was really significant to him. He paused and said, "You know, that's entirely possible."

We chatted on about Willis for another ten minutes, and Dr. Caldwell rose from his chair. I took that as a signal to leave and got up. He walked over and put his arm on my shoulder and said, "You know what we've just done? We just named Willis Casey as athletic director."

Two of the reasons I turned down the athletic director's job to stay in coaching were Bobby Heuts and Paul Coder, two exceptional young players just starting their careers at State. I thought they might even give us our first national championship. Instead, they gave me my first brush with the drug culture that was just starting to invade America's locker rooms.

The Coder-Heuts incident is one of the hardest parts of doing this book, for Joan and for me. I think the world of Bobby Heuts. He and his wife, Cindi, are close friends with Leslie and Biff Nichols, our daughter and son-in-law. But this story needs to be told. It needs to be told, even if he was a good kid and has become a fine and prominent citizen with a responsible job.

Coder was a hulking six-foot, nine-inch, center from just outside Washington, D. C., who led our 1968—69 freshman team with points and 12.6 rebounds per game. Heuts, a six-foot, nine-inch forward from Bloom Township High School near Chicago, led our freshmen in rebounding the next year.

We won the ACC in Coder's sophomore year, struggled through extensive graduation losses the next season, and then appeared to be set for another title run in the fall of 1971 with a front line that included Coder as a senior and team captain, Heuts as a junior, and seven-foot, four-inch, Tom Burleson as a sophomore.

Talk about amphetamines, or "uppers," would come up in conversation, but that was the extent of it. Marijuana was something used by hippies, not athletes, and the more serious drugs like cocaine and heroin were in another galaxy from Raleigh, North Carolina.

On Monday morning, September 23, 1971, I received a thunderclap call. I was needed at the city jail; Coder and Heuts were being detained there for possession of marijuana. I rushed to the jail and was standing beside them when the police went through their personal effects.

There is a place adjacent to the State campus called the College Inn, which is now the athletic dorm. It was common knowledge that marijuana was being grown in the field behind the College Inn. We found out that several players on the football team and these two on the basketball team were getting together to smoke pot. Some were doing amphetamines.

Bob and I were pretty close. When I plucked him out of jail, I began lecturing him on the seriousness of what he had done. He was adamant that I was out of step, that in five years marijuana would be sold over the counter in the drug store. I said, "Bob, I don't think you're right. But even if you were, right now it's against the law. You're breaking the law."

The front page of the Raleigh *News and Observer* the next morning confirmed that in cold, black type:

Two members of the North Carolina State University basketball

> team, one the team captain, were arrested Monday by Raleigh police in felony warrants charging possession of marijuana.
>
> Arrested were Paul Coder, the 6 foot 9 senior center and team captain, and Bob Heuts, a 6 foot 7 forward who started some games for the Wolfpack last season.
>
> Detective Lt. E. L. Randolph told a reporter Coder and Heuts were apprehended by police in Pullen Park, adjacent to the NCSU campus.
>
> Randolph said about five ounces of marijuana were found in a 1964 Ford registered to Norman Bruce Coder, and on the two students. Possession of one gram or more constitutes a felony in this state. . . .

So much for the innocence of intercollegiate athletics. I went to Earle Edwards, the State football coach, to tell him there were guys on his football team involved. His attitude was what mine had been. "I don't believe you," he responded.

The matter became a celebrated case in Raleigh and throughout the Carolinas. Claude Sitton, who had come to Raleigh from the *New York Times* to become editor of the *News and Observer,* took a hard-line stand against any leniency toward Coder and Heuts. In editorials he hammered it and hammered it. I went down to the newspaper's office to talk to him about his position, but to no avail.

"You have to realize, Coach Sloan," Sitton told me, "this is a Carolina paper." Carolina, as in the University of North Carolina, the alma mater of just about every member of the Daniels family that owned the *News and Observer.*

After several campus meetings, it was decided to have the two players voluntarily withdraw from the team until they were cleared. The day of the opening game of the season, I had gone to the YMCA to get a rubdown and steam, which was my standard practice. I was on a rubdown table when one of the attendants handed me the phone. The news was that Judge George Bason had just thrown the case out of court for illegal search.

Naturally, reporters came scurrying to me to ask if Coder and Heuts were going to be allowed to play. I talked to Willis and Dr. Caldwell, and we decided that if we suspended them, we would be prejudicing their case. So we decided to let them play.

Indignant over our decision, Sitton called his staff together and decreed that every story about North Carolina State basketball the rest of that season would have to include a disclaimer noting that Coder and Heuts had been arrested and charged with possession of marijuana.

The local prosecutor, W. G. Ransdell, Jr., then took the case before the grand jury and obtained an indictment against the two players. Now I was stuck. We had made a commitment to our players, so we decided not to back down. We would just tough it out. The media started getting on Caldwell, which exposed a soft spot universally typical of college presidents.

Of all the people who can't stand negative press, college presidents are at the top of the list. If the morning paper takes them to task about anything, they're apt to dump their corn flakes in their laps. After a short time, Dr. Caldwell called and said we couldn't continue allowing Coder and Heuts to play. We had to make a change, he said. I argued that we couldn't do that; we had made a commitment. "Are we going to allow Claude Sitton and other people in the media to run this program, or are we going to run it?" I wailed. "We got together and talked about what we were going to do. We did what we thought was right after Judge Bason threw it out. Now they've been indicted, and we decided we were going to tough it out."

Our information was that the case would be postponed and dragged out until sometime after the entire season had been played. We had a lot of conflict over this situation, and it marked the only instance in which I had a strained relationship with Dr. Caldwell.

The situation was aggravated by the fact that Dr. Caldwell's son was having drug problems. "Well, what about these other people who are paying the price, like my son, Andy?" he asked. "My son is out of school, and these guys are not only still in school, but playing basketball."

I hadn't known until that moment that Andy Caldwell had been convicted of possession of marijuana and had been kicked out of school. Dr. Caldwell felt one set of standards was being applied to his son and another was being applied to my players. The difference, of course, was that Andy had been convicted. The players were not guilty unless convicted, but I wasn't smart enough to make that argument at the time.

We finished the season with Coder and Heuts, and the case finally came to trial in June. Pleading guilty, they plea-bargained a suspended sentence, and I wouldn't let Heuts come back for his senior year.

You develop a special relationship with some people after you go through a difficult situation like that. Bobby Heuts is one of them.

Bobby grew greatly from his experience, and Cindi Heuts recently told Joan and me that Bobby has characterized this whole embarrassing incident as "one of the best things that ever happened to me."

Here was a young man from a fine family who was in college during the sixties and got caught up in the student unrest and experimentation of the times. He made a mistake and was severely penalized; he lost his senior season and his scholarship. Today you typically have to be found positive three times on drug tests before being permanently suspended; and after suspension, a school will pay an athlete's expenses to drug rehab facilities and, in most cases, keep him on scholarship. That is true at the University of Florida.

Bobby Heuts was banished after one mistake that proved a turning point in his life.

I don't know that we've made progress. You read every day about Lawrence Taylor or some other prominent athlete being given another chance. We keep bringing them back for second and third chances. There was such a difference in the attitude at that earlier time when I hit Bobby Heuts with such finality over marijuana, as compared to how we've become such forgiving bleeding hearts today in cases involving repeated abuse of drugs that are far more deadly.

Later in this chapter, we'll get into the case of Vernon Maxwell and the efforts to save him from himself. Yet, to this day, he blasts Florida and the coaching staff, the people who gave him the repeated chances that Heuts didn't have. Maxwell busted out of two rehabs and was found positive three or four times, and yet he doesn't appreciate a thing anyone did to help him.

Seeing former players mature and become successful in life is the most gratifying part of coaching. I'm very proud of Bobby Heuts.

David Thompson, the star player on our 1974 NCAA championship team at North Carolina State, was one of the finest young people I've ever known in my life. In college David was not a problem in the slightest way. He was an absolute model citizen. So when I started getting phone calls from guys like pro coach Hubie Brown telling me David had a serious drug problem, I refused to believe it.

Proof came late one night a few years after David had finished his career at North Carolina State. I was watching television in bed when a drug documentary entitled "Cocaine Connection" came on. Suddenly there before me on the screen was David, baring his heart about his deep-rooted drug addiction. I have never been more stunned in my life. I shook Joan and told her to wake up.

David said he had had a serious problem for a couple of years. He had two beautiful children, but when he woke up each morning he said his first thoughts were not of his children but of cocaine. We knew him as such a wonderful person that until I actually heard him say he had a drug problem, I couldn't accept it.

Broken hearts kept us awake for hours after that television show. Perhaps for the first time, it hit home with me the power and the grip that drugs can hold on a person. If drugs can get to David Thompson, we're all vulnerable. He got caught up in the drug scene as a pro and lost everything: his career, his money, his wife and daughters, his self-respect.

I was with David recently in Charlotte, and it was a terribly emotional experience for me to realize that he is fighting with every fiber of his body to stay sober. With an assist from the expansion Charlotte Hornets, David is making a stirring comeback in the NBA. And in life.

The Hornets gave him a community relations job, putting on clinics, golf outings, speaking to youth groups. He had a relapse, got into alcohol, and started missing work. The Hornets stayed with him and spent fifty thousand dollars to send him out to California to a rehab program similar to Alcoholics Anonymous that deals with both drugs and alcohol. When I joined David and his rehab sponsor for dinner, he told me he was attending as many as three meetings a day as part of the program. His sponsor expressed what a fine person David was and said it was especially tough because of the nature of his job with the Hornets, having to be around drinking because of the cocktail parties that are associated with many aspects of athletics.

Before he fell off the wagon, he had a nice private office. Now he has a little cubby hole. They're giving him a second chance, but he has to earn every step of it. That's the way it has to be.

David talked frankly about his opportunity. I think he wanted to do that. He was driving a small Chevrolet and living in a modest apartment. I admire him for what he is going through. He's having to adjust from the highest of life-styles. He was one of the world's top athletes and commercial properties when he first turned pro. He drove a Mercedes and a BMW, had a huge house, and was the first NBA player to make a million dollars a year. Now he owes

Uncle Sam about a million dollars. It's especially tough on him because he goes to work every day in a business where he sees all these guys making huge salaries, knowing he was a better player than 95 percent of them.

I thought I had had an experience with drugs at North Carolina State with Coder and Heuts. But that was innocent compared to what we walked into at Florida, where serious drugs like cocaine and bona fide dealers were on campus. It was a problem for the entire athletic department.

Athletic director Bill Carr and his staff authorized the school's first drug program for athletes. I'd never been around a drug program or policy before. The policy at North Carolina State was simple: you didn't drink. That was all. We didn't do any testing. I'd never heard of testing.

I'm confident that Carr and his people put a lot of time and thought into the drug program, but I guess it was typical of something you do for the first time. They didn't have many models to go by, and the resulting policy was full of loopholes and inconsistencies. But we did have a policy, and we did test.

Our first year of testing was 1984 when Vernon Maxwell, a guard from Gainesville who would go on to become Florida's all-time leading scorer, was a freshman. We had guys we felt sure had drug problems before that, but we couldn't prove it. We simply knew they had a problem because too much disturbing information was coming from too many different sources.

This, more than anything else, led the athletic department into drug testing. I don't think the intention was as preventive at the outset as it was just trying to nail the situation down so you could say, "Son—or lady—you've got a problem. Let's get some help."

We had a few positives that first year. The policy stated what the action was on the first positive and on the second positive and so forth. But it just wasn't tight and comprehensive. When we first pinned it down, Maxwell's problem involved a fraternity guy who was a dealer. I never understood why, but he gave Maxwell marijuana. Maxwell's girlfriend told me Vernon would get out of bed every morning and go to the guy's fraternity house and smoke a joint.

I asked Gene McDowell, one of our older players, to go talk to Maxwell, to tell him what a mistake he was making. Gene came back and said, "Coach, I didn't have any influence on him." Perhaps this was because Vernon was envious of Gene, who did everything right. Gene went to class; Gene graduated on time; Gene wouldn't do drugs. Vernon used to tell him, "You're Sloan's pet."

At the end of Vernon's freshman year at Florida, he introduced us to the trauma of having to send a kid to a rehabilitation center. We first sent him to a place in Miami. He violated some of the rules, and they sent him home after a week. The next summer, we sent him to another place in Ocala. He violated their rules, and they also sent him home after a week.

By trial and error, Florida's drug policy gradually began to tighten. I think the main thing that happened was a change of attitude on the national level. People started admitting to drug problems. You'd see the people in the NBA and NFL and major league baseball players being suspended and put into rehab. A pub lic mandate emerged to deal seriously and effectively with the problem.

People don't understand how much time and care you really expend when you're working with these kids. I spent a lot of time with Vernon Maxwell: working on skills, working on handling the ball. He always had great speed and great quickness, but the ball didn't always stay with him like it does with great guards, where the ball virtually becomes a part of them. Vernon fought the ball. He was a "pattie." He would "pat" the ball; you have to hammer it. When you dribble the ball, you're actually passing it into the floor. These are things you spend a lot of time on; in the process, you get close to players. Over four years you go through class problems and girlfriend problems. You go through Mom being sick, through a death in the family. Whatever. You become very close to these kids. A lot of people don't understand that.

After the first year of our drug program at Florida, the university upgraded to a full-time director. The man hired to head up our drug program was a former professor named Tom Harrison. I had known him when he was an assistant in counseling education, working under my back-door neighbor, Dr. Joe Wittmer. So I felt Tom and I had a good relationship when he became involved in our drug program, though I had nothing to do with his getting the job.

Under Tom we went to a revised policy with random and more frequent testing, but it was still riddled with loopholes. Earlier, in administering urine tests, we simply gave an athlete a vial and he went in the toilet and closed the door. Soon we started hearing rumors that guys were bringing urine with them, doing this, doing that. We had to tighten up the procedure to the point that somebody actually stood there watching them urinate in their bottles.

I made it very clear from the start that neither I nor any member of my staff was going to stand there and watch our players pee in a bottle. We weren't going to play narcs. That isn't conducive to the kind of relationship we wanted to establish with our players. From day one we established that as coaches we would have nothing to do with the drug program other than to administer the rules when they were violated.

We had a few players who tested positive, but they were warned and it became a one-time thing. But Vernon Maxwell's positives wouldn't go away. These tests prompted us to force Vernon under the threat of suspension into the Miami treatment program. At first he was reluctant to agree. We explained that he had reached the point in our drug program that he either agreed to it or he would have to be suspended from some games. So he went and after he busted out in a week, Tom Harrison showed up and told me we had a problem because Vernon hadn't satisfied the treatment aspect of our program. "I'm going to have to do something to him," Tom said.

I said I understood and made it clear that Vernon had been advised there would be consequences within our departmental drug program if he didn't complete the required rehab. I told Tom it was up to him and Vernon. Tom said he would handle it. I think he put Vernon in a counseling program that summer. Anyway, when Vernon's sophomore season began in the fall of 1985, Tom gave him the green light to play. Tom said Vernon accomplished just as much from the counseling as he would have from actually attending the rehab institution.

But it became apparent that Vernon's situation hadn't improved. After another positive near the end of his sophomore year, they again recommended that he check into the institute. I told them that it wouldn't work.

"Tom, that didn't work the first time," I warned. "I talk to this kid every day. He's not going to stay this time, either. When he comes out, what are you going to do?"

"We'll suspend him," Tom said.

"Why," I asked, "are you going to do something when you know it's a foregone conclusion how it's going to turn out? That doesn't make sense to me. Find some other avenue, or suspend him now."

They sent him back, and Vernon was out within a week. Tom announced he was going to find something else for Vernon to do.

Drugs were at the core of his problems, but Vernon's problems ran the gamut.

After North Carolina State point-shaving allegations broke in 1990, one of the networks dredged up footage of one of the games in question. The clips shown were of Charles Shackleford shooting. It wasn't pretty. Bad games happen, but there are times you wonder.

Vernon Maxwell was Florida's all-time leading scorer—second in the SEC only to Pete Maravich. He could put points on the board, but one of his performances late in his senior year had a fragrance of something between rancid butterbeans and cod liver oil.

In an upset loss to Tennessee at home in the O'Connell Center, Vernon played all twenty minutes of the second half and didn't score a point. It was surprising the number of people who came to me or members of my staff, stumbled around a little bit, and said, "You don't really suppose. . . ."

Many were suspicious that something was funny about Vernon being shut out in a complete half. Amongst ourselves, even we coaches were skeptical.

We had beaten Tennessee by twenty in Knoxville earlier in the season, so naturally we were favored on this night playing at home. With our star player inexplicably unable to make a single point in the second half, we lost, 65–63.

I suppose we'll never know how hard Vernon was trying to score in that second half. What we did find out when we looked into the situation was that Maxwell had been drinking heavily on the day of the game. I know that is true because I personally confronted him the next day. "You realize when you play twenty mintues without scoring, questions will come up. And they have come up. Did you, in effect, dump the game?"

He was very defensive, very indignant. He admitted to the drinking after I told him we had information from some of the other players that he and his buddy, Patrick Aaron, had been drinking that day.

We had had so many problems with Vernon. Throughout his senior year, we were having him tested for drugs four times a week. We had had him on three times a week at the outset of the season, but he got caught doing cocaine. So we went four times a week to eliminate any seventy-two-hour windows. Within that range, you can do cocaine and beat the test. Using diuretics, you can even beat a forty-eight-hour check by washing out your system.

That's when his alcohol problems became very prevalent. He was arrested for having an open container, beating up on his fiancée, getting into fights in bars. The alcohol problem started manifesting itself when his cocaine use had been blocked.

The average fan might want to ask why I didn't know he had been drinking that day. I couldn't smell it. I couldn't see anything unusual, except in the fact that he didn't score a point in the second half. He was quick. He did all the things he usually did, except he couldn't get it in the hole.

After that, I'd had it with Vernon.

When I called him in, I started laying down the law to him. He started that same routine: "No, not me. . . . I wouldn't do that." That only made me angrier.

"This is the last time I'm talking to you," I barked. "This is not a threat. This is a promise. If you have one more drinking problem or anything to do with drugs, I'm going to make three phone calls, and I promise you any pro career you think you have going will be gone."

That statement would come back to haunt me. When he had problems later and they became public, he automatically thought I had blown the whistle to fulfill my promise. All I was trying to do was scare him into going straight. A coach isn't going to intentionally sabotage a player's future, but neither will he go around covering up for a player with lies.

However, I did come as close to lying for him as you can when Spurs Coach Larry Brown had an assistant, Alvin Gentry, call me on NBA draft day 1988 to ask about Vernon's drug use. He set it up for me. Alvin said, "He doesn't have a drug problem, does he, Norm? It's just a recreational thing, right?"

I said, "Yeah, that's right."

Well, that wasn't just close, was it? It was a lie, because it wasn't a recreational thing. Vernon Maxwell had a drug problem with oak leaf clusters. I'm not proud that I told Alvin and Larry Brown what they wanted to hear. A few minutes later, they drafted Maxwell.

When I threatened to ruin Maxwell's pro career, I really struck a nerve. His mother came to see me the next day. We had a good relationship, but she was really angry with me. She was dressed for work. Ironically, she worked for the probation department.

She repeated what I had said to him about making three phone calls. "You mean that, don't you?" she said.

Probably at that point I should have admitted to her I was just trying to scare him, but I didn't want her going back and telling Vernon not to worry about it. So I told her, "You can count on it."

"You would, wouldn't you," she said, "because you're white and he's black."

Now it was my turn to get mad. I jumped up and called Kenny McCraney, a black assistant, into the office. I said, "Kenny, Vernon's mother is laying black-white stuff on me. I don't deserve that."

Kenny began to lecture her about how off base she was by trying to throw up the old racial barrier into our conflict. But the race complaint probably is always going to be there, no matter how wrong it is.

After I went to bat for Vernon with the San Antonio Spurs, I called and found Vernon in a hotel in Miami. I told him of my conversation with Alvin Gentry and my closing words were, "Please, please don't let me down."

Athletes are young men who can make decisions on their own. The cheating by coaches that everybody seems to believe is going on is just not happening. Vernon Maxwell claimed that I gave him thousands of dollars, but my gosh! If I had given him all that money, then why did he need a sports agent?

There had been two or three instances during the last half of his senior year when we were on trips and waiting in an airport and Maxwell would bring out a big roll of money. I saw this myself on two occasions. The third time, our trainer, Tony Sutton, came to me and said, "Coach, I gotta tell you this. This kid is carrying a lot of money. I don't know if there is anything wrong. But I thought you needed to know."

It is important to remember where Maxwell came from. He never had had any means of financial support, but all of a sudden he was flashing a lot of money, wearing expensive warm-up suits, wearing expensive dress suits.

When this happens there are three things that you don't want to think about but which, nevertheless, immediately come to your mind. First, you hope to heaven that he hasn't gotten involved with someone fixing games and gambling. Second, you hope he hasn't been selling drugs. And, finally, you worry about an agent putting a lot of money in his pocket. In this day and time, it makes sense to be concerned about these things, particularly with someone who has a history of being in trouble and suddenly demonstrates signs of having access to a lot of money.

In Vernon's senior year he bought a new car and a brand-new color television set. On the car, we had him and his mother sign a letter, explaining where the money came from and saying that they did not have an agent. As coaches and athletic administrators, that's all we could do. But Vernon couldn't pass off a mysterious "uncle" in Miami or generous "homeboys" as his vague explanation when the Drug Enforcement Administration turned up the heat, pressing him about where he was getting all this money. They strongly suspected it was coming from agents or drug dealing, or both. So instead, Vernon told them I was giving him huge stacks of green. Me. The guy who was asking him the same sticky questions.

It later came out in court that the money—or at least a large portion of it—was from agents he had engaged while he was competing at Florida.

When Bill Arnsparger came aboard as athletic director, I went to him and said, "Bill, this drug program isn't being handled properly. I don't know what Tom is trying to do, but in my opinion Tom Harrison is in over his head. So am I. I don't know how to do this. But I don't think Tom Harrison is capable of handling the program."

"What are you saying?" Bill asked.

"I'm here as the head basketball coach requesting a change in the leadership of our drug program."

"Oh," he said. "I don't agree with that."

"Well, why don't we meet with the athletic department drug committee and talk about it. I think this is a serious matter."

The committee included Dr. Richard Shaara, team physician, Chris Patrick, the head trainer, and Jeremy Foley, associate athletic director. Tom was there and so was I, voicing my objections and concerns. The same problem was happening in football. An end on the team had been in and out of three or four rehab centers. "He's an example of what is going on. We've got another case of this with Vernon Maxwell. I just think this thing isn't being handled properly," I said.

The committee supported Tom 100 percent. And Arnsparger came down hard on me in front of the group.

So I said, "Well, I hope if my ass is ever in a crack that you'll defend me as strong as you have Tom."

That was the end of it.

In November of Vernon's senior year, he tested positive for cocaine for the third time. Under the guidelines of our program, I thought that meant he was through for the year. We were all confused because the guidelines for each phase were constantly changing as the drug program was being refined. But I was sure this was adios for Maxwell.

I got the message to go see Arnsparger and Foley. They told me Vernon had tested positive, and I said I knew.

So Foley said, "Well, I'll tell you one thing. He's *got* to miss some games."

I thought to myself, *Oh, shoot. I thought he was done.* I said out loud, "Yeah, I know that. I thought he was going to miss the whole season."

Foley mentioned that Vernon had not yet been assessed the 10 percent penalty, meaning suspended from 10 percent of the regular season games for that sport, which in our guidelines was supposed to come on the second positive. They said he would have to miss three games. If he tested positive again, he would be out for the season.

As the head coach, what was I going to say? Was I going to argue that he must go right now? I had already questioned the administration of our drug program and had been slapped down for it. So I agreed it was fine.

I called Vernon in and told him, "Young man, you just dodged another big bullet. I thought you were finished, but they are suspending you for three games with the understanding that the next time you test positive, you're gone." That was when we instituted the four-times-per-week testing.

At one point I told Vernon that I was tired of putting up with all of this. We had worked so long and so hard to get the program going. When Vernon couldn't play in those three games at the start of the 1987–88 season, he was smug until we beat Georgia Tech by eleven points without him in the second round of the preseason NIT. That blew him away. He was so certain we'd fall flat without him. When we reached the semifinals and final at Madison Square Garden and his suspension had run its course, he was awesome on the floor. He had to prove that we were better off with him, even though we won in the early rounds without him.

At the end of the season, we made the NCAA tournament and were assigned to a subregional at Salt Lake City. I knew the tournament policy was to test the top seven players, plus one reserve at random, after each game. Within our own program at Florida, I had the right to call for a test of the entire team. So I did, figuring I would rather head this off in Gainesville before we discovered any problems in Salt Lake City. I didn't want to get out there and be embarrassed.

We tested the team on Friday, and I got the results on Saturday. Sure enough, we had a couple of positives in the tests on campus. We were lucky in that one of the guilty players had a sprained ankle and the other had a bad knee, so we could leave them at home and spare them from embarrassment by simply explaining that they were injured.

Tom Harrison contacted me on Monday, not long before we were supposed to leave for Salt Lake City. He said that one of our players, Patrick Aaron, had failed to show for the Friday testing. Aaron already had tested positive once, and one more meant a three-game suspension under our program rules. I called Patrick and told him he had to give a specimen before he could get on the plane. He gave a specimen, but there wasn't enough time to have it analyzed before the flight.

I told Tom we would take Aaron with us and that he was to call me in Salt Lake. If Aaron tested positive, I'd send him home. That night at dinner in Salt Lake, I got a call from Harrison who said Aaron's test had turned up positive for cocaine.

I pulled Patrick out of his room and put him on a plane. He was hollering and cursing, claiming it was all a mistake, but I shrugged and said he needed to plead his case with Tom Harrison, not me. "The program guidelines say you go home for a second positive test," I told him.

It turned out that Patrick and Vernon had done cocaine together. So after we beat St. John's in the first game, Vernon was tested positive by the NCAA's technicians. What I couldn't figure out was how Vernon had tested negative before we flew to Salt Lake.

In the meantime, Patrick had gone home and had told his mother that the coaches and Tom Harrison had switched Maxwell's and his specimens to keep Vernon eligible. Now he, Patrick, was being made the fall guy. He charged that I was manipulating the drug program to keep Vernon playing and was persecuting innocent Patrick in the process. Believing all this, Patricia Aaron went right through the roof.

Above: Playing at North Carlolina State under Coach Everett Case (second from right) provided a powerful role model for my own coaching career. I'm number 75. *Right*: A publicity photograph taken while I played at North Carlolina State.

Left: Graduation day, June 10, 1951. Left to right: Charles Sloan, my grandfather; Marvin; Joan; me; Dad; and my grandmother. *Below*: Each year players from my Presbyterian College teams got together, including my last year at Florida.

Above: In the back yard with my family in Gainesville. Left to right: Debbie (age 14), Leslie (age 10), me, Mike (age 12), and Joan. *Below*: Pancake Day in Gainesville for a Boys Club fundraiser.

Above: Posing with the ACC championship trophy in 1971 with Mom and Dad. *Below*: On the sideline at the ACC tournament with Sam Esposito.

Above: David Thompson and Monte Towe. *Left*: David Thompson at Monte Towe Day in Converse, Indiana. *Below*: Tom Burleson and I pose by his car.

Above: My 1974 North Carolina State team on tour in the Orient. *Below*: David Thompson, Tom Burleson, and I on tour at the 1972 World University games in Moscow.

Above: It was a delight to cut down the net after defeating Marquette for the national championship in 1974. *Above right*: Objecting to a call on the way to the championship. *Right*: Joan and I at the basketball banquet after the championship season.

Left: Leslie, Mike, and Debbie in Raleigh, about 1968. *Below*: Joan, Mike, Debbie, me, and Leslie on my fiftieth birthday.

Courtesy Orlando Sentinel

Courtesy Orlando Sentinel

Games brought a wide range of emotions and reactions on my part. I never was one to hide my feelings.

Courtesy Orlando Sentinel

Left: Vernon Maxwell in action. *Below*: Giving instructions to Andrew Moten during a time-out.

Courtesy Orlando Sentinel

Above: I continue to have the highest regard for my friend Lefty Drisell.
Below: Dwayne Schintzius and I at practice during his freshman year.

Courtesy Orlando Sentinel [Watson Tracy photo]

Courtesy Orlando Sentinel [Eileen Samelson photo]

Left: Golfing at the Lake County Gator Booster tournament at the Pine Meadows Country Club in Eustis. *Below*: I was delighted with the Florida fans' response to the six hundredth victory of teams coached by me.

Courtesy Orlando Sentinel [Angela Peterson photo]

Courtesy Orlando Sentinel [Joe Burbank photo]

Above: Chancellor Charlie Reed. *Right*: University of Florida president Marshall Criser during his resignation speech. *Below*: University of Florida president John Lombardi (right) and athletic director Bill Arnsparger (left) at a 1990 press conference in which they responded to NCAA charges.

Courtesy Orlando Sentinel

Gainesville, Florida

October 30, 1989

Dr. Robert A. Bryan
Interim President
University of Florida
226 Tigert Hall
Gainesville, FL 32611

Dear Dr. Bryan:

After considerable personal reflection and consultation with my family, I have concluded that the forthcoming basketball season should be my last season of coaching. I have, therefore, decided to retire at its conclusion.

I have achieved most of the goals which I had set when I returned to the University in 1980. The team has won its first conference championship and has participated for the first time in the NCAA tournament. Indeed, it has now begun to do so consistently, having played in the last three NCAA tournaments. As you know, I have been in active coaching for 40 years. The stress of coaching has increased to the point that I do not wish to shoulder the burdens longer than these next few months. Other off-the-court events, with which we all are familiar and for which

Text of the letter drafted by University of Florida officials, proposing that I retire one year early after the approaching 1989-90 season. Handwritten editing is by University of Florida attorney Tom MacDonald during a meeting with my attorneys to fine tune the agreement. Within an hour, school officials reneged on their own offer after a mysterious threat from U.S. attorney Michael Moore.

I am not responsible, only add to that feeling. Moreover, I am clearly at the point in my life when it is increasingly important to me to enjoy quality time with my family. Taking all of these factors into consideration, I am satisfied that my decision is clearly in the best interests of all of us. I also believe that it is in the interest of the team to announce this before the season begins, both to avoid distractions during the season and to permit the University to begin the process of selecting my successor.

Therefore, effective immediately upon the conclusion of the final game played by the basketball team in the 1989-1990 season (including post-season tournaments), and in no event later than April 2, 1990, I resign my position as head basketball coach, and voluntarily terminate my contract with University Athletic Association, Inc., ~~dated November 10, 1981, as amended~~, on the following conditions, which I ~~understand are~~ believe will be acceptable to the University:

1. This resignation, ~~and all of the conditions hereafter~~ to

-2-

~~set forth, are subject to reservation by~~ recognize that the Association reserves ~~of~~ all of its rights under sub-paragraphs 14(C) and 14(D) of my employment contract dated November 10, 1981, as amended, ~~which it now possesses or may possess at any time prior to the date on which my resignation would otherwise be effective~~ and that it may exercise them at any time before this resignation becomes effective.

1. This resignation is irrevocable, as I recognize that the University will begin a search for my successor before its effective date.

2. Within ten (10) days after this resignation becomes effective, I will be paid a lump sum of $99,575 by the Association, (less appropriate withholding of income and FICA taxes) such sum to be reported by the Association on IRS Form W-2.

3. Upon the effective date of my resignation, I will be entitled, at my own expense, to continue Association group medical insurance for my family and myself as legally required by COBRA.

4 I will fully account for all travel, ticket and other expense advances and charges incurred by me as of the last day

of my employment. In turn, the Association will pay me for any appropriate and previously incurred but unreimbursed expenses.

5. I will return ~~all~~ the two automobiles provided by the Association for use by me or my family on or before May 1, 1990.

6. Within ten (10) days after this resignation becomes effective, I will vacate my personal office and return all Association credit cards and keys to the designated representative of the Association.

7. The Association will make the appropriate pension fund contributions on the sum described in item 3.

8. On the effective date of this resignation, the Association and I will exchange releases in forms approved by our respective counsel. ~~These releases will effectively terminate all agreements which I have with the Association~~.

9. I will continue to cooperate with the present investigation of the basketball program by the University and the NCAA, and will provide complete and accurate information to both the University and the NCAA in response to their inquiries.

11. This resignation will be announced at 7:00 p.m., EST, Monday, October 30, 1989. Prior to that time, there will be no public comment either by me or the University concerning the resignation.

I acknowledge that I have no other agreements with the University, the Association or their respective representatives regarding this resignation except as expressly set forth herein.

Sincerely,

Norman L. Sloan
Head Basketball Coach

Left: Joan Sloan, the delight of my life, singing the national anthem at Florida. *Below*: Writing this book has provided me with an opportunity to reflect on what is most important to me in college basketball and in life.

Courtesy Orlando Sentinel

She was from Montgomery, Alabama, but at this time she was in Gainesville attending school. She was single, bright, attractive, and articulate, with a noticeable racial chip on her shoulder. If Patrick had a problem in a class, her attitude was, "Well, it was a white professor." She was ignoring the signs she should have been reading.

Patrick was a pretty good talent and a decent kid until he began running around with Vernon and became a mess. He sank to the point that he stabbed one of his teammates, Tony Williams. One summer, Tony and Patrick shared an apartment that, as I understood it, had a metal spiral stairwell leading up to a bedroom. Kenny McClary, another of our players, had stopped by and was talking to Tony, who said things weren't going well. He said he'd given his share of the money for groceries to Patrick, who'd spent it on crack cocaine. About that time, Patrick came in and, as the three of them talked, honed a knife on the metal stairwell. Tony and he got into an argument about the grocery money and the crack, and according to McClary, Patrick suddenly screamed like an animal and lunged at Tony's stomach with the knife. Tony grabbed the knife, saving his stomach but slicing his hands. He was rushed to the emergency room where the cuts required quite a few stitches.

I had several conferences with Patricia about little indiscretions, like her son getting drunk at a football game and attacking a police officer. At the start of that year, after we won the preseason NIT in New York, he was so drunk he couldn't answer the bell the next morning to get on the plane. We had to send an assistant coach, Kenny McCraney, up to his room with a pass key to help him get dressed and get him on the bus and the plane. He was stinking drunk, and when we got home, we kicked him off the team for a month. He made some progress, so we put him back on the team. Then he tested positive for cocaine. I went through hell trying to send that kid a message.

Patrick and his mother wouldn't agree that he had a problem. "He doesn't have a problem," she said. "College is a place for experimentation. That's being a college student."

Earth to Patricia, Earth to Patricia: your son has a problem. Alas, Patricia had tuned out, and it became obvious that he never had a chance. She was never going to let him stand up and face his responsibilities.

I said I wasn't going through this again. I explained I already had one player I couldn't help because he kept insisting he didn't have a problem when he had a big one. I wasn't able to help. "Two years with your son," I told Patricia Aaron, "is all I'm going to put in unless you agree that he has a problem and get some help. I'm just not going through all that again." They wouldn't agree, so I declined to continue his scholarship.

At that point Patricia Aaron came unglued and hired Aaron Greene, a black attorney in Gainesville whom she was dating. He wrote me a letter saying he was going to have the state investigate me on various charges.

Obviously, in these later years of my career I went too far in trying to help kids get straight. During my first turn at Florida in the early sixties, I sent two of my players home from Vanderbilt just for staying out past curfew. Now here I was trying to help guys with alcohol and drug problems. It was a stupid decision on my part, but that was the decision I made.

I always tried to avoid making terminal decisions. By terminal I mean taking away somebody's scholarship. When a kid gets into drugs or some other problem, the knee-jerk reaction is to get rid of the bum. That's the easy way out.

At North Carolina State we had a player named Rick Anheuser. I was awakened one night at 3:00 A.M. after Rick had been jailed for drunken driving. When I went down to get him out, he kept trying to talk to me but I said, "Shut up! You're drunk! I don't want to talk to you. When you sober up tomorrow, we *will* talk then."

The next day I told him: "That's one time. You were wrong and you know it. There's no point in my suspending you. But I'll tell you this. The next time, there is no suspension. You'll be gone, no discussion." I never had another minute's trouble with Rick. He became the best player/coach I ever had. If one of his teammates slept in and cut class, Rick would go take the guy's mattress and throw it out the window.

He became a heckuva player and a leader on the team. I never enjoyed coaching anyone any more than I did Rick Anheuser. Rick now has his own business in Atlanta. He's a successful person.

How do you know how far to go with a kid before you say it's enough? It's a tough decision. It's easy to make it a week, month, or year later. Looking back, I might have made some changes, but not many.

So I told Tom Harrison he would have some trouble with Patricia Aaron. She was raising hell.

"Screw the bitch," he said. "I'm not going to worry about her."

I said, "Well, it's your problem. And by the way, how did Vernon not test positive? The word is that Patrick and he were doing cocaine together."

When Tom Harrison responded, I could have killed him.

He said, "I've been weaning Vernon away from the testing program. I took it upon myself not to test him at that time."

I was furious. "Are you telling me that before we go to a national tournament and I call for a test of the whole team to prevent this from happening, you take it upon yourself *not* to test Vernon Maxwell?"

He nodded.

I began screaming. "You stupid s.o.b! You realize what you've caused us!!??"

Even I didn't realize the full scope of what this would touch off. This incident became the basis of Patricia Aaron's going to the Drug Enforcement Administration (DEA) and claiming that I was manipulating the drug program. I'll give her the benefit of the doubt and say she really may have believed that. But from this grew the whole ugly scenario that affected the NCAA investigation and ultimately led to my own unceremonious and shameful dismissal by school and state officials anxious to believe what Patricia Aaron and Vernon Maxwell said.

Instead of going after the kids and their drug connections, the DEA thought they had something big with us. Soon the rumors began coming back to me that Vernon and Patrick were saying all sorts of wild things to the DEA.

I confess I do not have the answer to the drug problem that is crippling America and, all too often, athletic programs. Based on my personal experience, I believe taking a hard line has been best for the individual caught doing drugs and is in the best interest of everyone in his circle of influence. Too many people get hurt when the offender is given second and third chances. The hard line is the best.

I'm not advocating permanent suspension after the first positive test, but I do believe temporary suspension and serious counseling should take place immediately. The worst signal we can send out is that an athlete has one free shot before being held accountable for drug use. The message that *must* be sent is that chemical abuse is unacceptable. Period.

CHAPTER 8

Captain Loose Screws

Before I wade into the bizarre and mysterious events that precipitated my forced retirement from Florida on October 31, 1989, I am compelled to make a stab at trying to explain Bill Arnsparger, easily the most incompetent and Machiavellian character I encountered in nearly four decades of collegiate coaching.

It was common knowledge that Arnsparger became athletic director at Florida immediately following the 1986 football season at the behest of former Governor Bob Graham. When Arnsparger was an assistant on Don Shula's Miami Dolphins staff and Graham an ambitious young Miami attorney, they were neighbors in Miami Lakes. They frequently played tennis and talked sports. Graham was the consummate jock-sniffer and quickly befriended Arnsparger, his ticket to the Dolphins' locker room and intimate parties that included Don Shula and prominent Dolphins players.

Graham, now a U.S. senator, has publicly acknowledged that he "lobbied" for Arnsparger in his bid for the University of Florida athletic directorship. Most insiders suspect it went much farther than that. Graham and Dr. Marshall Criser, then president at Florida, apparently cut a deal in the summer of 1986 when interviews for the athletic director job were being conducted. Then head coach at LSU, Arnsparger skipped pratice just days before the Tigers were to open the season and flew to Gainesville for an interview with Criser, who hired him at the end of that season despite the fact that he was sixty-one years old and had not a single day of experience as a collegiate athletic administrator. When Criser resigned a year later, after Arnsparger had plunged the department into turmoil and had wrecked staff morale, his last act was to give Arnsparger a new five-year contract.

Senator Graham must be a lobbyist of infinite skill.

In his book, *Sacked*, former LSU athletic director Bob Brodhead described Arnsparger as a guy who would do anything to make himself look good at the expense of others. From Brodhead's book:

> In my dealings with Bill Arnsparger, I found him to be a shallow man with an unfriendly personality. His interests were few; in fact, if a topic didn't appear between the front and back covers of his playbook, he didn't want to talk about it. He'd rather transcribe it into the notebook he carried for recording all events as he interpreted them, which may or may not be as they actually occurred.
>
> He was a poor public speaker who didn't try to hide the disdain he felt for anyone who might question his coaching expertise. I would spend a considerable amount of time, as would his wife, B. J., attempting to repair the burnt bridges he left in his wake. B. J. would prove better at it than I was. But she had more practice.
>
> Arnsparger also had a deep-seated contempt for authority. Perhaps the years he spent watching Shula and Dolphin owner Joe Robbie at each other's throats rubbed off on him. . . . His [LSU television] shows were artistic and financial flops. His personality came through loud and clear, unfortunately, and the programs were proving to be a tough sell. According to several people involved in the production process, Arnsparger was extremely difficult to work with, and his lack of consideration was a constant source of irritation.
>
> By the time the broadcast contract [which Brodhead negotiated at $120,000 a year for radio and TV] expired after two years, WJBO had seen enough. Management notified me, and Arnsparger as well, that in the future they would carry only the radio portion of the deal. . . . When Arnsparger learned that his TV show had been canned, he made a desperate attempt to negotiate another package on his own. But his negotiating skills, like his on-the-air talents, left something to be desired and he was finding it tough sledding. . . .
>
> By this time, my administrative staff was beginning to show signs of revolution under Arnsparger's bullying tactics. The open hostility between several of my staff members and the coach caused me a great deal of concern.

The picture Brodhead painted of Arnsparger was exactly the sort of person I came to know and despise at Florida.

Maybe prominent Florida booster Leonard Levy put it more succinctly. Levy, owner of a successful printing company in Tampa, is one of the school's most faithful and influential supporters. Like so many others of Orange and Blue loyalty, he quickly became distressed with Arnsparger's heavy-handed disruption of Gator harmony. At a cocktail party during his first summer on the job, Arnsparger approached Levy and asked about the source of his reported irritation.

"Bill, you're acting like a football coach," Levy said in his blunt style. "You're paranoid, and you're autocratic. And you can't be either as an athletic director."

The first recollection I have about Bill Arnsparger becoming athletic director at Florida was after Bill Carr announced he was leaving the position. This is really ironic. Football coach Galen Hall and I were talking one day, speculating about who might be the next A.D. I confessed I didn't have a clue and really was not very concerned about it. I suppose I should have been.

Galen said he had heard that a number of big names were rumored to be interested and said I would be surprised at one of the names he had heard: Bill Arnsparger, the football coach at LSU.

I scoffed at the rumor, saying I didn't believe it.

"I'm telling you, Norm," Galen said, "I think he really wants the job. And I think he would do a great job."

The irony is that Galen was the first of four Gator head coaches that Arnsparger would railroad out of town. Yet Galen was the person who convinced his closest friend on the athletic board, Lloyd Blue, to cast the deciding vote in favor of hiring him.

Shortly after this conversation with Galen, the word was out that Arnsparger was coming on campus for an interview. Jeremy Foley, the interim athletic director, called and said he would like for Bill to come over and visit with me while on campus. This was in August 1986.

I agreed but told Jeremy I really didn't think it was necessary. I certainly wasn't going to have any influence on the decision. In fact, they brought three guys in: Arnsparger, Fred Gruninger from Rutgers, and Bucky Wagner from Georgia Southern.

I told all three of them right up front that I was happy to talk to them and to discuss anything they wanted to discuss, but I didn't really understand why they had to take their time to sit down and talk to me. I told each of them, "Look, my contract runs through 1991, and after that I'm gone."

Arnsparger said, "Well, I just want you to know one thing. If I were to come here, you would hardly know I'm here. I wouldn't want to interfere with anything as successful as your program is. I'd just be there to help you."

The next thing I knew, there was a lot of conversation about whether he would get the job. Some people on the committee had been heard to declare Arnsparger was the one guy they would not hire. He was not impressive at all in his interview, according to the late Bill Elmore, who was chairman of the Athletic Association for years. Randy Reese, Florida's wonderful national championship swimming coach later run off by Arnsparger, also confided that he had been assured by the school president, Dr. Marshall Criser, that a football coach would never be hired as athletic director.

Not long after that, at dinner one night at The Yearling, Fred Montsdeoca, an Ocala booster who was well-plugged into Gator politics, said he heard that Arnsparger was all set to come in as athletic director. I was surprised, but I still was not all that concerned about whomever they decided to hire.

When Bill took the job, he told me, "This is a successful program. You'll never know I'm here. If you need me, call on me. I wouldn't interfere with anything as successful as this."

But in no time, a flood of papers and memos from him started flowing across my desk, recommending this, recommending that. It was frustrating and annoying. I'd been in the business all these years, and here was a guy who was on the job as an athletic administrator for the first time in his life wanting me to try things I had discarded during the first five years of my career.

I finally had enough of it and made the mistake of going over to Bill's office to express my annoyance. He had been at Florida about three months. I had no intention for this to turn into a confrontation and didn't anticipate that it would. I just wanted to discuss the matter.

"Bill, I've been in this business a long time," I said, "and I've tried most all of these things you're suggesting. They aren't going to work."

"Well, we've got to try something," he snorted and immediately jumped on the academic record of my players at Florida.

I explained that I had taken over a very bad situation, but it was getting better every year. I told him there were some things I didn't like about it, either, but in order to get some players good enough to win, I had to take some that didn't belong academically. I explained that I had discussed all this with Dr. Criser, and we were in agreement. I explained that we were working at it and had turned the corner. We could see evidence that we were beginning to attract enough good students who could also play to avoid accepting many of the other kind.

He scowled and hit me with a phrase that every coach at Florida would come to despise. "Well, you can do better," he snipped. That ticked me off, and I made the mistake of losing what little cool I had.

"You know, Bill," I retorted, "I'm going to be very frank with you. What I really want to tell you is that I'm sick and tired of all your memorandums."

He bowed up. "Well, throw them away," he shot back.

We had a few more terse exchanges, and I finally said, "Bill, at my age, sixty-one, I don't think I deserve to have an ex-football coach come in here and go through on-the-job training as an athletic director."

Arnsparger jumped out of his chair and lurched across the room, his face flushed and his fists doubled up. He completely lost control. I was sitting on a couch across from his desk, and he was dancing around in front of me like a school kid picking a fight. "Well I'm sixty-one too! And I've never had anybody talk to me like that!" he screamed and began babbling. "I'm not gonna take that shit! I'm not gonna take that shit!" I was torn between laughter and anger. Was he trying to be an athletic director or Hulk Hogan?

"Well, you're going to take that shit from me," I answered, "as long as you continue to talk down to me and make me angry. I'm not going to bite my tongue. I'm going to talk to you just like you're talking to me." I've been known to use poor judgment in times like that, but I said what was on my mind. I would have been better off biting my tongue, but that wouldn't have been me.

From that point on, our relationship went rapidly downhill. As I look back, there is no question in my mind that after that day, Bill's every move in dealing with me or the basketball program was designed to get rid of me. This was the first of three memorable meetings I had with Bill. Jeremy Foley, the associate athletic director, was present for the other two.

At this first meeting, I learned how to cope with the big, soft couch on which Bill insists his visitors sit. If you sit back on it, you sink and have to look *up* at Bill. If you sit up on the edge, it's as if you are sitting at attention and giving off body language that suggests anxiety. So each time I went in there, I just kind of sprawled on the couch. I got comfortable to make sure he didn't think he was intimidating me. That was one thing you learn very quickly with Arnsparger: he wants to intimidate you.

He yells and points his finger in your face. I never have liked for anyone to point their finger in my face. He did that repeatedly.

Bill has a habit of finding something critical to bring up about you so he can put you on the defensive. He would tell me, "You've got dormitory violations going on up there. Can't you get your players under control?"

I asked what he was talking about, noting that I hadn't had any complaints from Howard Brown, who was in charge of Yon Hall.

"Your guys have cats up there."

Well, that was true. A couple of our players adopted stray cats and kept them in the dorm as pets. I'd seen signs of the cats and had tried to reason with the players without making a federal case out of it. "C'mon, guys, get the cats out of there. You're going to get in trouble, and it isn't worth it." They'd go off and leave them in the room over a weekend, and the cats would urinate on the carpets.

But it was still hardly an indication that our players were out of control. It irritated me that Arnsparger would throw that up in my face, using something so piddling to try to put me on the defensive. "You're getting on my case about my guys having a couple of cats up there. What about the athletes in other sports who have guns in the dorm?" I replied, and he squirmed because he knew I was right. "Am I to understand we equate cats with guns?"

That's how silly our discussions became.

In that first meeting, he jumped my bones about the basketball team's academic record, which, in truth, wasn't bad at all. A year later, I even got a bonus because the percentage of basketball players that graduated was above a certain level. At this meeting he also complained that "certain people" over at Tigert Hall, the university administration building, were unhappy about the way I conducted myself on the sidelines.

"People in Tigert Hall? Who? They must have names. Who said that?" I challenged.

"Well, I'm not going to tell you. That's confidential."

That's another little endearing quality that would soon drive every Florida coach to the brink of screams. Each time Bill wanted to have something over your head or manipulate a situation his way, he would come up with "confidential" tidbits about the coach or the program or, as in the confrontation that sank Galen Hall, about a player the coach wanted to recruit.

Desperate to recruit top players under the adversity of the football probation that he had inherited, Galen and his staff were heartened by the signing of a junior college transfer linebacker named John Clark. As a freshman at the junior college, Clark had faced sexual charges brought by a coed but was tried and acquitted. Hal Cuddy, his high school coach in Mount Dora, and Dr. Kim Karvasale, a prominent leader in the community familiar with Clark and his family, spoke highly of Clark's character.

However, just days before the 1989 preseason practice began—months after Clark had been signed to a grant-in-aid—Arnsparger revoked the scholarship offer, claiming he had other damning information about Clark. When Hall asked what the information was and where it came from, Arnsparger would only say that it was "confidential."

Frustrated, Hall helped set up a face-to-face meeting with Clark, Cuddy, Dr. Karvasale, and Arnsparger in a futile attempt to get Arnsparger to reconsider. He was a stone wall. The collective pleas on Clark's behalf didn't budge him. Afterward, Karvasale revealed that he had been appalled in the meeting to witness Arnsparger's demeaning treatment of Hall. Each time Galen tried to speak, Arnsparger interrupted, refusing to hear anything his own head football coach had to say.

I thought of that each time Arnsparger made his shallow public claims that he was 100 percent behind his coaches. Yeah, he was back there okay, with a dagger in his hand.

John Clark, by the way, opted for Akron University where his play on the field earned him defensive MVP that very first season and recognition as a Butkus Award candidate the second season. His deportment off the field, according to Coach Gerry Faust, was exemplary. Following that second season, however, Clark was arrested and convicted of a felony, trying to pass off crushed Tylenol as cocaine in a sale to an undercover cop. He was dismissed from Akron and served thirty days in jail. Perhaps Arnsparger indeed had spotted a legitimate character flaw worthy of denying Clark a scholarship, but his atrocious handling of the matter was the absolute Brand X example of working in concert with your head coach.

Arnsparger likes to project the notion that in keeping his "sources" confidential, he is being very noble; he's taking the heat himself rather than revealing the identities of these mysterious critics. My feeling was that he was expressing his own opinions but was cowardly masquerading them as the confidential criticisms of others.

"Well, I can't tell you who my informers are," he'd say. Now doesn't that create a warm, fuzzy family relationship!

For a long time, I thought it was just me. Honestly, I didn't talk to a lot of people about the deteriorating working atmosphere. I talked to my staff, but that was about it. Then, gradually, I heard from Randy Reese, the swimming coach, and Jim Weaver, one of the assistant athletic directors. They had reached the point where they were looking over their shoulder. The same was true of the people working in the cafeteria and those working in the gift shop. I gradually realized that everybody was unhappy. Many were starting to say, "I can't work under these conditions. I'm going to leave." A co-worker would have to calm them down and tell them not to let Arnsparger get to them. The man destroyed the morale of the entire department.

It was best put by a coach in another sport. I'm not going to identify him because he is still there, toughing it out. "We are afraid to talk to one another, afraid it might get back to Arnsparger," he told a booster. "The situation has become so bad, we just go to work, stick our key in the door, and hope it will turn."

Everybody was scared but me. I was the one guy who should have been scared, but I wasn't. I knew Arnsparger was after me, but I didn't think he could get me. Not for the remaining two years on my contract. It just didn't make any sense to create that kind of stink in *his* program.

But then, Bill Arnsparger did a lot of things that made no sense.

Arnsparger and I were at loggerheads from that very first meeting, when his personality and tactics came through to me with frightening clarity. He had a terrible temper and was ultrasensitive to any questioning of his decisions. He could not take it and reacted violently. He couldn't communicate, and had no experience in or understanding of college athletic administration. I would go to his office to discuss something with him, and the longer I was there, the more angry his mannerisms and body language made me. Bill is gifted with the antagonistic knack of making you mad just by saying, "Good morning."

After the memo meeting, I went back to the O'Connell Center and called my staff together, including my secretary. "I want you to know the kind of guy that we're working for now," I began. This was before anybody said anything critical about him; it was still the honeymoon time, but I knew from that first meeting that we were in for big trouble.

When these problems first became apparent, I talked to Dale Brown, the basketball coach at LSU. Arnsparger had tried to get the athletic director's job there, but Dale and others on the staff headed it off. "The school president, Dr. James Wharton, told me he had signed off on it," Dale said, "and I told him, 'I am not going to let this happen.'" Dale and other staffers made the school administration aware of how Bill was splitting the department, trying to fight other coaches in staff meetings. Dale said he even threatened to air out a few skeletons in Arnsparger's recruiting closet if he became athletic director. So Wharton reversed his field, paving the way for Arnsparger to become Florida's problem. Thanks a lot, Dale.

In 1985 I sat down with Bill Carr, Foley, and Richard Giannini (then an associate athletic director and later a top executive with Raycom Sports) to work out my final contract at Florida. They suggested a four-year contract, which was fine except that it would take me one year short of my sixth-fifth birthday. I explained that I had always targeted age sixty-five as when I wanted to retire and suggested a five-year contract. I said that, hopefully, as the program continued to improve, it would be automatic that we could just turn it over to Monte Towe, my top assistant. That way there would be continuity in coaching personnel and philosophy.

They agreed on the fifth year and said the intentions regarding Monte sounded fine, although it was too early to make a specific commitment. We all seemed in accord, and the resulting contract would take me through the 1990–91 season. I discussed all of this with Dr. Criser who, like Carr, said he couldn't make a commitment regarding Towe but saw "no reason why that wouldn't be a logical thing to do." Monte felt good enough about it that when a couple of head coaching opportunities came along, he rejected the feelers.

Two years later, with Arnsparger on board, I went in to suggest it was time we made some movement toward nailing all this down. I explained that it was starting to affect our recruiting; prospects had begun to realize that I would be stepping down during their college careers.

That's when I got the first of many shocks from Arnsparger. "I can't make that commitment," he said. "As a matter of fact, I can tell you right now there will be a national search for the new coach."

I told Bill I didn't understand that. I understood that we had to accept applications because that's the law. But I reasoned that since this program was doing well, establishing some continuity would be the natural thing to do.

Shock number two. Many more were to come.

"I don't know," he said. "It isn't doing all *that* well."

He started telling me all the things he didn't like about our program. We got into a hell of an argument, and I shared with him the same conversation I had had with Criser about understanding what happens when we take some players who are not excellent students. I pointed out that he hadn't been at Florida during the development of the program and didn't understand how far we had come, that at this particular time we were doing better academically and were also competing with Kentucky at the top of the league. I told him he didn't understand the contribution and hard work that Monte and Kenny McCraney, my other assistant, had put into that progress.

Bill didn't want to hear it.

I asked him, "When you left LSU, didn't you recommend Mike Archer as their next football coach?"

He conceded he had.

I said, "Why didn't you recommend a national search there?" Bill mumbled something, and I said, "Well, what's the difference? Archer was an assistant coach. Monte Towe is my assistant coach, and he's a qualified man for the job. He's been a part of building this program, and he's earned this job. We don't deserve for somebody else to come in and profit by what we built. That isn't right, Bill."

He held firm on a national search, and that was the end of that.

A few days later, Monte came roaring into my office. He was furious. He threw a newspaper clipping on my desk and angrily demanded, "What the hell is this supposed to mean?"

It was an article about how assistant coaches usually improve their financial status by jumping to other schools. Arnsparger had clipped it and sent it to Monte in the interdepartment mail. As you might expect, it had a wonderful effect on Monte's morale. He called and requested a face-to-face meeting with Arnsparger, then went fuming and sputtering over to the stadium where Arnsparger's office is located. Jeremy Foley sat in, which didn't help matters any, except maybe to make it clear that Monte wasn't going to succeed me as head coach.

Monte reiterated the growing questions from recruits.

"You can tell them," Arnsparger said, "that I have a contract, and I will be here."

Monte shook his head and chuckled a bit at that one. "Bill, that's fine with me if you're here, but I don't think that's what the prospects are interested in hearing."

Earlier, Foley had assured Monte that he was aware of the plans for Monte to succeed me and indicated he was in full support of that scenario. On more than one occasion, Jeremy privately told Monte that he thought Monte was the right man for the job. "You're the next basketball coach," he said.

Now, in this showdown meeting with Arnsparger, new and startling words began tumbling out of Foley's mouth. "None of us have any guarantees around here," he told Monte in front of Arnsparger. "I don't either."

Monte was dumbfounded and stunned by this self-serving shift. Weather Vane Foley. Whichever way the wind was blowing. The distasteful handwriting was on the wall.

Meeting number three with Arnsparger came in summer 1987. It concerned Vernon Maxwell's acquisition of a new car just before his senior season. I had looked into it, and he and his mother gave me the cock-and-bull story about the money for the car coming from an uncle and "homeboys." I had confronted him and had made it clear I didn't believe him. I didn't know what else I could do.

Foley sat in on this meeting, and when he was present, Bill hardly would say anything. He let Jeremy do the talking. Bill sat there and glowered until he was so mad that what he finally did say came out in sparks. That was how far our relationship had deteriorated.

I explained that I was aware of the car and related my conversation with Vernon and his mother.

"We're just concerned about the possibility of an agent," said Foley.

"Yep. That's one of the things I challenged them about," I said.

Jeremy and I went on discussing the matter, and finally Bill got his voice. "Here's what we're going to do," he said. "We're going to bring them in and talk to them."

"Bill, I've already talked to them," I said.

"*We're* going to talk them," he said, meaning he and Jeremy.

"Fine," I said. "Do you want me to sit in on it?"

"No. Isn't necessary," he said, curtly.

I realize I'm not easy to deal with when I'm upset, but this just wasn't handled right. He made me feel like I was the enemy as much as Vernon and his mother.

So Arnsparger called Vernon in to talk about the car without me present, which, frankly, I didn't appreciate. This was typical of Arnsparger, as it turned out. He doesn't want you to be informed. He wants to hold things back and touch base with the president and legal counsel, get a case built up, and then bring you in and ambush you with it. That's what he did with Randy Reese, the national champion swim coach who had made the same mistake of standing up to Bill and fighting for his turf. Bill summoned him and demanded his resignation, humiliating him in front of Foley and university counsel Pam Bernard. "And they enjoyed doing it," Randy told me.

Arnsparger operated on terrorism, intimidation, threats. But he wouldn't confront anyone openly. When there was a confrontation, he lost control and flew all over the place.

When I would ask him why he thought a particular suggestion was sound, he would attribute it to some study or commission. I'd say I didn't care what such-and-such a service said. "What do *you* think about this, Bill?" He wouldn't commit himself.

He once called me over to discuss business matters that were going to be brought up at a Southeastern Conference meeting, cost-cutting measures like cutbacks on the number of scholarships and number of games. I told him that sort of thing made sense only to school presidents who don't know what is going on and athletic directors who are out of touch—people who would think such cosmetics would look good in the media.

"Bill, if you want me to cut costs," I told him, "I can walk down this hall with a few pink slips, and before I get to the end of it I'll save you a hundred thousand dollars and make this place more efficient by weeding out a lot of people who are unnecessary and don't belong here." That was true. They were terribly overstaffed. Secretaries had secretaries who didn't have a job to do.

In fact, before Arnsparger was hired, Dr. Criser conducted individual meetings with the coaches and asked our concerns about the administrative setup. I told him we were vastly overstaffed. "Oh, I agree with that," he said. "We have to address that." But the staff kept getting larger and larger.

Bill came to my office one Sunday just before the start of our 1988–89 season. It was right after Criser had made a statement of lukewarm support for Galen, saying they would give him one more year to prove himself. This was not long after the 1988 Georgia–Florida football game. With Georgia's 26–3 victory sealed and Galen's future growing more tenuous by the minute, Criser was interviewed in the press box by *The Orlando Sentinel*. Criser's comments were equivalent to: "I'm not throwing my body in front of an alumni lynch mob."

Galen was struggling to save his job with a team that was shorthanded to start with, and now was uncommonly beset with injuries. Stacey Simmons, the team's best wideout, and Emmitt Smith, the Heisman-Trophy candidate tailback, were both lost to midseason knee injuries.

Many boosters and alumni were disappointed in Criser's callous comments, and a sympathetic backlash of support for Galen developed quickly. When Criser received a batch of letters criticizing him for his unfair stance toward Galen, he and Arnsparger issued a hollow statement of support filled with hazy phrases but no meaty commitment regarding Galen's future beyond the next season.

So in this Sunday meeting, Bill started getting onto me about something or other and I brought up the budding Drug Enforcement Administration investigation that was beginning to undermine basketball recruiting. Because of the investigation, rumors about our basketball program were everywhere. The school administration sat mum, thus creating in the eyes of the public something of a confirmation.

"Bill, I wish you would take a stand on this DEA thing," I said. "The perception out there is killing us."

He mumbled something about how he was supporting me.

"Yeah, you're supporting me just like you did Galen," I snapped. "You're an ex-coach. How would you like to have had your athletic director and your president say, 'We'll give him one more year.' Do you *really* think he can go out and recruit now? My God, you know enough about recruiting to know he can't recruit under these circumstances."

He stalked out of the office.

The most bizarre and juvenile of our meetings came in April 1989 shortly after the end of what would turn out to be my final season as Florida's basketball coach. By now we were battered with the uncontested rumors and allegations leaking out of the DEA and NCAA investigations. Foley requested the meeting three days in advance, but he wouldn't tell me what it was all about. "We'll talk to you about it when you get here," he said mysteriously.

"What's wrong with now?" I challenged. I didn't want to wait three days with words like that hanging over me.

So I showed up, and we sat there, Bill in his chair, Jeremy in his chair, and me on the couch. There was a long, uneasy silence. I looked at both of them. Jeremy looked down; Bill looked up. After several more moments of silence, I had the impish notion to jump up and say, "Well, if there's no further business, I have to go back to work." But I had tweaked enough noses in this personality conflict, so I broke the silence by saying, "What's this all about?"

Bill just glared.

Jeremy spoke up, saying something about Bill and me needing to get things worked out between us. "You're both important people around here, and you need to be able to work together and get along," he said.

"Fine," I said. "But what do we have to get along better about?"

"Well, you don't think Bill supports you."

"That's only because he doesn't," I replied. "He's been here a year and a half, and there has not been one word of support from the University of Florida for me and my staff about all these ridiculous charges out there. Not one."

What I know now makes it clear why Jeremy thought a peacemaking meeting was in order. There was a provision in my contract that during a window from February 15 to March 15, I could be terminated without cause. It later came to light that Arnsparger had tried to exercise that option two months earlier, right in the middle of our SEC championship season, but he was rebuffed by Criser.

Bill said nothing. He sat there, scowling and shaking his head.

Since he wasn't entering the conversation, I began referring to him in the third person as if he weren't in the room. "Jeremy, you can tell Bill so-and-so. . . . Jeremy, if Bill is concerned about such-and-such. . . ."

He sat there, seething. Once again I explained that by stonewalling me and my staff, by telling us to get our own attorneys, the school had created a terrible perception of the rumors and allegations about drugs, alcohol, money, and NCAA violations. People were taking these wild claims as the truth because my own athletic director wouldn't stand up and say the school is behind the coaches.

"Yeah, but he does support you," said Jeremy.

"He does *not* support us," I insisted. "As a matter of fact, I've gone to him and tried to talk to him about this DEA investigation. And he just said, 'I don't know anything about it.' I said to him, 'If you say you don't know anything about it, you're either lying or you're a damned fool. It's the most important thing going on in this athletic program right now, this investigation and these problems and the perception that's coming out of it.'"

Still not a peep from Arnsparger.

"Well," stammered Foley, "maybe if you would just *believe* he supports you. . . ."

"Jeremy," I said, becoming impatient, "you want me to tell you I believe something is true when it isn't true? He doesn't, he hasn't, and he won't support me. But I can live with that. I only have two more years here, and I can do two years standing on my head. I don't care whether he likes me or supports me. What he has done has created a perception out there that we can't erase no matter what we do. In order to erase it, he would have to be put in a bad light. He would have to admit he hasn't handled this properly, and he isn't going to do that. So we're hung out here fighting our own battles. And I'm not going to lie and say I understand, because I don't understand."

Back and forth we went like a cat chasing its own tail. I estimate that this went on for a full fifteen minutes before Bill finally came to life and joined our little tea party. He sat up, pointed his finger at me, and angrily snorted, "You got one! One!"

I blinked and looked at Foley, bewildered. I had no idea what in the hell he was talking about. It turns out that what he was saying was that I had only one Proposition 48 scholarship to use. Under rules of the conference and the state at that time, we could have three. The schools we had to play could sign up to three, but Bill decided he was going to cut us down to one. Until this point in the meeting, nothing remotely relating to that subject had been mentioned. But right out of the blue, "You've got one!"

Bear in mind this meeting was taking place in April. We had already had a signing period in November, and spring recruiting, for all practical purposes, was over. We wouldn't find out for another month or so—after final high school grades and entrance exams were in—if any of the players we signed would fall into Proposition 48. This was something we should have talked about in the fall. In other words, Bill was now declaring that if we had, say, two of our signees turn out to be Proposition 48s, we would have to cut one of them loose.

"That's fine. That's your decision," I said. "But the only thing I'm going to say to you is that if an outstanding recruit doesn't meet Proposition 48 and we don't get him, then I'm going to let it be known that's your fault, not mine. That *you* said we couldn't take him. I'm not going to have it out there that Norm Sloan and his staff couldn't recruit the kid."

"You got *one*!" he shouted again, his face contorted into a menacing mass. "I like you. You won't let me be your friend."

I told him that wasn't true, that I wasn't keeping us from having a friendly working relationship—*he* was. I told him that he couldn't tolerate me disagreeing with him "and that was going to happen a lot. I'm going to say it again: you aren't qualified for this job, and you're taking it out on me. All I'm doing is telling you the truth, and you don't want that."

That infuriated him. I know I shouldn't have been so blunt, but it was the way I felt. I would like to think when I was working with my coaches, I wasn't so sensitive about them disagreeing with me. Our staff had arguments, but we batted our ideas around and sometimes they impressed me with a contradictory idea. Sometimes I made changes; more often I didn't. But we didn't stalk out of the room, forever mad with one another.

The first year Willis Casey became athletic director at North Carolina State, he made my life miserable. But we worked it out, face-to-face, in an adult manner. He sent every expense account back to me and was on my case about everything. Finally I walked into his office, shut the door, and said, "You know, Willis, you're driving me crazy. And it isn't deserved. I have the distinct feeling that you think I'm going to take advantage of the fact that I turned the A.D. job down and recommended you. Hell, you know me better than that. You're the boss. Now if I have to stop in here every morning, stick my head in the door, and say, 'Good morning, boss,' I'll be glad to do it. But get off my ass. You're driving me crazy."

After that, we got along just fine. We had a few problems, but they were normal problems. We talked a lot. I had a lot of confidence in Willis.

I'd like to think that if I were a top administrator of a program as large as the athletic departments at North Carolina State or Florida, I would want people who would share their opinions and experience. Not Arnsparger.

I resisted the temptation to bring up Bill's paranoia about staff loyalty. I wanted to say, "I understand in your staff meetings, loyalty is a big thing with you." I had been told by several of his aides that he brought it up at almost every meeting, saying how important it was for each of them to be loyal to him.

Anytime damning information got out, he accused them of leaking it to embarrass him. He tried everything he could to intimidate Norm Carlson, the longtime publicist. He'd glare at Norm in the staff meeting and say, "There's a little birdie that's been cheeping in here, and I'm gonna squash that birdie!" There is not a more loyal or capable member of Gator athletics than Carlson, but he was constantly made to feel like he was sitting in an electric chair with Executioner Bill fingering the switch.

Everyone in the department nodded in agreement when one state newspaper columnist borrowed an old Ted Turner description and labeled Arnsparger "Captain Loose Screws." It was sad, but true.

Back to our childish meeting. With no warning and for no apparent reason, Arnsparger leaped to his feet, fuming and spitting. "You come in here, and you sprawl out on that goddamed couch! Nobody has ever talked to me the way you talk to me! Sprawled out there, trying to intimidate me!"

"Bill, I'm not trying to intimidate you," I said. "But I'm not going to let you intimidate me, either."

Once again, he charged up to me in a rage, his fists balled up, his face all screwed up in anger. "Goddam you! Goddam you!" he shouted. "I'm not going to take that shit!"

Bill finally got hold of himself and walked back and sat down. "I like you," he barked. "I'd like to sit down and have a drink with you and talk about coaching. But you won't allow that. You aren't going to allow that. I'd like to get along with you."

He mentioned five or six things he would like to see happen, but he followed each with the declaration that I wouldn't allow them to happen.

"Bill, I don't think our relationship will ever change," I said and turned to Jeremy. "I don't see where that has anything to do with our working relationship here. I'm not going to lie and say I believe Bill supports me when he doesn't. But it's not a problem for me on a daily working basis. I'm not out talking about Bill. I'm not out crucifying him. But I will say this: there's a lot of talk about him and a lot of people are asking me about him. And Bill, when they ask me about you, I tell them the truth."

With that he puffed up again.

"I knew you've been talking about me!" he snapped. "I knew you've been talking about me!"

"Bill, if you think I've been walking up to people and saying, 'Hey, let me tell you about Bill Arnsparger,' that isn't it at all. They say, 'What's the problem with Arnsparger?' Then I tell them you're not qualified for the job."

Bill glared off into space, and I excused myself.

As it turned out, I would spend about six more months, not two years, at Florida. That was the last meaningful conversation I would have with Arnsparger, if you consider it meaningful.

CHAPTER 9

University of Investigations-Gainesville

In early July 1988 I found out by accident that the Drug Enforcement Administration was looking into our program at Florida and, in particular, into the activities of the coaching staff. Ex-players Kenny McClary and Andrew Moten were working as camp counselors at our summer basketball camp, and one afternoon McClary stopped by my office to tell me he would have to miss camp the next day.

"I have to go to Tallahassee," he said. "I've been subpoenaed to go there."

I asked what on earth for.

"I don't know. I've got a couple of outstanding traffic tickets. I guess it's about that," he said with a shrug.

I offered to help him arrange legal counsel, but he said it wouldn't be necessary. Upon his return, I asked him about it.

"No big deal," he answered. But I could tell he was nervous and evasive. When I pushed him on the matter, he walked away.

Kenny's wife, Lolita, came to my office that afternoon and leaned in the door. She made small talk for a minute, then asked if I knew what had gone on with Kenny in Tallahassee. I said I didn't have a clue.

"Oh, Coach," she said, "they're really after you."

"What are you talking about?" I asked.

"You really don't know? Coach, they're after you," she said again. "And they got you, too."

I kind of laughed uneasily and told her to come on into the office. I asked her again what she was talking about.

"Coach, they know about you swapping urine specimens," she said.

"That's ridiculous, Lolita. Nothing like that ever happened."

"Oh, Coach, they know. And they're after Dr. Criser, too. They're after everybody over here."

She began to tell me about Kenny's DEA interview, about allegations of rampant drugs and manipulation of urine specimens. "And they know, Coach," she added, "about y'all giving players money."

I tried to tell her that no one had been tinkering with the drug program and no one had been giving players money. But she insisted the players were telling DEA agents all this.

I promptly called Arnsparger, who told me I should call Pam Bernard, the school staff attorney. I did and proceeded to tell her what Lolita had said. "Yes," Pam said, "we've known about this investigation for some time."

You could have knocked me over with a shoelace.

"You *what*!!??"

"Oh, yes. We've known about this since the latter part of May," she replied.

"Why in the world wasn't I informed?" I demanded.

"Well, we just didn't think it was a good idea for you to know."

"My God! They think I'm right in the middle of it, and you're telling me you didn't think it was a good idea to tell me about it? I don't understand that at all."

"Well, it was just a call we had to make at the time," she said.

"Well, I think you made the wrong damned call!"

I would discover that Bill Arnsparger, Dr. Marshall Criser, and Jim Quincey, an outside lawyer retained by the university, had been meeting on this for some time. In this first conversation with Pam Bernard, she said words to me that still haunt me. "We think," she said, "there's a hidden agenda here." She pointed out that U.S. attorney Mike Moore and assistant U.S. attorney Lyndia Barrett, under whom the DEA works, were Florida State graduates.

Naturally, I was very disturbed by this wonderful first exchange with my own school's legal counsel. Trying to catch up with the facts, I talked to some of the players and asked them what was going on. They told me the DEA agents had been interviewing Vernon Maxwell for a couple of months and that Patrick Aaron had said, "We're going to get Sloan fired, and when we do, I'll get my scholarship back."

I flashed back to something Kenny McCraney, one of my assistant coaches, had told me a few weeks earlier. Kenny said he received a call from Patricia Aaron, Patrick's mother, warning him to cover his flanks and distance himself from me and the rest of the staff. "There's going to be some big problems, and I don't want to see you get hurt," she told him. I chalked it off to just another frustrated basketball parent.

During that encounter, Patricia had told Kenny something else, far more chilling, that he did not relay to me until more than a year later. I'll get back to that.

Time to fight, Norm. Battle stations. Except that I didn't know who or what to fight. Suddenly, I seemed to be in the middle of something I knew nothing about. I was being shot at by an unseen enemy. It was frightening and frustrating.

Throughout the early summer, Vernon Maxwell had strolled into the office, glib, friendly, chitchatting. He asked Sharon, our staff secretary, or one of the other coaches how I was doing. I would later discover that on two of those occasions he had come directly from Sloan-scuttling interviews with the DEA and once on the day after he had testified before the grand jury. Pointedly asked to explain his sudden affluence, Maxwell testified that he could get money from me or the rest of the basketball staff anytime he wanted. When that reached the school administration, Arnsparger had the ammunition he coveted to run me out on the plank and begin sawing.

I pulled Vernon aside on his next visit and challenged him. "Vernon, I'm getting reports that you told the grand jury we gave you big money anytime you wanted."

He denied it. "Oh, Coach, no, I didn't say that."

I said, "I'm telling you, if that's the case, it will come out."

"Oh, Coach," he said, "this whole thing's secret."

I think that because Vernon was told that nobody would ever know about his testimony, he really believed nobody would ever know what he was telling them. I told him if the agents' trial went to court, he would wind up having to give public testimony. Would he continue to lie then?

"It'll never go to court," he assured me.

He was right about that. Unfortunately, the agents copped a

guilty plea and the trial was over almost before it began, leaving Maxwell's allegations floating out there to be believed by our own people.

It was frustrating as the devil. I don't think any of the pain and disgrace that followed would have been necessary if our administration had talked with me about these things and had taken an objective look at the charges. Instead, when the first allegation hit, they promptly circled their wagons and instructed us to get our own attorneys. Norman Sloan and his assistant coaches instantly became the enemy, and because the school cut us off, we were made to look guilty in the eyes of the public.

Patricia Aaron had assembled all the unhappy players: Patrick, Vernon, McClary, Tony Williams, Andrew Moten. They contrived a portrait of manipulation in the drug program. Incompetence, yes. Manipulation, no.

The coaches never had anything to do with the administration of the drug program. This was how it *should* be. Coaches should never become drug counselors because it destroys the relationship they need to build between coach and athlete. But Patricia Aaron was alleging that we not only controlled the drug program, but we manipulated it so that it was unfair to her son. And she convinced the DEA.

So instead of going after the kids and their drug connections, the DEA went after us. Soon, I was getting feedback that Vernon and Patrick were charging all sorts of wild things to DEA agent Carl Lilley.

I went to Huntley Johnson, a local attorney who had represented players at Florida over the years. He had been in the state attorney's office and had represented people in federal cases. Huntley is an aggressive criminal lawyer, a Florida grad in his early forties. He has Humphrey Bogart and Marilyn Monroe pictures hanging in his office, and his desk is made out of a huge cypress tree with a lion at each end of it. Huntley sits behind it on a big chair that looks like a throne. The B-movie setting left me wondering if I had gone to the right man, but he did a good job.

Huntley said he had heard rumblings about what had been going on. I said I wanted an interview with the DEA. I felt, and Huntley agreed, that it was important to sit down with Lilley and find out what was going on. We were getting too much information secondhand.

In the meantime, the DEA already had interviewed Kenny Mc-Craney for two and one-half hours. They asked Kenny if we had supplied drugs to the team and if we knew about players using drugs. Kenny was taken aback and asked why in the world they would ask questions like that. He was told, "Let's face it, Coach. You fit the drug profile. You're black, you're from Miami, and you drive a BMW."

When Kenny told me that, I went back to Huntley Johnson and said I wasn't asking, I was *going* to talk to the DEA. He said I shouldn't go unless I received immunity from prosecution. At first Assistant U.S. attorney Lyndia Barrett (now Padget) agreed, but about an hour before we were to meet, Huntley called me and said, "I've got some bad news. Mike Moore won't allow you to have immunity. I don't think you should go in there."

"No, I want to," I argued. "I'm not worried about immunity. I've got nothing to hide. I'm anxious to talk to these people." I wanted to clear up the wild allegations being bandied about, some in print.

On Monday, August 1, 1988, Huntley and I walked into the DEA's Gainesville office on the second floor of a small state building just off the square in the center of town. A young woman greeted us in a simple reception area, and we waited there for Lilley, who ushered us into a small conference room.

Lilley is a man about forty years of age, of average build with a full beard. He had his coat off and wore a gun in a hip holster. While waiting for Lyndia Barrett to arrive, we engaged in pleasant, idle conversation. He originally lived in Williamsburg, Virginia, was a big fan of ACC basketball, is the father of two children, and says he has dedicated his life to fighting the drug scene.

The moment Lyndia showed up in the conference room, his whole demeanor changed. Instantly, it was hardball time. What I had hoped would be a cooperative exchange of information became an adversarial interrogation. He opened with, "The first time that I have any indication that you're lying to me, this interview is off."

It was like a cold slap. I thought it a strange comment. I had gone there in a spirit of cooperation, and suddenly I was on the defensive. Later, I would find out that he ran that line by everyone he interviewed. Further, with some of our players, including Kenny McClary, Lilley would take his gun out and lay it on the table in an obvious effort to intimidate them. He'd tell them, "I could put you in prison, and you'll never see your son. He'll be a grown man before you get out." It worked.

"The man scared me," McClary said. "Scared me to death."

Lilley asked me if I used drugs, then asked if I supplied drugs to players. I was stunned. We went into Florida's drug-testing program, and he seemed surprised when I told him that the coaches had nothing whatsoever to do with the mechanics of testing.

We got into a discussion of Maxwell, and I had to explain how I viewed Vernon Maxwell. "Vernon is a compulsive liar. He doesn't know the truth from a lie. He says whatever is helpful to him and immediately believes it," I said.

Lilley nodded. "Yeah, he's a liar," he said. "No, he's a *goddammed* liar!"

Not to mention, a talented one. Vernon is a member of that cunning segment of mankind that can beat a lie detector test. It's amazing how many people still believe that doctors can save every patient, that the government doesn't cheat, and that you can't mess with a lie detector test.

Vernon Maxwell can. And did.

During his freshman year, there was an ugly incident in an intramural football game on the Florida campus. Playing against a team of dental students, Maxwell and Andrew Moten were going all-out, rough-and-tumble, as if they were all wearing pads and this was the Super Bowl. Vernon was trying to tear peoples' heads off. He would have been a great secondary player in football; he's a great athlete, and mean.

When the dental students went out for passes, instead of chucking them, Maxwell would unload, trying to hurt them. Tempers became short, a fight broke out, and Maxwell and Moten brutalized a couple of the dental students, who then filed charges with the student judiciary.

Vernon and Andrew got a lawyer, Huntley Johnson, Bogie pictures and all. Things weren't looking good, so Huntley suggested we submit them to a lie detector test. I expressed some concern about what would happen if they didn't pass, but Huntley said, "Doesn't matter. If they don't pass, nobody will ever know they took it." He explained that with the right operator and the right questions, anything is possible. They secretly took the test and returned, grinning up a storm.

"We passed it with flying colors," Vernon announced. Their contention was they were provoked into the fight when the white dental students called them "niggers." There were many witnesses at the game who said that never happened, but that was Vernon's and Andrew's story. The lie detector results unveiled at the hearing supported the claim, and the student judiciary council accepted the test as powerful evidence. There was no punishment.

During the DEA interview, I observed that, based on what I heard in that room, Patricia Aaron had convinced them of her vindictive account of things that had never happened. Lyndia Barrett stiffened noticeably. "Oh, no," she said. "Patricia Aaron had nothing to do with this."

Time for another lie detector test, Lyndia. Even then I knew that Patricia Aaron not only had fed misinformation to the DEA, but frequently called several newspapers in the state, especially the *St. Petersburg Times.* She had gone to Pam Bernard and stated flatly that she was going to get Norm Sloan fired, and it was becoming clear that she had set into motion the machinery to make it happen, all because her son had a serious drug problem that she refused to face.

That Friday, August 5, 1988—four days after our meeting in Gainesville—I went before the grand jury in Tallahassee. As Huntley and I awaited the call on a hallway bench just outside the grand jury room, an attorney named Bob Harper kept emerging from the jury room to pull Huntley aside. "Lilley just told me they've got Sloan in a perjury trap," was his whispered first announcement.

Next time out, Harper said, "Lilley just told me in there that somebody in Washington, D.C. wants Sloan's ass bad."

At the time, I laughed at that, but as the whole bizarre episode began to unfold, that laughter gave way to almost a cold sweat. I began to wonder if maybe there wasn't someone in Washington connected to the U.S. attorney's office or the DEA who was after me. If not, why would federal agents be calling one of my former players, Ronnie Williams, in Belgium to say, "We're turning up the heat on Sloan"?

I flashed back to something that had happened earlier that summer. Dwayne Schintzius was trying out for the U.S. Olympic team at Georgetown University. Right in the middle of a practice, Lilley walked out on the floor and flashed his badge to John Thompson, the U.S. Olympic coach. Lilley identified himself as a drug agent conducting an investigation of the Florida basketball program and said he needed to talk to Schintzius.

Dwayne Schintzius was cut from the trials and put on a plane home that night. Thompson had made some other cuts that day, but those kids already had their airline tickets for home. Dwayne's ticket didn't materialize until after Lilley burst in on the practice. I don't blame John. He was picking a team for the Olympics, and if there was any possibility that one of his players was going to be involved in a drug investigation of a college program, he couldn't run the risk. I don't hold him responsible for what happened. Carl Lilley made that cut. If he wanted to interview Dwayne, it was totally unnecessary for him to barge in on the middle of the Olympic trials to do it.

The fact that Lilley was in Washington tied in too snugly with his remark that someone in D.C. wanted to get me. Why was I the target when nothing pointed to me about drug trafficking, nothing even close to committing a crime?

This was an investigation of suspected Gainesville drug trafficking in which the names of some University of Florida athletes had surfaced, but the U.S. attorney's staff and DEA agents seemed more intent on getting them to talk about me with regard to NCAA infractions. Even if there *had* been NCAA violations, why was the federal government trying to dig them up?

This riddle was not lost on all the grand jurors. Reconvening after a break in my testimony, one juror posed that very question. "Why are we spending all this time on these matters?" he asked. No one seemed to have an answer.

My sworn testimony before the grand jury was largely a re-enactment of my interview with Lilley earlier in the week, except that Lyndia Barrett was now asking the questions. We went over the school's drug testing procedures, positive test results on players, Maxwell's new car, and other sudden signs of affluence, the recruitment of and problems with Aaron and Tony Williams, hiring practices for our camp staff, and, of course, the allegations of cash payments to players.

From the transcript:

Barrett: Were you ever aware of any player receiving payments from either anyone on the staff or any alumni?

Sloan: No, ma'am.

Barrett: Other than the scholarship?

Sloan: No, ma'am.

Barrett: And you're telling the grand jury that you didn't direct that anyone make any payment like that or cause any payment to be made?

Sloan: I certainly am.

She asked me about detecting drug or alcohol abuse by the players. Again, from the grand jury transcript:

Sloan: When I became aware that [Maxwell] had a problem, I started noticing some practice habits, effort, alertness, techniques that indicated there was something wrong. When somebody in basketball, at the level we're working at, when you work as hard as we do and strive for the level of perfection that we do, if you have a big drop-off in the way a player plays, you say there's something wrong. He's disturbed mentally about something, or dissipating or maybe he's drinking or maybe he's involved with drugs. And I did start noticing some erratic play that bothered me. . . .

* * *

Barrett: Did you have problems with Patrick Aaron?

Sloan: He would be number two of all-time problems I've had behind Vernon. I had a lot of trouble with him, trouble on trips, violations of training rules. I called his mother in and we talked about it. She wasn't much help. She's very strong in defending her son, and she never was much help. . . . At the end of his freshman year, I called them both in and said I recommend he go somewhere else. He is not going to ever become the kind of player that's going to be successful here, and I have a policy that I'll go two years with [a problem player]. I told him he had the option of staying another year, but advised it was a waste of time. He said, "I want to stay." I said, "Fine."

Barrett: What was your perception of what most of his problems were caused by?

Sloan: Alcohol and drugs. . . .

* * *

Barrett: Tony Williams just came last year?

Sloan: Yes, ma'am. He came on board, and shortly after he was there he started demonstrating some problems with alcohol. I called his [junior college] coach at that time. We didn't know much about it because of the [last-minute] way we recruited him, and he said [Tony] does have a problem with that. Shortly after that, he had a ruptured or perforated ulcer. He was rushed to the hospital. He had an emergency operation like 4:30 A.M., saved his life, literally, and then the doctors called me and said this was brought on by excessive alcohol use [and that I] should know that. . . .

* * *

When I testified that our staff felt the school's drug program was not being properly administered by Tom Harrison, Lyndia went into a long line of questioning that included these exchanges:

Barrett: I just want, in that vein—what do you mean by beating it to death?

Sloan: [Players] were beating the test. When we first started this thing, the person taking the specimen would come over there and sit down, give them a vial, and they would go behind a closed door, say, in the restroom behind the closed door. We had reason to believe, because of the things we heard and the results we were getting and some of the things we were suspecting, that they were doing funny things behind that door. Maybe switching specimens or bringing—you know, it got to the point it was pretty obvious, a guy would walk in, see the man there to take the specimen, and somebody run out, make a phone call, and people would show up. You know how kids will do, make a funny little remark. We tightened that up and got to the point where somebody sat there and actually observed the specimen being taken.

Barrett: You weren't involved in that aspect of it?

Sloan: No, ma'am. One of the things I made clear from the beginning is I'm not going to sit there and watch that, and neither is any member of my staff. So we never even watched it. I wasn't going to do that.

Barrett: But when you say beating the test, you had reason to believe people were using drugs and not coming up positive?

Sloan: Yes, ma'am.

* * *

Barrett: What was your relationship with Tom Harrison?

Sloan: Wasn't very good. Wasn't very good because I'm not very good at argumentation. I'm a little too intense, and a little too frank maybe. I always felt he was taking some liberties that he shouldn't take in terms of the way he talked to the kids. It got to the point where he and I had a run-in over something, and I actually called for a meeting of the (drug) committee and asked them to replace him. They emphatically told me that wouldn't happen. And I told them, "I don't want him working with Vernon any more." They said, "That isn't your decision and he will still do that."

Barrett: Who told you that?

Sloan: Arnsparger. I remember clearly because I told him, "I hope if my butt is ever in a crack you're going to be as tough defending me as you are him."

* * *

I found out later that Harrison also testified to the DEA and was given transactional immunity, which requires permission from Washington. I think they thought that by giving Harrison immunity, they would get the true story on all the awful things my staff and I were doing. They figured he had an ax to grind since I had tried to get him fired. They kept peppering Tom with pointed questions, getting nowhere. Finally, he told them, "Look, Sloan and I don't get along. But I can't tell you anything bad about him."

I think that was the first piece of the puzzle that fell apart for Lilley and the DEA.

Their biggest setback, however, came two months later when Kenny McClary went before the grand jury on October 24, 1988, and exposed Patricia Aaron's choreographed efforts to discredit me and my staff. In interviews with Lilley and Barrett that summer, McClary had gone along with Patricia's party line about manipulation of the drug tests and cash payments. But under oath before the grand jury, McClary stunned Lyndia by suddenly and unexpectedly admitting that he and other disgruntled players had lied in the DEA interviews to get back at me for lack of playing time.

He told the grand jury many of his allegations were lies that he fabricated after talking with the Aarons. Flustered, Barrett warned McClary that he could be charged with perjury if he were lying now.

The *Palm Beach Post* obtained a copy of the transcript a year later and quoted McClary telling the grand jury: "I assumed on my own he [Lilley] knew I was lying. And he wanted to take it as the truth. That's what he did. He was like—he wouldn't let me forget, you know, about Norm. And he told me the best way to get Norm fired was to cooperate with the DEA. Patrick Aaron and his mother also told me that, because she referred me to agent Lilley. . . . She would call me two or three times a day and tell me if I did this, if I do that, Norm Sloan would get fired. So the day before I met agent Lilley, I seen Patrick, you know. He told me, you know, if you can just make up anything and they would believe it because they want to get Sloan fired. . . . He told me he was trying to get Sloan—say Sloan was giving us money to buy drugs. . . . The agent said this would get Norm Sloan fired and I had a very high grudge against Norm Sloan at that time."

I couldn't help laughing at one portion of McClary's testimony.

McClary: We all kind of got together and talked about it.

Barrett: Oh, you mean a conspiracy?

McClary: No, we just got together and talked about it.

But there was no question that there was at least a loosely formed conspiracy. I know from having talked to Lolita McClary that Patricia Aaron made repeated phone calls to these kids, had meetings, took notes, put words in their mouths, and urged them to think of all the things the coaches did. There was a definite campaign on her part to get something done to us. I would have to say she was successful.

Much later, even Pam Bernard finally declared, "Patricia Aaron is crazy. I told her not to come back to my office again." But by then, the poison she planted had taken root in the university administration.

McClary's break from this little group in front of the grand jury was welcome affirmation of what I had vainly tried to tell our own people for nearly two years. I appreciated McClary's courageous turnaround. I wish the newspapers had flushed it out a year earlier, before we had been forced out under a broad blanket of public innuendo. But while the public was unsure just what to believe at that time, I have little doubt that our executioners in high offices were well aware of McClary's revelations as they plodded undeterred toward our ouster. McClary explained that his conscience started bothering him and that he realized he was being used for somebody else's purpose.

I remember as a player, when I finished a season and hadn't gotten to play as much as I thought I should have, I was depressed and ripe for outside agitation. Upset about my role as a reserve behind Vic Bubas at North Carolina State, I complained to Coach Everett Case at the end of the season. He countered with something I wasn't prepared to combat: logic. "But, Norm," he said, "we're winning."

"Yes, but if I were playing," I argued, grabbing at straws, "we'd be winning by bigger scores." He must have gotten a few laughs telling that one around the office.

But time goes on, and you get over the personal frustration. I think a lot of that was true in McClary's case. Also, he is married to a very fine young lady, Lolita, who encouraged him to do the right things. Kenny is basically a good person. He had over-optimistic dreams of going to the NBA, and his mother called about halfway through his senior season to complain about his playing time. "You're costing my son a chance to play in the NBA," she said. I realize parents view it that way and tried to explain that the way he played and practiced—relative to the other players—determined how much playing time he got.

As the DEA investigation crawled along during the 1988–89 school year, my staff and I became an island. We were cut off from communication with the school administration, its attorneys, the NCAA investigators that would soon be descending upon us, and, finally, the Chicago-based attorneys the school would hire on the recommendation of the NCAA.

In the face of all this, our players couldn't have performed more admirably. Led by junior Schintzius and sophomore Chatman, the team bounced back from a 1–3 start in conference play to win the regular-season SEC championship for the first time in the history of Florida basketball (with a 13–5 league record). With all the growing distractions and ugly rumors about my coaching—and criminal—status buffeting us constantly, the season was more gratifying than the 1974 national championship at North Carolina State. That team was expected to win. This team reached down for it.

In addition to the league trophy, we earned our third consecutive berth in the NCAA tournament but suffered a first-round upset loss to Colorado State, 68–46, in the Midwest Regional in Dallas. However, the 21–13 overall mark gave our program sixty-seven victories over a three-year span, the most in the Southeastern Conference during those years. For the first time in Florida's history, we were establishing a basketball tradition of success and momentum. Unfortunately, it was headed for a dead end.

As the rumors grew and the public perception worsened, my morale was buoyed by a few signals of support. My mother, who lives in Rock Hill, South Carolina, went shopping for shrubs one day at a nursery—A. B. Poe & Co. She discovered that the proprietor, Alvis Poe, was one of my players more than thirty years earlier at Presbyterian College. He said when the dark stories about rampant corruption at Florida began to surface, "I told my son not to believe what the papers were saying about Coach Sloan. Norm Sloan would not do something like that."

Tommy Burleson, the star center on our national title team at North Carolina State, read of Maxwell's claims and called Monte, his former teammate, to playfully ask when I had started giving players money. Tommy remembered the time he was a freshman and barged into my office needing money to pay a library fine. "He not only refused to give me the money," Tommy recounted, "he yelled at me and threw me out of his office."

Stewart Knight, the director of the Secret Service when President Kennedy was shot, had become a close friend when I was coaching at North Carolina State. When the Florida story broke, he sent me a wonderful letter. "I know that you have done nothing wrong," Stu began. "I have always admired and respected you for your honesty and integrity. I find it too difficult to understand all the rumors and innuendoes. But I know that you're right and therefore have to feel good about yourself. As long as you can feel that way and your family and friends feel the same, there is nothing 'they' can really do to you. Keep your head up and walk tall. You've earned it."

I was heartened to be reminded that some people still believed in Norman Sloan.

Apparently, none of them were on the staff of the NCAA, which in the summer of 1989 launched an investigation of our basketball and football programs. It began with allegations that had surfaced in connection with the DEA investigation and the approaching trial of the agents who had prematurely signed Vernon Maxwell and several Florida football players. The public perception was that all this was merely the tip of the proverbial iceberg; the full, seamy story would come gushing out at the agents' trial in September. There would be a sordid avalanche of revelations about NCAA irregularities.

Carl Lilley was out on the street telling people how his office was going to shut the program down at Florida. He boasted that we could sell season tickets if we wanted to, but there wouldn't be a season. All the time, I was trying to tell Arnsparger and Pam Bernard that we needed to do something about all this. When I became insistent, Pam Bernard told me, "We are not going to talk to you about this. I have never misled you. I represent the university, and you have to take care of yourself."

Dummy me. And I thought I was part of the university.

Obviously, the school administration made a decision early on that we were guilty and would have to defend ourselves. I don't think they thought I would go before the grand jury. I don't think they thought I'd stand up publicly and go before the press and say this whole thing was a fabrication, that the perception was wrong, and that spreading talk of an NCAA death penalty was ridiculous. I was out there saying all this and was making it clear that I was angry because I wasn't getting any support from the university. I think that upset the U.S. attorney, Arnsparger, and Dr. Bob Bryan (who by then had become Florida's interim president). I know it upset Charles Reed, the chancellor of the state university system, who just happened to be cozy with Arnsparger, and the man who got Arnsparger his job as athletic director: Senator Bob Graham.

Charles Reed was very much a part of what happened to me and to the Florida athletic program. I think he took a great deal of personal pleasure in having a major hand in orchestrating my forced, early retirement. I was at odds with his bosom pal, Bill Arnsparger.

On August 30 at 11:15 A.M., I called Pam Bernard to request a meeting to discuss what was happening in the DEA probe. She replied, "Norm, I have made it abundantly clear that I don't want to talk to you and you don't want to talk to me. Because if you talk to me, you may say something to me that I will have to use against you when you come to make a deal with me."

I said, "Boy, if there was any doubt in my mind, Pam, that you people have prejudged me and made your mind up, then you just eliminated it. What I want to talk to you about is what is going to happen at this agents' trial."

"Oh, oh. That's a different story," she said. She thought I wanted to talk about the NCAA investigation. So we had a meeting with Arnsparger, Foley, and university spokeswoman Linda Gray. In an earlier phone conversation, Linda had said to me, "Aw, Coach, I'm so sorry all this is happening. I do hope we aren't going to have any sacrificial lambs out of this." I told her not to worry about that, that there may be a lion roar in there every now and then, but there won't be any sacrificial lambs. Dummy me. Just call me Mutton Sloan.

This meeting would turn out to be the only time in my last six months at Florida that Arnsparger and I were in the same room together. It took place just before the agents' trial, and I thought it was in order to get our heads together to anticipate some of the things that might come out in the trial and how we could best deal with them. Maxwell was going to have to take the stand, and we anticipated that he would be asked about his grand jury allegation that he had received big money from me. That was going to be fine with me because I thought they would put me on the stand.

"I'm looking forward to this," I said in the meeting. "Finally, we're going to have a chance to air these questions in front of an impartial group and let them make a decision."

"Oh, you don't want that," Pam warned.

"Don't want it!?" I exclaimed. "I want it in the worst way. You people are killing us. You're killing us with the perception you're building by making us go get our own attorney and by refusing to talk to us. People know about that, and it makes us look guilty."

At one point during the meeting, Pam attempted to cut me down. When I said I could easily take care of some matter or another, she said, very snidely, "Oh, that's right. You're a special person. I forgot that, Norm."

So I just shut up.

Afterward, I asked Pam to stay a moment so I could speak to her. When the others left, I told her I had had it with her adversarial attitude toward me in front of others. "You're entitled to your personal opinion of me," I said, "but you have some professional responsibilities, too. The fact that you've prejudged me and the fact that you've made some of the statements about me that you've made to other people and in front of me is very unprofessional."

She went berserk.

"I fuckin' don't know who I am! I fuckin' don't know who my friends are! I fuckin' don't know who the NCAA are, what the fuckin' DEA is after!"

She absolutely lost it.

After the agents' trial was short-circuited by a plea bargain, I began to fear that the truth might never come out in time to save our program. Those doubts increased in the first week of October when Arnsparger and Bryan forced an in-season resignation by Galen Hall over what one Florida columnist equated to "NCAA parking violations." Galen confessed that he had supplemented the salaries of two assistant coaches out of his own pocket (when he couldn't get budget support from Arnsparger), saying he didn't realize that was an infraction. Several prominent coaches around the country promptly echoed Galen's contention. Also, Galen admitted providing transportation for defensive back Jarvis Williams to his hometown, thirty miles away, to settle delinquent child support charges.

For this, Galen was spectacularly beheaded in midseason by our supportive administration, again spawning the perception and rumors that he must be guilty of much more. Slush funds? Rampant cheating? Galen's vain bleats that there was nothing else hiding in the closet would not be substantiated until the combined investigations ended nearly a year later with only one more football allegation, a one-hundred-dollar loan from a former assistant coach so a player could go home for Christmas. Even the NCAA scrooges officially shrugged that one off as a "minor" infraction.

With Hall having been fired essentially over nothing, the administration now had to answer the question of how they could keep a basketball coach accused of handing out stacks of cash and drugs to his players. When Galen was fired, I sensed I was in big trouble.

So did Bob Brodhead. Reached in Louisiana by the *Florida Times-Union,* the former LSU athletic director reacted to Hall's dismissal with these chilling comments: "As soon as Arnsparger got the job, I predicted right then that Galen Hall was gone. I also predicted that Norm Sloan would be gone when Bill got the job. Norm is definitely no valentine, but he is his own man and is a good basketball man. And a guy like Arnsparger is going to clash [with him] because Arnsparger wants to control him. Arnsparger wants to control his people. And nobody's going to control Norm Sloan, or Galen Hall for that matter, or tell them what to do."

Brodhead's comments came into sobering focus just a few nights later—October 14—hours after the Gators football team had played its first game without Hall. Joan and I and a number of Galen's friends went to his house that night to lend support through the tough moment. Lloyd Blue, a member of the Florida athletic board, said he needed to talk to me privately and escorted me outside by the pool.

"Norm, you've got to be careful," he warned in hushed tones. "They got you in their crosshairs. They're really after you. I was in a group where Bob Bryan made the comment, 'Sloan will be difficult to get. He's smart and he's tough.'"

That was confirmation of just how strongly they were moving to push me overboard.

I wish that I had known early in my career what I learned the hard way through this experience: perception is all-important.

Facts and truth are not as powerful as public perception, and the reason coaches and media have such a difficult relationship is that the media creates perception. All young coaches would be fortunate to make this discovery early.

CHAPTER 10

Halloween Massacre

Four days after the party at Galen Hall's house, Tallahassee attorneys Dexter Douglass and Julian Clarkson arranged a meeting on my behalf in Tampa at the law offices of Tom MacDonald. Also in on the session were Pam Bernard, the university's general counsel, and Bob Josefsberg, who represented Florida interim president Bob Bryan. MacDonald is a staunch Gator booster who frequently represents the Florida athletic department as an outside counsel.

Douglass had come highly recommended to me as a man with the connections both in the university hierarchy and state government to help cut through the scrawl I was now reading on the wall. Dexter is an accomplished trial lawyer and a loyal Gator. I was not unhappy with Huntley Johnson, who had represented us to this point, but he had an adversarial relationship with the U.S. attorney's office, and friends, including MacDonald and Dr. Criser, recommended that Dexter's higher profile would be valuable.

Dexter associated with Clarkson, his close friend and fellow Gator who had become versed in the disclosure of grand jury testimony through a case he was presenting to the Supreme Court. Both were long-time friends of MacDonald's.

They made something of a legal odd couple. Dexter is a feisty, swaggering, sometimes profane, banty rooster who can go for the jugular with the best of them. Clarkson is the classic genteel southern barrister with a wide streak of compassion. On October 18 they flew to Tampa in an effort to determine from MacDonald, Bernard, and Josefsberg just what was needed to bridge the growing gulf between the University of Florida and its beloved and esteemed basketball coach, one Norman L. Sloan.

Dexter reported, "Josefsberg made it clear that we had a problem with U.S. attorney Mike Moore, and we should go see him and find out for ourselves what he would want us to do. Josefsberg was more direct than I expected. He was like saying, 'Listen, dumbass, this is a criminal case so you'd better get over there and see the prosecutor.' It really woke me up. We were talking about big-time stuff. I don't believe, even for one minute, that MacDonald, or Pam Bernard, or Bryan wanted to get Sloan. I really don't. I think they were wanting to protect the university. They kept telling us Arnsparger wanted to fire Sloan by exercising a clause in Sloan's contract whereby between February 15 and March 15 he could have been terminated without cause. But Marshall Criser, the school president at the time, refused."

At this time, days into preseason practice for the 1989–90 season, I had two years left on a five-year contract designed to take me to retirement. When that contract had been worked out, I had stressed the need for a commitment to Monte Towe, my top assistant, to keep continuity to the program. But when Bill Arnsparger came aboard as athletic director midway through that contract, he made it clear that Monte had no chance for the job.

"Hey, players don't come to a school because of the coaches," he told me. "They come because of the university." That's the kind of ridiculous statement he would make. I tried hard to work out something that would avoid a disruption in the program when I retired, but Arnsparger refused to listen to me.

By then we weren't able to recruit. There was just too much hanging over us. Rival coaches were whispering "death penalty" in the ear of every prospect we contacted. We were the defending SEC champions with a strong team returning for what figured to be our fourth consecutive NCAA tournament bid, but whatever momentum that should have provided in recruiting was being buried under the cloud of the various investigations and the question of who would succeed me. And, more important, when.

Back in Tallahassee, Dexter and Julian arranged an appointment with U.S. attorney Mike Moore for Saturday morning, October 28. Dexter and Julian walked the two blocks across downtown Tallahassee to Moore's office, where assistant U.S. attorney Alan Burrow, assistant U.S. attorney Lyndia Barrett, and DEA agent Lilley also had assembled for the conclave.

Dexter remembers thinking it odd that agent Lilley had his gun on. "But I reasoned that Julian and I could probably have whipped all of them," joked Dexter, "and maybe that was why he felt he needed the gun."

Moore sat behind his desk, with Burrow and Barrett on one side of the table that extended from Moore's desk and Dexter and Julian on the other. Lilley hunkered in a corner and mostly just listened. But he was at the ready if he had to shoot any guerillas or menacing Gator boosters that suddenly stormed the office.

"The reason we are having this meeting today," Moore began, "is because the grand jury is coming in on Monday." Dexter and Julian thought that was odd, too, considering they were the ones who requested the meeting. But who's to quibble.

After a few preliminaries, Moore made his second thunderclap announcement of the morning. "Look," he said, "I am the person who will make the decision on whether there will be an indictment of Sloan."

Indictment? Indictment!!?? Never mind that grand juries, not U.S. attorneys, are the ones who are supposed to hand down indictments.

"These people all have their input," Moore continued, "but the decision will be mine. I am going to go over it with everybody and consider all the circumstances."

"Well," said Dexter, "what in the hell are you going to charge him with? I know you don't have a case for perjury because the only thing you've got is some scumbag dope-dealer [Maxwell] you've granted immunity to against an upright guy like Norm Sloan."

It was all Lyndia could do to keep from laughing. Alan Burrow then airily said, "No, in drawing our indictment, we plan to cast our net a bit more broadly." He mentioned mail fraud. Fourteen counts, he said.

"Mail fraud?!" Dexter shrieked. "What did he do, write his mama a letter and lie about when he was coming home?"

"Well, no," Burrows replied. "He signed statements to the NCAA saying his athletes were eligible, knowing they weren't. Therefore, he defrauded the university."

The reference was to the required NCAA compliance forms. Each coach must annually certify that his program is squeaky clean and that all players are agent-free, academically sound, and thus eligible to compete in NCAA-sanctioned competitions. The premise here was that, for instance, if Maxwell had an agent prematurely and was thus ineligible, then I had sent fraudulent forms through the U.S. mail. Around the courthouse, this is what is called a frivolous indictment. Highly questionable, but often effective.

Dexter sensed that Moore and gang wanted a certain action out of Sloan. "Are you saying that Norm Sloan should resign?" he asked. "And further, what is the U.S. government's interest in all of this?"

"One of our functions is to protect young people from bad influences," Moore replied.

"You mean whether our client would resign or retire?" Dexter asked.

"That would certainly enter into the equation," Moore agreed.

In looking back to that meeting, Dexter and Julian say Moore never specifically said that if I didn't resign, I would be indicted. But he clearly implied that if I *did* resign or retire, the U.S. attorney's office would go on to greater callings and leave me alone.

The discussion shifted to how much time I would have to make this career decision. "Moore said two things were going on," Dexter later recalled. "Their people were having to pick a jury over in Gainesville on the DEA/agents' trial the next week. And they had the grand jury coming in at Tallahassee. We asked if we had until Wednesday. Moore squirmed a little and said, 'Tuesday afternoon would be better, but Wednesday would do.'"

Julian and Dexter walked back to Dexter's office and called Tom MacDonald. They reported on the meeting with Moore and began discussing various options, one a plan for me to retire one year early, at the end of the 1989–90 season that was about to begin in just eleven days with a November 8 exhibition against a touring Soviet team. "That would darn sure be satisfactory with the university," assured MacDonald, who said he would run the plan past Josefsberg and the other university bigwigs.

After talking to Bryan and others, MacDonald called back later that day and left a message on the answering machine at Dexter's home that such an arrangement was acceptable to all parties at the university. He said he was going to have Josefsberg run it past Moore, but that Josefsberg already was saying he thought that would be acceptable.

Now it was time to see if it would be acceptable to one other party with a casual stake in all of this: me. Keep in mind that I had no idea of the wheels that had been set in motion during this busy October Saturday.

Dexter called my house and walked me through it. He reasoned that if I stayed and coached this one last season, then I could go off into the sunset with not only my plaques, but also my salary for the second season. If I had to go out, he argued, this would not be a bad way to go. "Knowing that this was the last year," he said, "you would have a lot of emotion on your side." Not to mention a good team with Schintzius in his senior season. I also thought about the stagnant recruiting situation, and it made even more sense.

Joan and I talked about it and agreed it would be best for everyone concerned. MacDonald and Dexter talked again on Sunday, and all systems were go. MacDonald and Pam Bernard would fly to Tallahassee on Monday and work out with Dexter and Julian all of the paperwork for the early retirement agreement.

When they met in Julian's office on Monday morning, there was an air of relief. An amenable solution had been reached to spare the university and me a lot of needless embarrassment. MacDonald joked about the sign hanging over Julian's desk: Fix Bayonets. Julian explained that the sign was his personal motivational message.

"I was sitting here one day not being able to motivate myself," he explained to the group, "and I thought, 'What are the words you have heard uttered in your lifetime that revved you up more than anything else?' Well, nothing else even came in second." The foursome had a good laugh.

MacDonald and Bernard presented prepared drafts of the entire package: the revised financial agreement, my letter of retirement at the end "of the forthcoming season," Bryan's letter of acceptance, and legal releases from me and the university to one another. All were dated that day, October 30, 1989. The draft of their deal is reproduced here in the picture section, complete with MacDonald's handwritten editing added there in Julian's conference room.

In the meantime, Bernard went into Julian's private office to call Josefsberg, who hadn't been able to reach Moore on Saturday. He had promised to run the whole agreement past Moore first thing Monday morning. Josefsberg stunned her by saying my retiring one year early might not be acceptable after all.

Panicky, she called Bryan. Josefsberg, Reed, and Moore were having a conference call. MacDonald said Bryan already had cleared the plan with Reed, whose reaction was, "If this is what the university wants, fine."

But now there was this conference call with Josefsberg, Moore, and Reed. Immediately after it, Pam Bernard was told, as Tommy

MacDonald put it, "Moore wouldn't accept that, and Reed was agreeing with Moore."

The group suddenly was thrown into a quandary. MacDonald suggested that Julian and Dexter go talk to Moore. "We already talked to Moore," Dexter said irritably. "It seems to us that the university attorneys should go talk to Moore." MacDonald called and set up a meeting with Moore at 1:00 P.M.

Dexter returned to his office, and Julian ordered in sandwiches for himself and the two befuddled university attorneys. He drove them to Moore's office at one o'clock, let them out, and said he would return to pick them up when they called. MacDonald told Julian they would need "only about a half-hour." At 3:30, two and one-half hours later, they called. Both were grim when Julian plucked them from the sidewalk in front of Moore's office. They swung by Dexter's office to get him and returned to Julian's firm.

With the four attorneys seated around Julian's conference table, Tom MacDonald took a deep breath. "Mike Moore told us," he somberly announced, "that Norm Sloan would not walk on the court for the first game of the season unindicted."

Julian and Dexter blinked and collected their thoughts.

MacDonald revealed that the only "credible" evidence the university had of any wrongdoing at that point was the alleged giving of a plane ticket to a recruit's mother.

"You got another one of those superhonorable black guys to testify to that?" Dexter challenged.

"No, I used the word *credible* because this is a white player," said MacDonald.

"Well, who is it?"

"I'm not going to tell you because Norm might go get the guy to change his story," MacDonald answered. "Whoever gave the plane ticket told the boy and his mother those timeless words we have heard so often: 'What the NCAA doesn't know won't hurt them.'" McDonald did later say the player was from "Indiana or Kentucky."

Recalls Dexter, "We began discussing what the options were. We could suggest Norm tell Moore he could kiss Norm's ass, that Norm wouldn't resign and he would be indicted. And if he were indicted, the university could then fire Norm with cause under the provisions in his contract. Then again, there was the chance these bastards were bluffing and maybe we ought to see if the university had guts enough to tell Moore to stick it and just see what happened. But on the other hand, if they weren't bluffing and did indict

Norm, then we've killed our client. We might as well go pick his pallbearers, because I had been through two or three of these before and it's unbelievable what it does to a person. Norm may have thought he wanted to stand up against them—and I would have, too—but God knows we've got to do what is best for Norm.

"My sense of who was pushing the pedal on all of this was Charlie Reed. Bryan and Arnsparger and the others directly connected with the University of Florida seemed thrilled to take the one-year deal. Bryan was very happy with that solution. I think you can rule out Josefsberg as the major motivator behind the whole thing because he was representing Bob Bryan. That only leaves Charlie Reed and Mike Moore.

"My first contact with Reed," Dexter continues, "was when he worked as a lobbyist for the state education commissioner Ralph Turlington and that contact was unsatisfactory. I was late for a meeting with the task force for the School for the Deaf, which I worked with for years. I walked in, and Charlie Reed didn't know I was there. He started alleging all these things that had happened during a Senate committee meeting which I also had attended. I knew he was lying. When he got through, I said, 'I'm not on yet, but I want to tell you people that what he just said is not true.' Reed just about fell dead on the spot."

Reed moved from that post to become Governor Bob Graham's educational adviser, then chief of staff for Graham, and finally became chancellor of the state university system.

Dexter continued: "When Reed became chancellor, I had a conversation with Dr. Marshall Criser when he was then president at UF. I said, 'Hey, this guy Reed is trying to become something of a superpresident and the chancellor's office was never set up that way.' Criser agreed and expressed concern. I knew Reed was trying to set himself up in that role when he publicly dressed down the president of Florida A&M for not doing something Reed had suggested he do. Nobody on the Board of Regents said a word. I knew right then that he had filled a power gap and was taking advantage of all the weaklings on the Board of Regents who weren't going to lift a finger to oppose him."

Julian added his comments: "If Dexter's theory is correct about Reed being the architect of Coach Sloan's ouster, then that decision must have been communicated during that Monday morning conference call. Bob Bryan had signed off on the one-year deal on Saturday and seemed happy with it. We had no reason to believe that the one-year deal was unacceptable to Mike Moore. Otherwise, we would not have gone to the trouble of having MacDonald and Pam Bernard fly up on Monday to cut the deal."

"Then when they have the three-way conversation on Monday with Charlie Reed," Dexter reported, "all of a sudden the deal has changed."

Now the time had come, again, to inform me of all the new and exciting wrinkles.

We were in the middle of basketball practice when Dexter placed an urgent call to my office at 4:45 P.M. I had alerted Sharon Sullivan, my secretary, that Dexter would be calling, fully expecting him to report the few remaining details of the retire-at-the-end-of-the-season agreement. Instead, he said he needed Joan and me to drive over to Perry, a little town about halfway betweeen Gainesville and Tallahassee, the next morning to meet him and Julian for breakfast. He said he'd rather not go into details over the phone, but followed with words that set off all the alarms.

"There's a problem," he said. "They want blood."

Those ominous words ended what turned out to be the last practice of my thirty-eight-year college coaching career. I staggered back upstairs and dismissed the squad early.

That night and all the next morning—Halloween morning—as we drove to Perry, Joan and I kept guessing, trying to imagine what the new plan would be. Who could possibly have a problem with me coaching out the year and retiring a year early? Why was this suddenly unacceptable? Who was really pulling the strings here? Why?

Dexter remembers, "At the same time, Julian and I had talked all the way from Tallahassee about what was going down. When we got there, to Pouncey's Restaurant, Norm had just gotten his breakfast, a helluva stack of hotcakes, enough to feed us and every redneck in Perry."

Dexter broke the news and recommended my immediate retirement with the university paying in full my remaining two years' salary. The virgin mound of pancakes suddenly didn't look so tempting.

My first reaction was that we would fight it. I still couldn't remotely imagine anything that I could possibly have done that would merit a federal indictment. The whole thing was so ludicrous, like a bad dream. Joan was livid.

Dexter later said he thought Joan was going to hit him. "I wouldn't have blamed her either," he said.

"Norm," said Dexter, "you don't want to be indicted."

"Hell, we've been indicted all over the world for the past two years," I snapped back angrily.

Very slowly and carefully emphasizing each word Dexter answered me. "You. . .haven't. . .been. . .indicted. You don't know what you're talking about."

Years earlier, Dexter had represented a famous Florida politician, Malcolm Horne, against a similar frivolous indictment. They won an acquittal, but the rigors and expense of the case stripped Horne of his political career, his health, and most of his financial resources.

I looked over at Julian, and he had tears in his eyes. Not only was he doing what had to be done professionally, but he cared and was deeply hurt by the injustice of what was unfolding. That helped me make up my mind.

To this day, I don't think Joan thinks we did the right thing. She was more willing to fight it than I was.

The meeting at Pouncey's lasted about an hour, and I never touched the pancakes. When we left, Dexter told Julian they should go back in there and get a doggie bag for all those pancakes.

Back in Tallahassee, Julian and Dexter called MacDonald in Gainesville at 11:30 and told him I would be willing to have my immediate retirement announced that afternoon, but that I wanted to personally break the news to my team when they reported for practice about two o'clock. MacDonald advised that he was sharing a speaker-phone at the moment with Pam Bernard, Arnsparger, and Jeremy Foley and all were nodding in agreement to hold everything until after three o'clock.

Dexter read the new, revised letter of agreement to MacDonald, who said he would have to get it approved by Dr. Bryan. Not long after that, he called back and said Bryan had approved the new arrangement, which stipulated a lump sum payment of the salary called for in the remaining nineteen months of my contract: $139,000. Dexter insisted we get it all up front so they wouldn't have anything left to hold over my head if I wanted to do something dastardly, like tell the truth to the reporters or, heaven forbid, write a book.

During the noon hour that Monday, Monte Towe, my top assistant, was playing tennis with Dr. Steve Goldfaden, a dental specialist in Gainesville, on the university courts. Sharon Sullivan knew she could reach Monte during the lunch hour by calling the pay phone just outside the end court. When he answered, Sharon advised that I needed to see him at my house ASAP. Goldfaden knew this was something heavy because there had never before been anything urgent enough for Monte to leave in midmatch. Certainly not with him up a set.

When he arrived at my house, my first words were, "You won't believe this, because I didn't either. Reed wants all of us out here." I gave him the dizzy highlights of the previous seventy-two hours.

Monte called his wife, saying he still wasn't certain how all of this would impact him and Kenny McCraney. "But I'm not going to resign," he vowed.

At 2:00 P.M. Monte rejoined me at my office as I was calling some special friends to tell them what was happening. I called Sam Esposito at North Carolina State and Dr. George Neder, an Orlando allergist who had been especially supportive of our program, then walked into the locker room to meet with the players.

I told them some things had happened that I didn't understand but thought it best that I resign, then I walked out of the arena with Monte at my side. "Norm, we've walked into a lot of coliseums together," he said, tears forming. "If this is the last time we walk out of a coliseum, I want it to be together."

"We don't deserve this. We don't deserve this," Monte recalls me saying, over and over. I was in shock. I shook his hand. We hugged, and I drove away in a daze.

Monte went back inside and was a trouper. He told the players they had still chosen the right university and that they should remember all I had said about the players making things happen, not the coaches. "But who's gonna be coachin' us?" Livingston Chatman kept asking.

"I don't know," Monte answered. "I don't know."

When Monte stepped out of the locker room into the hallway leading to the basketball offices, he discovered Bob Bryan, Bill Arnsparger, and Jeremy Foley in the reception area. Sharon, sobbing, had advised them I had departed, and the threesome started toward the dressing room to address the team. When Monte realized they were going to walk right past him and Kenny McCraney without speaking, Monte lurched into action.

"Hey, wait a minute, Bob! Let me tell you what I told the players," demanded Monte, who was hoping there was some chance they would have the good sense to name him or Kenny as the interim coach to keep some modicum of continuity in place. At this point, Monte admitted he was confused about all that was happening, but nevertheless he informed the trio that he had urged the players to hang together and keep playing for whomever was named the head coach.

"At that point," Monte later admitted, "I guess I was hoping in the back of my mind that they would say I would coach out at least the rest of that season."

Arnsparger, however, sent all the signals necessary with his response there in the hallway: "I need to see you both, individually, in your offices, after we've spoken to the team."

Bryan confirmed to the team that I would not continue as their coach. He referred all questions to Arnsparger, then left. As Arnsparger addressed the team, Chatman broke in and asked again, "Well, who's gonna coach the team?" When the athletic director began talking in circles, Livingston promptly peeled off his practice gear, put on his street clothes, and left. Arnsparger told the remainder of the squad, "You might have your assistant coaches."

But directly from the team briefing, Arnsparger walked into Monte's office wearing an expression the guy at AAMCO might use if he were about to tell you the transmission can't be saved. "Tough times," he said. "Tough times in Gatorland. I'm gonna have to ask you to resign." Obviously, he had blatantly lied to the players at a time when they were groping for words of trust.

"On what grounds?" Monte challenged.

"I'm gonna have to ask you to resign," Arnsparger repeated.

"On what grounds?" Monte repeated.

"Well, uh, I-I'm just gonna have to ask you to resign."

"And if I don't? What then?"

"Well, I'll have to fire you," Arnsparger said. "We'll honor your contract for the rest of this year, either way."

"Well, I'm not going to resign," Monte stood firm. "I'll have to talk to my attorney."

It had become a common phrase. That was the depths to which things had sunk. Everytime there was a touchy issue, it was, "I'll have to talk to my attorney."

With that, Arnsparger rose, reached across the desk, and extended his hand in a shallow gesture, a repulsive notion to Monte at this shattering moment. Monte's eyes narrowed to pencil strokes as he looked at Arnsparger's empty hand.

"Bill," he said tersely, "get out of here!"

Arnsparger later had someone call Sharon to say they wanted my office cleaned out and all my keys turned in by the next morning. She relayed the message to Joan and me at home, where we were sitting around the pool with friends, sorting through the trauma. Some of them stayed late, and finally about 2:00 A.M., one of them went over to the O'Connell Center with me while I cleaned out my desk. I was pretty upset, and he was too.

I threw away more than I should have. At that point, I thought that I didn't want to have too many memories of all this. I should not have made decisions on sentimental items in that state of mind, but I loaded up two cardboard boxes and threw the rest in a dumpster. I've had people tell me what a bad feeling it is when you are told to clean out your desk. For the first time in my life, I found out just how hollow it felt. I never dreamed I'd get fired in this business.

While sorting through my things, I was startled by a crash in the outer office. I jumped through the door to discover the large, framed photo of Vernon Maxwell that had hung in the reception area along with those of other significant past Gator players, lay shattered on the floor at the feet of my friend. He looked up and smiled. Must have been an ill wind that blew it off the wall.

Within days, many of the Florida newspapers had dug past the party line and reported the true story, that I had stepped down under the threat of a frivolous indictment from Moore. They variously intoned that Reed, Arnsparger, and/or Senator Bob Graham had been pulling Moore's strings.

Perhaps the tight little circle was too much to dismiss. It was Graham who greased the athletic director's job for Arnsparger. When Graham became governor, Reed was his top aide. Now Reed was chancellor and singing Arnsparger's praises.

Reed freely admitted to reporters that he had been conferring with Mike Moore on the Florida situation since June 1988. "We've been working on this, and we're going to clean up athletics," he grandly proclaimed. Pat McManamon of the *Palm Beach Post* called Dexter for his reaction to Reed's statement.

"Charlie Reed," he said, "is trying to be a national hero—clean up college athletics and go to Washington and save the country."

I later had a call from an attorney in Gainesville, Jim Clayton, who wanted to come see me about all this. He said, "There are rules governing the conduct of U.S. attorneys, and what they are doing isn't right. What you've gone through is wrong. I want to talk to you about your options on this."

In summer 1991 Moore was nominated for a South Florida judgship, and a Miami magazine, *Miami Review*, published a lengthy article critiquing his legal career and asserting that his questionable handling of this case was the one glaring blemish on his record. Moore declined to be interviewed by the writer, Valerie Greenberg Itkoff, for the story.

As far as the fallout goes, I have said all along the people who were really hurt were Monte Towe and Kenny McCraney. Knowing the mentality of college presidents, particularly today with the pressures on them to scrub up their schools' images, Monte and Kenny's careers are dead for all practical purposes. They are unfairly and unjustifiably tainted, and no one has wanted to touch them. Both have been passed over for several coaching jobs. Monte was even snubbed by a North Carolina junior college that chose to hire a high school coach instead.

The Florida basketball program and star players Dwayne Schintzius and Livingston Chatman were also dealt setbacks that may take years to overcome.

As the events of that season unfolded—the hiring of interim coach Don DeVoe, Schintzius and Chatman quitting—Bill Arnsparger and other officials kept trying to blame the disastrous season (5–21) on Monte and Kenny, intimating they had influenced those kids to quit. I know for a fact that was not true. They talked with both of those kids because Chatman and Schintzius both needed a friend; they felt they didn't have anyone at Florida to talk to. But Monte and Kenny advised both of them to stay in school and stay on the team and work out their problems. Monte even told Dwayne to get his controversial "lobster cut" trimmed, keep his mouth shut, and finish out the year.

I'm not coming down on Don DeVoe, who was thrust into an almost impossible situation, but I would hope that if the situation were reversed I would have handled it a little better than he did. I don't think he understood what a great relationship we had with the players. I think he believed too many of those stories about how tough I was on players.

He could have gone in and said, "Hey, all of you got a bad deal—the players, the coaches, everybody. Now I'm here. Let's make it happen and try to put it all back together and have a good year." Instead, he came in with "my way or the highway." You can't deal like that with many players today, and you certainly couldn't deal with Schintzius and Chatman that way.

McCraney discovered his new and unshakeable stigma kept him from getting jobs at Cal-Berkeley, Stanford, and Iowa. I have a close relationship with Iowa coach Tom Davis, and I called him on Kenny's behalf. But nothing seemed to combat the scarlet letter.

Kenny called David Berst at the NCAA and requested a meeting. He explained that no one from the NCAA had talked to him during the investigation, yet he was being circumstantially branded by it. Berst set up a meeting with Carrie Doyle, the principal investigator on the Florida case.

Mike Glazier, the attorney from Chicago that the university had hired, called and wanted to be in on the meeting, too. Glazier, however, was not working to try to help us find the facts and come up with a good defense where it was merited. He told us early on that he had a special relationship with the NCAA enforcement staff and that he was going to protect that relationship. Glazier and his firm have developed an expertise in the NCAA enforcement process, so the NCAA recommends them to schools under investigation. They, in turn, help convict those schools; so the NCAA keeps recommending them, and Glazier keeps making big bucks off college administrations suddenly on the carpet. Those schools are running scared and are willing to jump through whatever hoops the NCAA suggests. In the end, Glazier winds up representing the interests of the NCAA more than those of the school because that's where his bread is buttered in the long run. Knowing all that, Kenny wasn't too keen on having Glazier in on the meeting.

"You know, I don't think I want to talk to you," he told Glazier. They talked it out, and Kenny finally agreed to let him sit in on the meeting.

So Kenny talked to Carrie and Mike and told them the rest of the story about being approached by Patricia Aaron, which I didn't know about. He said Patricia and Aaron Greene, her attorney-boyfriend, came to him and said, "We want you to join us. We have the players organized. We're going to get Sloan, and we don't want you to get hurt." I think Carrie was beginning to realize that some of the things she had been told didn't hold together very well.

Could there have been a hidden agenda in what Patricia and some of the players were saying?

I wrestled for the longest time trying to think of who the white kid from Indiana or Kentucky was that I supposedly supplied with an airline ticket for his mother, but I couldn't remember anything. The only thought I had was Rob Harden, a player from Kentucky, but to my knowledge Rob's mother had never been in Gainesville.

Walking with Joan on the beach at Daytona one day in early March, it hit me. "Reed Crafton!" I blurted, jolting to a stop in the sand. Joan asked what on earth I was talking about.

"Reed Crafton! Reed Crafton!" I sang out. "That has to be the player in the allegation."

Back in our beachfront condo a few minutes later, I made a call to the Florida basketball office, and Sharon sheepishly confirmed my suspicions. Urging her not to say anything to me, NCAA investigators had questioned her about the airline ticket arrangements when Crafton, a guard we had recruited late out of Indiana, made his official visit in July 1985. We signed him, and because he had to stay and enroll in the last half of summer school to become eligible, his mother wound up using the return portion of the round-trip ticket we had provided him—an NCAA infraction. At first Reed alleged that I instructed Sharon to make the arrangements for Nancy Crafton to use the return portion, something neither Sharon nor I could remember doing.

Nevertheless, this turned up as one of the two heinous allegations that were used as justification to snuff out my career in infamy and fracture a lot of other lives in the process.

The other charge, which I freely admitted and had made no effort to hide, was that I had provided Vernon Maxwell with a round-trip ticket to Boston the summer after his junior season for him to participate in a camp run by the Celtics' Red Auerbach and K. C. Jones. I thought NBA luminaries might get through to Vernon and his drug problems where assorted rehab centers, counselors, and one exasperated coach had failed. I openly ran the ticket through on my expense account, not really thinking—as I should have—that it was an NCAA infraction.

The depth of the NCAA's "case" against me and my staff after two years of digging—the Crafton claim and Maxwell's ticket to Boston—was affirmed by the line of questioning that occurred when I was finally interviewed by Carrie Doyle. Remarkably, this due process came nearly five months *after* I had been forced to retire.

I had openly offered to talk to NCAA investigators throughout the probe, but when they got around to me in the eleventh hour, they balked at Dexter Douglass's stipulation: a court reporter must be present. Carrie said that was against NCAA policy, and she would have to request special permission from the infractions committee to conduct an interview in that manner.

"This is the same tactic used by the FBI and DEA agents," Dexter told me. "They prefer not to have an interview recorded. They want to take notes and then interpret those notes in whatever manner is expedient two years later when you're not sure what the hell you said. That's their technique. They will say recording an interview is against their policy. Of course, the answer you should give to that is, 'Well, screw you. You'll do it this way or we won't do it.'"

On March 26, 1990, in Dexter's office in Tallahassee, Carrie, Mark Glazier, Dexter, Julian, Norm Sloan, and court reporter Julie Doherty tackled the business of the NCAA's feverish concerns with Florida Gators basketball. In a two-hour, five-minute interview, I came to respect Carrie Doyle more, Mike Glazier less.

Carrie convinced me during those two hours that she was after the truth, that she was not just out to hang me. And I think I convinced her that some of the wild claims she had heard from Patricia Aaron and disgruntled players were just that. She also confirmed that all the players she had interviewed discredited the allegation that I had been passing out big money.

From the transcript:

Sloan: You've talked to a lot of my former players. Did anybody ever say I gave them money?

Doyle: No. I mean, not that I can recall off the top of my head.

I think we can agree that she would have remembered "off the top of her head"—if they had.

Shortly before this, SEC Commissioner Roy Kramer, a member of the infractions committee, was quoted in the papers implying that I was guilty and that Arnsparger was doing the right thing. When I questioned Kramer's ethics in such a public prejudgment, Carrie had the backbone, bless her, to agree his remarks were "totally inappropriate."

Glazier was not the same tower of strength. He became flustered when I had an opportunity at one point in the session to question his role in all of this.

Sloan: Mike, there have been a lot of things that have really upset me, that indicated to me a deal was cut on us a long time ago by a few people: Pam, Arnsparger, and Squeakie Bryan. And Reed got involved. Last August 30, at 11:15 A.M., I called Pam and said we have to talk. . . . She said, "I thought I made it abundantly clear to you, I don't want to talk to you. You're on your own. I'm representing the university." . . . That's what we've lived with. The university turned their back on us. And I think they've relied on you as their expert. I get the impression from her that you're the one that advised them about a lot of things regarding us. She laid it on you, anyhow, that the reason we don't talk to you is, "We've been advised by Glazier not to talk to you." Is that true?

Glazier: I asked them not to talk to you about the substance of the investigation here because, for one reason, I haven't reported complete information to them, the final results of my—our investigation.

Sloan: Why shouldn't they talk to me about it?

Glazier: I haven't asked them not to talk to you about whatever your relationship was with the university.

Sloan: No, it was about these charges, these allegations. Why couldn't they talk to me?

Glazier: Well, for one thing, the university has not received formal charges.

Sloan: Hell, the university, Mike, should be defending us. We worked at the university. See, they, acting on your advice, they put us on the outside and made it look like to everybody on the outside that we were guilty and the university believed we were guilty. Can you see that? When they forced us to get attorneys, when they wouldn't talk to us, they make it look like the university believed we were guilty.

Glazier: Coach, I'd be happy to talk to you about that, but after this interview.

Sloan: I just think that was totally inappropriate and wrong. I had to find out everything accidentally. That's wrong. What the hell am I? Why did we get treated like that?

Glazier: Let's visit about that after we finish here.

Sloan: Why not now? [Carrie's] doing something else. Why not now?

Glazier: I'd just rather wait until we finish with the interview.

But he didn't then, either.

Two months later, on May 21, the NCAA formalized its case against the University of Florida, alleging three infractions connected with basketball. They were the two I have mentioned—the airline tickets involving Maxwell and Crafton—plus the revelations spilling out of the agents' trial that Maxwell had taken money from agents while still competing at Florida, as we had suspected all along. However, I knew that my coaching staff and I, as well as the athletic department administration, had done all we could do to challenge Maxwell on that matter.

Soon we received new information on the Crafton allegation, but in a new manner. In midsummer, a couple of weeks before Florida's hearing before the infractions committee, I was on a telephone hookup with a sports talk show on WQAM in Miami. The host, John Moynihan, and I were discussing the NCAA allegations when a most noteworthy listener called in.

It was Reed Crafton. He was working in South Florida and happened to tune in the talk show as he was driving along I–95. So he picked up his car phone and dialed the station. Reed, Moynihan, and I batted around the subject for nearly an hour, during which Reed admitted that he only "assumed" I knew about his mother's use of the return ticket. He stated that I had not been involved in the discussions about its use. Moynihan sent Carrie Doyle a tape of the conversation, which led to a significant move when we all gathered in Colorado Springs in early August for the infraction committee hearings.

Though invited to appear at the hearings at my own expense, I had all but decided not to bother until Florida released its 1,100-page response to the NCAA allegations. Essentially, it said that the university's administration was simon pure and in full compliance now that the "last of the renegade coaches," as Pam Bernard so delicately described us, had been booted out. Dr. John Lombardi, the new Florida president who came aboard after I left, likened Galen and me to "people who cheat on the IRS."

Our great learned men and women in the University of Florida administration had made matters worse throughout the investigation by giving the media buzzwords like "death penalty" and "rogue university." Now they were adding to the shameful Gator Glossary "renegade coaches" and "IRS cheaters."

That upset a lot of Florida supporters terribly, many of whom indicated to me that they were now seeing this whole, ugly scenario in a totally different light. Before, they told me, they thought I wasn't treated fairly and felt badly for me. After the blatant overkill and character assassination, their remorse turned to anger. I'm sorry that happened, but it opened a lot of eyes to what had been going on.

It also revived my ire enough that I was now by-damned determined to show up in Colorado Springs and look the s.o.b.'s in the eye. Just once before, some seventeen years earlier, I had appeared before the same committee under contrasting circumstances. That time, I went in with the full support and backing of my North Carolina State president and administration.

This time I knew that the Florida ground rules were different. This was every man cover his own keister.

CHAPTER 11

Undue Process in the Rockies

Saturday, August 11, 1990, broke bright and blue in Colorado Springs, a warming sun splashing over the elegant Broadmoor resort at the foot of Pikes Peak. Overprivileged adults comfortable with paying $210 a night for a double room strolled beneath the Gothic arches in casual vacation attire, unhurried en route to an appointment with one of the Broadmoor's golf courses, tennis courts, or breakfast buffets.

The all-star rodeo in town had been relegated to second billing on the local sports page by a thunderclap development just up I–25 in Denver. Broncos coach Dan Reeves had suffered a slight heart attack two days earlier, and Broncomania was awash with the grim prospect that Dan might not be sending in plays for months. (Happily, he returned the next week to whisper sweet X's and O's into John Elway's ear.)

Resort guests in the vicinity of the Broadmoor golf clubhouse paused, curious at the sight of a television news crew stationed at the door. Encouraged that he might get a glimpse of some international celebrity, a man in white shorts and a Pebble Beach golf shirt was disappointed that the noteworthy occasion was merely a session of the NCAA Committee on Infractions.

"Yeah? Who they got on a carpet?" he asked a reporter.

"Today, the University of Florida. Tomorrow, Illinois."

The man stepped back and watched with interest as the television camera duly recorded the arrival of two somber men in suits:

Galen Hall and his attorney. The coach and his counsel nodded toward more reporters milling in the clubhouse lobby and began padding up toward the second floor.

An old-fashioned, carpeted stairway rises from the lobby of the Broadmoor clubhouse to a landing that serves three meeting/banquet rooms. The infractions committee hearings were booked in the Copper Room on the west end of the two-story building, directly above Dow Finsterwald's pro shop. A wedding rehearsal was scheduled in the adjacent room, a sunny, airy expanse overlooking the putting green. (A member of the wedding party, camcorder in hand, would wander up the stairs later in the morning and innocently poke his head into the Copper Room while the hearing was in progress, setting off a momentary panic of paranoia. Two young NCAA staffers scrambled to the door to interrogate the interloper almost as if he were Edward R. Murrow and they were Hitler's general staff.)

The third room, unbooked on this day, would be commandeered by the press delegation of about a dozen, mostly Florida-based reporters. Directly across the landing from the Copper Room, the media was thus positioned to observe and intercept any principals emerging from behind the closed doors of the hearing.

Inside the hearing room, conference tables had been arranged into a large horseshoe with the open end near the main entrance doors. In the near left corner was a lavish buffet spread with cereal, Danish, snacks, fruit, coffee, cold drinks, juices, and more. The Florida delegation would sit along the left leg of the horseshoe. The NCAA staff was positioned directly across along the right leg, and seats for the five committee members were reserved across the front. At the open end of the horseshoe was a sophisticated tape-recording console, where a technician wearing earphones sat, occasionally interrupting the proceedings long enough to change tapes. Scattered about the tables were a series of curious, flat microphones resembling thin hockey pucks. Wires from each mike led to no man's land in the middle of the horseshoe and plugged into a junction box that had a thick, black connecting wire running back to the console. At the outset of the hearing, committee chairman Alan Williams told us the mikes were very sensitive and there was no need to speak above a normal conversational tone.

Dexter Douglass and I were in the room nearly an hour ahead of the nine o'clock hearing time. Wanting to visit with each of the committeemen and NCAA staffers, he made small talk, getting a feel for each individual and developing a rapport that helped soften the hard exchanges that would follow. Dexter is a shrewd man with a glib, down-home patter and infectious laugh that can charm the socks off anyone with a pulse. Unfortunately, I'm not sure all the committee members had a pulse.

I didn't quite know how I would handle meeting the University of Florida delegation: Arnsparger, Lombardi, Foley, and others. If they spoke and wanted to shake hands in some plastic display of cordiality, I didn't feel I could go along with the act. I didn't feel cordial toward them. I don't feel badly toward the Florida Gators program and supporters or even toward the university in general. I love Gators, and I feel Gators love us. But these, after all, were the handful of people who shot us down, treated us unfairly, hurt the university's athletic program, and mishandled the entire situation.

Dr. Nick Cassisi, the faculty athletics representative, was the first to pass. Nick frequently bumps into my son, Michael, in Gainesville. For the first few times after I had been forced to retire, Michael would speak and Nick would ignore him. That hurt Mike. So when Nick leaned forward, smiled, and stuck his hand out to me, I stiffed him. Most of the others took their cue and cut a wide path around where I was standing, but Arnsparger walked up and stuck his hand out to me. I acted like he wasn't there. Recoiling awkwardly, he then poked his hand out to Galen, who also turned away. "Hmmmph. . . . So that's the way it's gonna be," he grunted and walked away.

How the hell did he expect it to be? The man should have had sense enough to just walk on by. He knew how he had burned us, stabbed us in the backs. Did he think we were going to give him a hug and a kiss on the cheek? He had needlessly destroyed our careers and those of our assistant coaches, and now he wanted to pretend this was like a high school reunion of long lost buddies?

(Later my daughter Debbie was disappointed to learn that I hadn't decked Arnsparger during the hearing and had only refused his hand. She shook her head and said, "At least you could have puked on his shoes!")

The exceptions were new coaches Steve Spurrier and Lon Kruger. They are fellow coaches and had no part in all of this. I was only too happy to greet them and shake their hands. I appreciated the way Lon had handled questions from the press about me. He would say he wasn't involved in all that had transpired and simply regarded me as a friend and a fine coach. I told him right here that I appreciated his posture.

At the center of the head table, or the closed end of the horseshoe, chairman Alan Williams presided. He is a history professor at the University of Virginia, and I've known him for years. He is also the longtime faculty athletics rep at the university, and he attended the ACC meetings when I coached at North Carolina State. He probably played hardball with me more than anyone else on the committee, sternly challenging that as a coach with thirty-eight years of experience, I should have known that providing Maxwell with a plane ticket to Boston was clearly a violation.

Indeed, I probably should have. But at the time, when I was dealing with a kid with alcohol and drug problems and was desperately trying to get him straightened out, the letter of NCAA law was not the pressing factor that perhaps it should have been. Maybe I should have pleaded temporary insanity.

To Williams's left sat Beverly Ledbetter, vice chancellor and general counsel at Brown University, then Dr. John Nowak, professor of law at Illinois. On the other side were Dr. Milton Schroeder, professor of law at Arizona State, and Tom Niland, former coach and athletic director at LeMoyne College.

As all of us connected with Florida deployed on the left leg of the horseshoe; the official delegation—Lombardi, Arnsparger, Foley, Cassisi, Jim Weaver—gravitated toward the front near the committee. Galen and I and our attorneys gravitated toward the end. At first, Steve Spurrier started to pull out the chair next to Dexter, but I stopped him, musing that "all of us convicts need to sit down here together." He kind of smiled and nodded, ambling off to a chair up the table.

Across the way, the NCAA staff was headed by enforcement chief David Berst, closest to the front, then Carrie Doyle, who had been the principal investigator on our case—Case No. M32.

Interestingly, when we sat down, all of the men on the committee and the NCAA staff took their coats off. The Florida delegation and the "convicts" all kept their coats on. Mike Glazier and his partner Mike Slive, took their coats off, just like two more members of the NCAA clan. But they were working for us, right?

The irony was that here we were at an NCAA hearing, debating whether I had behaved unethically over a $240 item, and the committee and staff was being housed in a $200-a-night hotel for a week. In Kansas City, the NCAA has vast facilities in a magnificent complex, paid for in the main by basketball television money, that could have been used for this purpose. They could have saved thousands of dollars, but the reason they go to places like the Broadmoor is that it buys people like Alan Williams. You get them to serve because you're giving them free airplane trips, free lodging in an exclusive hotel, expensive meals, and liquor. They aren't doing this because they care about college athletics. If you want to find out whether they are or not, take the perks away; you'll soon discover how many of them suddenly don't have the time to give.

The same is too often true of faculty advisers on athletics. Nick Cassisi kissed fanny and did everything he could do to get the appointment as faculty athletic rep at Florida for one reason. He didn't care about upgrading the program or making life better for the athletes. It was the lure of making all those trips. That has been going on for years, and it isn't going to change.

Lombardi's opening statement rambled on for about ten minutes, the whole thing a defense of Arnsparger. He named Arnsparger repeatedly. He said the media keep implying he should fire Arnsparger. "In traveling around the state and speaking to our constituents, I keep getting asked if I am going to fire Bill Arnsparger. I'm telling you," he said, "that Coach Arnsparger is carrying out the template of now the third president he's worked under. He's not to be fired. He will not be fired. That's not even a question here.

"You put in place a template at a university, and people have to meet the requirement of the template. It makes no difference who the coaches or athletic director are. The template controls the people. And if they don't adhere to the controls, you swiftly eliminate them. Coach Arnsparger is doing a fine job. He is carrying out our mandate."

Dexter leaned over and whispered, "You don't need to say anything to the committee about Arnsparger." I wasn't going to do it, anyway.

Lombardi's tack really surprised me. His entire presentation was to take Arnsparger off the hook. Only to a lesser degree did he defend the administration on the institutional control question.

In the course of the two years that the NCAA dealt with Arnsparger in this whole mess, the NCAA people lost a lot of respect for him. At the end, I sensed from the NCAA staff some growing empathy for me. They realized that I hadn't been treated right and had been cast as the scapegoat. The one thing that Lombardi is going to have to face up to is that the situation at Florida will not heal with Arnsparger still there. Whether he has been right or wrong—whatever the perception—the anger and mistrust toward him is such that business will not return to normal while he is there.

I deferred my opportunity for opening comments to Dexter, who made a fine presentation based on the assertion this whole thing was more about a man's reputation than anything else. He noted that, to his knowledge, there had "never been a program more thoroughly investigated with the subpoena power of the DEA and the U.S. attorney's office. The media have scrutinized this and, as a matter of fact, the principal allegation against Coach Sloan was brought out by a reporter for the *Miami Herald.* And after all this scrutiny over the years—grand jury investigation, DEA, U.S. attorney, NCAA, internal investigation by the university—we have two allegations. I think that speaks well of my client. I don't know how many other programs could undergo that and come out with just two allegations, neither of which involved a recruiting or competitive advantage.

"I am a Gator," Dexter continued. "In one way or another, I contribute money to the various programs of all these people you see sitting over here. And there are many other Gators out there who feel about Coach Sloan as I do. And by the way, Coach Sloan is still a Gator. He isn't mad at Gators. He does have some difficulty with certain individuals about the way they've handled this."

I thought his remarks were excellent and concise. They set a good, noncombative tone.

By contrast, Galen's attorney, Jimmy Judkins, threw down the gauntlet. "We're going to have some hard confrontations," he said, "because we have some hard differences about one of the allegations." That allegation was that Galen supplied not only transportation, but the $360.40 for defensive back Jarvis Williams to satisfy delinquent child support at a hearing in his hometown of Palatka, some thirty miles from Gainesville.

We took a five-minute recess, after which we would go into the basketball-related allegations. Galen, his attorney, and former football assistant coach Larry Kirksey were excused during that portion of the hearing. Once the basketball issues had been deliberated, Dexter and I would depart and the football people would rejoin the proceedings.

During the recess, I didn't leave my chair, which gave me the opportunity for something I was determined to do at some point that day. As the recess began, all of the people seated along the table between me and Arnsparger stood up and walked back toward the buffet table. I sat there and stared at him. I wanted to see what he would do.

If someone is staring at you, sooner or later you can almost feel it. I could see that Bill was feeling my eyes. Squirming, he glanced up briefly, saw me staring, and quickly looked back down as if suddenly busy with the papers on the table in front of him. As he rose, he turned away toward the front of the room to avoid making eye contact and walked over to the windows overlooking the golf course. My eyes followed him every step, and he knew it. Eventually he turned back toward the center of the room and cut his eyes back in my direction to confirm what he suspected. Our eyes met again for a flicker of a second, and he looked away, quickly, self-consciously.

This may seem a childish exercise, but I wanted to see if he could still look me in the eye after all that had transpired. As I suspected, he couldn't. I loved it.

After the break, Carrie Doyle introduced the allegations involving basketball.

"Before we get started, we want to make an amendment to Number four," she said. That was the allegation that we had knowingly allowed Mrs. Crafton to use the return portion of Reed's airplane ticket. "We are deleting Coach Sloan's name as knowing and permitting this to happen." She explained that there had been conflicting statements from Mrs. Crafton and that in his final interview, Reed admitted that he only *thought* I was aware of the ticket use and that I indeed had not participated in any of the discussions about the ticket. Carrie requested that the word *staff* be substituted for my name in the wording of the charge where it was alleged who had allowed Nancy Crafton to make use of the ticket. "We're dropping any charge of Coach Sloan acting in an unethical manner in this particular instance."

Dexter nudged me with his knee and whispered enthusiastically, "Them taking you out of that one leaves you with just one allegation."

During the next two-plus hours, I thought Beverly Ledbetter was the most professional, concerned, and attentive member of the committee. I thought Schroeder was trying as best as he could to be fair, but I thought Nowak and Williams were arrogant, power-hungry individuals who seemed to enjoy brokering peoples' lives.

When the proceedings started, chairman Williams was eating a bowl of cereal. Often, when one of the other committee members or NCAA staffers was making a point, Nowak would get up, yawn, and stroll back to the buffet table to chomp on a roll or a piece of fruit. You'd hear him pouring a cup of coffee back there, and he'd stroll back, slurping his coffee. I was appalled at the constant stream of traffic to the buffet table.

These were deliberations in which it would be determined if coaches could remain in the profession, whether people would be branded as unethical. They were very serious deliberations. I thought Nowak's and Williams's attitudes were demeaning. During some of the deliberations, Nowak and Schroeder would drop their chins in their hands and fight sleep, the way you might do in a long lecture or church sermon.

Thankfully, SEC commissioner Roy Kramer, another member of the infractions committee, could not sit in on our case because Florida is a member of the SEC. Knowing Roy, he would have been right at home. In another life, Roy Kramer and John Nowak and Alan Williams would have been stacking kindling around my ankles while I was being prepared to be burned at the stake.

If I were a member of the NCAA council, I would be very embarrassed by the conduct of some of the committee members.

I thought Tom Niland, being a former basketball coach, had a grasp on what we were talking about that far exceeded the other people on the committee. He is a man who has been in the trenches. The NCAA should make sure that there is always one member on the committee like Tom who has had coaching experience and has had to recruit. But he was there only by happenstance, a substitute for another committee member who had resigned. Throughout the hearing, he injected what I considered a breath of fresh air—common sense steeped in reality.

"Norm," he would say, "didn't you talk to Maxwell about his problems?"

"Certainly," I replied.

I got the impression he knew what I had done to help the kid and prevent problems, but he also knew that here we were dealing with a couple of law professors, a legal counsel, and a history professor. He knew that the mentality was different from that of people who are out on the athletic frontlines.

I made a colossal mistake in flying Maxwell to Boston. But our contention was that if anyone in the athletic department had picked up on this and red-flagged it as a violation, we would have made Maxwell refund the money and would have self-reported it to the NCAA. But that didn't happen. My statement to the committee was, "I really wish someone had caught this, and maybe we all wouldn't be sitting here today."

This made Arnsparger and company more than a little nervous, because it flew in the face of their self-serving claim that despite all the institutional controls in place, these scumbag coaches had circumvented the system. Dodging the ominous charge of lax institutional control on their part and blaming everything on "renegade" coaches was the whole basis of the school's game plan.

Williams pressed for why I had put Maxwell's ticket on my expense account.

"I'm glad you asked that," I said, "because this shows I wasn't trying to hide anything. My thinking was, 'Where can I put this in the budget?' I couldn't put it in team travel. It certainly wasn't recruiting. So I instructed my secretary to charge it to my personal expense account."

At first the committee dwelled on the fact that the ticket was delivered to my house, like that was some surreptitious act of concealment. Niland picked up on that and asked Foley, "Jeremy, to your knowledge has Coach Sloan had other tickets delivered to his house?"

"Well, yes," Foley admitted.

"Well, what's significant about this ticket being delivered to his house?"

With that, Dexter jumped in. "Doesn't change a thing. The important point is that the expense account was in channels."

In the end, Alan Williams said he simply could not "accept that you didn't know this was a violation. Giving a player an extra benefit is the most fundamental violation of the rules."

"Dr. Williams," I said, "I agree with you. But I have to tell you what my frame of mind was at that time, and that's all I can do. If you don't accept that, then you don't accept it. At that time, I had a young man in serious trouble. Drug abuse. Alcohol abuse. Lifestyle. Beating up on his live-in girlfriend. Problem after problem after problem. We had had him in two rehab institutions, and he flunked out of both in the first week. We had taken him to psychiatrists and counselors, and nothing was working. I had an opportunity to send him up to this camp. The one thing I knew meant something to him was the NBA. My thinking at that time was I would get in touch with Red Auerbach and K. C. Jones and say, 'This kid has a tendency to self-destruct. Please give him some words of advice that might wake him up.' That was my thinking. The kid had finished his junior year. He wasn't going up there to become a better player. I was trying to get this kid some help to get his life straightened out."

Nowak was having none of it. "Coach, Coach, you had to know this was a violation," he harrumphed. "A man of your stature had to know."

"I probably shouldn't say this," I responded, "But I'm here trying to tell you what my frame of mind was then, and I'm trying to be as open and fair about this as I can be. As I look back now, I can say, 'Norman, that was a stupid thing to do.' But I wasn't looking at it from the point of view of, 'Is this a violation or not?'"

Tom Niland spoke up and said, "Mr. Weaver, you're the compliance officer, right? Coach Sloan ever call you to check whether something was a violation or not?"

I thought Weaver gave a great response. "Anytime he was in doubt, he called me," he said. "He obviously wasn't in doubt about this."

Indeed, that was exactly the situation. I wasn't in doubt about it. But I wasn't thinking properly, either.

Later, Niland asked Jeremy Foley if, now that this instance had been discovered, he had gone back and checked all of my other expense accounts.

"Yes," Foley answered.

"Well," said Niland, "did you find other violations?"

"No."

"Any irregularities of any kind?"

"No."

"In other words, this expense item of Coach Sloan's, through all the scrutiny, is the only one you've turned up as a violation."

Niland also put Weaver and Arnsparger in something of a box. Pointedly noting they must have been aware Maxwell was "a problem child," Tom asked Weaver if he had ever personally met with Maxwell to discuss those problems. Weaver hesitated and looked around at Arnsparger, who had told the staff that he, Bill Arnsparger, would take charge of the Vernon Maxwell case.

Arnsparger spoke up and related this to the committee. This was the only thing Arnsparger said the entire time I was in the room.

At the outset of the hearing, the NCAA staff had recommended the charge of insufficient institutional control be dropped, but all during the questioning I had to wonder if the committee was buying that. So much of the time was spent pointedly questioning how my expense account for Maxwell's ticket and the change of Reed Crafton's ticket to his mother could have gone through all channels unnoticed if proper institutional controls were in place. Afterward, the media concentrated on the matter of the institutional control allegation being dropped, but it was interesting that Dr. Lombardi made a point of noting to them that it was only the staff recommendation and that the committee had the prerogative to resurrect the charge.

There was a discussion of the Maxwell agent matter, although none of it was directed to me. One interesting exchange did come up. When the NCAA staff presented its findings that the school and I had done all we could do to determine if Maxwell had an agent, David Berst stated that Florida might still be subject to repaying all or a portion of the revenues from postseason games in which Maxwell competed. Berst said the NCAA council would determine that percentage, and Nowak noisily challenged him.

"You mean that we, on this committee, don't have the right to say that we think they should be penalized 80 percent or 90 percent or whatever?" Nowak indignantly asked.

Berst responded by telling Nowak he had the right to say whatever he wanted, but that only the council is empowered by the bylaws to make the final determination in such a matter. I thought the exchange was very telling as to Nowak's attitude. There were a couple of other instances in which he talked "down" to the staff. I didn't get the sense he cared about what was right or wrong. He was on the committee, by God, and whatever the committee did was sovereign and to be accepted as gospel.

Finally we got into the matter of whether the committee would find that I had acted unethically. At the beginning of this, Dexter again made an impassioned presentation, referring to me as "a man who has been thirty-eight years in the business, blunt, outspoken, accepted by his peers as a great coach. We're talking reputation here."

I could see this turned the committee off. They didn't care about my reputation. Most of them were dotting i's and crossing t's here. I wasn't a human; I was a case study that was either in compliance within the rules or not. Black or white; no grays. I couldn't shake the question of why all of this was going on over a $240 ticket to Boston. The trappings and the heavy discussions seemed to suggest something of greater significance to mankind. I didn't want to go out of my career being branded as unethical. The average fan out there reads that and thinks you're stealing or handing out cars or rewriting transcripts or bribing game officials.

Dexter and Nowak lapsed into a spirited exchange about what ethics are and how they are defined. I nudged Dexter with my knee. "You want to say something?" he said.

I nodded.

He got Williams's attention and I was given the floor.

"I came here for one reason—to try to get you people to understand that I didn't intentionally violate a rule," I began. "At no time was my thought process: 'I know this is a violation. They have checks and balances here I'll need to circumvent.' That wasn't the case. If I thought it was a violation and still wanted to do it, I would have given the kid the money and told him to keep his mouth shut. And this never would have come up. I didn't do that. All I can do is tell you that from my heart, and if that can't help me, then nothing can help me."

Those were my last words in the hearing.

Afterward, one of the young NCAA staffers walked up to Dexter and shook his hand. "I just want to compliment you on the way you and Coach Sloan handled yourselves. I think you guys helped yourselves. I don't think I've seen a coach and legal counsel acquit themselves in one of these hearings as well as you two did." (I'll withhold his name to spare his being hit with a charge of consorting with the enemy.)

I think there were a lot of people who expected me to go down, guns blazing. I think Dexter was a little concerned about that. "People at Florida think you're going to get up there and hurt yourself by blasting the NCAA and everybody," he had told me, coaching in his sly way. Some people view me as a loose cannon. But I wasn't going to do that. I felt my blood pressure boil up just one time, and that was when Lombardi said in his opening remarks that "coaches can violate rules regardless of our compliance program." I took that as just one more self-serving shot at Galen and me, and I could feel the blood rush to my ears. But I said nothing.

I thought on two or three occasions the enforcement staff stepped in and made positive statements on my behalf. And some of the committee members didn't agree. Basically, I felt the committee had its mind made up before the hearing. They read all the reports from the staff and formed their opinions. We might have swayed them on a point or two, but when I walked out of the Copper Room, I had the feeling that the matter of whether they would declare me unethical would come down to a 3–2 vote, one way or the other. My sense was that Niland and Schroeder would not declare me unethical and that Williams and Nowak would. That left Beverly Ledbetter as the swing vote and I couldn't get a reading on her.

She struck me as a sharp, intelligent, perceptive, independent-thinking person. She gained my admiration in that room, and I felt I could respect her decision, whatever her vote. When the findings were announced a month later, we would learn that she apparently chose to join the others in painting a scarlet *U* on my chest. With Florida abstaining on the matter, the committee chose to accept the staff recommendation that I be officially declared unethical.

Florida's callous abstention is in sharp contrast to the way Notre Dame reacted a year later when its football coach, Lou Holtz, appeared before the infractions committee to account for infractions virtually identical to the ones used to hang Galen and me.

Holtz admitted that while he was the coach at Minnesota, he gave $250 in cash to a football player so he could pay the cost of a correspondence course in the summer of 1985, thus enabling him to be eligible for that approaching football season. Additionally, he admitted giving "twenty-five to forty" dollars to a recruit that same year, supposedly because the recruit had lost his wallet. This means Holtz provided cash to players slightly more than the $240 airplane ticket I had provided Vernon Maxwell and only slightly less than the $360.40 that Hall was accused of giving Jarvis Williams.

Yet, Holtz didn't receive so much as a wrist slap. The statement of Notre Dame athletic director Dick Rosenthal afterward indicates the kind of support Notre Dame gave Holtz during the investigation:

> I would first like to express our appreciation to the NCAA In-

> fractions Committee for the professional manner in which it handled Coach Lou Holtz's connection with the University of Minnesota inquiry. The Committee worked quite diligently in providing Lou with a full hearing on the matter and giving lengthy consideration to his factual presentation. . . . We felt strongly all along none of the allegations involved any attempt to gain a competitive advantage of any sort, and we believe the NCAA has concurred with that stance.
>
> All of us at the University continue to have great faith in Lou Holtz, his integrity and in the manner in which he has conducted the football program at Notre Dame. We appreciate the forthright way in which he has dealt with this matter both with the NCAA Infractions Committee and with University of Notre Dame officials.
>
> It's appropriate that the Committee has recommended no further actions of any kind relative to these matters, in light of all the information provided by Lou and others through the course of the inquiry. . . . The University has fully supported him at every turn, and we're pleased that he can now focus full attention on his primary task.

Lou gave a kid $250 cash, and he is ethical; I gave a kid a $240 plane ticket, and I'm unethical. Lou helped a kid with his academic shortcomings, and he is ethical; I helped a kid with his drug problems, and I'm unethical. Lou says he sought no competitive advantage (although his player *did* become eligible the next season), and it is ethical; I gained no competitive advantage by helping Maxwell (who was already eligible), and I'm unethical.

I'm not pointing all this out to suggest that Holtz should be run out of college coaching. He helped kids in need, as he should have, just as I attempted to do.

The difference was that Lou worked for a school and administration with the backbone to stand behind him, and I worked for one falling all over itself to offer me and Galen as human sacrifices in a pitiable and unsuccessful attempt to avoid any sanctions.

An interesting thing happened during the Colorado Springs hearing involving Beverly Ledbetter. In Dexter's prehearing response to the NCAA on my behalf, he attempted to point up the irony that if I had been selling drugs it would have been permissible under NCAA rules. When I read that I took exception, explaining to

Dexter that we still had a moral obligation to report something like that to the NCAA.

Ms. Ledbetter picked up on it and challenged us in the hearing. "You mean that unless it's a violation of the letter of a rule, you wouldn't feel a moral obligation to take a stand on this?" she asked.

I didn't know what to say because she had flat nailed us to the wall on this. Dexter jumped up and said, "Oh, no, no, no! In fact, when Coach Sloan read that he corrected me and said, 'That's not true.'" When he said that, the whole committee kind of chuckled.

She kept on, and Dexter finally said, "I apologize to you for putting that in there. And I withdraw it. And I'll be glad to walk out there and tell all the press that I apologize for putting that in there, but I was simply trying to make a point that wasn't well presented." She was fine then.

Afterward, I walked to the front of the room, shook her hand, and told her I understood perfectly where she was coming from. We had a nice little exchange on the matter. Since I considered her the swing vote, I left feeling we had a shot, in part because of that exchange.

I also shook hands with the other members of the committee and thanked them for the opportunity to defend myself before them.

The NCAA staff members in particular were very cordial toward Dexter and me. I appreciated that. I didn't go into the hearing with an adversarial attitude toward them. I really was there just to establish that I was not an unethical person. I came to respect and appreciate Carrie Doyle and told her so. I think that anybody who has a problem with the NCAA and is investigated by Carrie will get a fair shake.

The two new Florida coaches, Spurrier and Kruger, came by, wishing me well in Greece, where I would go a week later to begin coaching a professional team. I wished them and the Gators luck for the coming seasons. It was a warm, sincere exchange consummated with firm handshakes.

But to the rest of the Florida delegation, I might as well have been a leper leaving the room.

We were into our exhibition season in Greece when the infraction committee's decision was announced on September 20. Obviously my hopes for Beverly Ledbetter had been misplaced. With my dear, supporting former Florida employers abstaining on the matter, the committee went along with the NCAA staff recommendation that Galen and I be declared unethical.

Significantly, though, the only penalty placed on the basketball program was a temporary and virtually meaningless reduction of the scholarship cap from fifteen to thirteen. Football, the repeat offender in this case, was hit with a two-year probation and prohibited from postseason play following the 1990 season, a sanction that would cost Florida millions of dollars and a possible national championship for Spurrier's very fine 1990 team. Spurrier and school officials reacted with shock, but what did they expect? With Arnsparger and Bryan spending two years characterizing minor misdeeds as heinous crimes and taking the dramatic action of firing Galen in midseason, the NCAA could hardly turn the other cheek.

My reaction to the news was interesting. When you are in a country where English is not the predominant tongue, there is the tendency to think you're invisible. If you cough, you imagine that they don't notice because you've coughed in English.

I quickly came to enjoy working with the Greek players. They really made me feel good the way they accepted me and responded to my coaching. After being branded "unethical," even if only as an NCAA categorical definition stemming from a single incident, my first reaction was this: "My God, I hope none of these people in Greece read that story."

I was anxious to get to practice the next morning to measure the reaction. Not one soul asked me about it. It never came up.

Again, I thought there was a whole lot of to-do about nothing. The penalty was a farce. To take away a few scholarships affects only a couple of walk-ons down on the end of the bench. In my last stint at Florida, I would venture to say that we never used more than thirteen scholarships for recruited players. The few times numbers fourteen and fifteen were utilized were only to reward some walk-on during his senior season for his perseverance.

I interpreted the penalty as the committee saying there were no serious violations committed. When you're not kept off television or out of postseason play, you're involved in a minor violation that had nothing to do with gaining an advantage or skewing the recruiting process.

Angered at the injustice of the unethical tag and the lack of due process in the committee proceedings, Dexter Douglass was anxious to pursue an appeal, but I thought that would be an exercise in futility. I had reached the point where I wanted the whole thing behind me. Family and friends who called parroted the same theme: There you are: nothing.

Sadly amusing were the comments of Dr. Lombardi, who intoned that Florida would weigh the merits of a suit against me to recover the $287,561 the school would have to return to the NCAA because of Maxwell's participation in the 1988 postseason tournament. Obviously, Arnsparger, Bryan, and their colleagues had failed to inform the new president that in their haste to run me off they had voluntarily given me a full legal release.

I would be tempted to dredge up the old saw about the left hand not knowing what the right was doing, except that this was definitely an administration of two left thumbs.

CHAPTER 12

Battling Woodward, Bernstein, and the Zebras

Of the many adjustments required of college basketball coaches over the years, I probably lagged behind the times the most in dealing with game officials and with the contemporary media. Oddly, my failings in both areas usually stemmed from my coaching strength, the intense, competitive zeal that enveloped me at the start of a game and continued to pulse hours after the final horn. Diplomacy and Norm Sloan were hardly bedfellows when one of the zebras made a questionable call in a close game or when a roomful of reporters were before me with my sideline adrenalin still pulsing at flood stage.

Two quick examples:

After our Florida team beat North Carolina State and Purdue in the first two rounds of the 1987 NCAA tournament in the Carrier Dome in Syracuse, I was ushered into the postgame press conference. The latter victory qualified us to advance to the Sweet Sixteen, and I was filled with emotion and a sense of vindication from what I had felt was a grave injustice to me and to our team during the hype leading up to the tournament.

I foolishly used that press conference to jump all over commentator Dick Vitale for his constant promotion of the Italian coaches. He had been stumping for North Carolina State coach Jim Valvano all week before the game, extolling Jimmy's virtues as a great motivator, great this, great that. It gnawed at me. What people have to understand, however, is that late in a game—late in the season—coaches are emotionally raw. I said what I thought was the right thing at the time, which was something to the effect of needing a vowel at the end of your name to be considered a worthy coach. I didn't even get back to the hotel before I knew it was the wrong thing for me to have said. Needless to say, the media were none too kind to me in reporting my remarks, and rightly so. I had made a mistake. For the most part, I deserved the lashing that came with it.

I was upset because I didn't think our team was getting the kind of credit they deserved for the year they were having. Vitale was glorifying these other coaches and their teams; yet here was a Florida team that was playing in its first NCAA tournament, and it was as if we were an afterthought.

Years before that, when I preceded Valvano at State, there was a game in which one of the officials was Dan Woolridge, a very fine person and a highly principled, capable referee. We lost the game, and I was very upset with a call or two that Dan had made near the end.

Unfortunately, the game officials used the coaches' dressing room at Reynolds Coliseum, just down the hall from our team locker room. At the end of the game, I flew down the stairs, my blood boiling. Honest to goodness, I don't remember what set me off, but the next thing I remember I had charged into the officials' dressing room to give Dan a piece of my mind, yelling and screaming at him.

Dan was startled, his eyes like saucers. He finally found a moment to get in a response. "Norm! Norm!" he exclaimed. "Do you realize where you are?"

I was standing, fully clothed, in the shower with Dan, raking him over the coals. Shower water was cascading down over both of us. He and I have laughed about that for years.

Perhaps the best piece of advice I ever received about how to cope with officials came from C. M. Newton, now the athletic director at Kentucky. A longtime basketball coach, Newton was associate commissioner of the SEC and supervisor of officials at a time when we were struggling to build the program at Florida early in my second stint at Gainesville. Having just come from the ACC, I was accustomed to the high level of officiating in that conference and was a bit too intolerant of the whistle blowing in the SEC. I called

Newton often, complaining about the quality of his bumbling officials.

It upset me at the time, but a comment he made really put it in perspective. "Norm, when you get a better basketball team," he said, "I think you'll find you get better officiating."

I think that's definitely true. I know I've always been toughest on officials when I had teams that weren't so good; I was trying to squeeze every ounce of help I could get. Officiating is a tough, thankless job, and we don't pay those guys enough.

That's something else the NCAA could do with that billion dollars from television in the next seven years: pay the officials more. The ideal situation would be that we would pay them enough that it becomes their primary profession, rather than having a banker or an insurance salesman officiating not so much for the money but for the thrill of being involved in athletics. I would have liked for their living to depend on their performance, just like mine did. That pressure is at the very root of some of the outbursts we've seen from coaches following particularly frustrating defeats where inept officiating was a factor.

A few years back, when the SEC tournament was at Kentucky, the championship game came down to Ole Miss against Kentucky. Ole Miss was something of a surprise finalist under Coach Bob Weltlich. They played well enough to win the title, Weltlich felt, but they lost in the final because of the officiating. On national television, sitting there at his postgame conference, he broke down and cried. "What do you have to do?" he agonized. He was ripped in the national media for blaming his defeat on officiating.

Gene Keady, the coach at Purdue, made the same mistake in the 1991 NCAA tournament. Keady said you run a clean program, you graduate everybody, and "the goddamn officials don't know the game." He pounded a table when he said it, and it was roundly criticized as sour grapes.

I don't think coaches should be the ones to evaluate officials. They should have a little input, perhaps, but they should not have the power to blackball officials that has long existed in college ball. That sort of power should only be the province of a conference commissioner or supervisor of officials.

For a long time in both the ACC and the SEC, it was understood that each coach in the league had one blackball; he could eliminate a guy from working games involving his team. Well, if you have a ten-team league, you might blackball ten different guys out of a pool of maybe only twenty-four officials. If you have a blackball, you're going to use it. I never failed to use mine. If you have a chance to scratch the guy you thought was the worst official, you'll scratch him.

It created a situation where, in the heat of a game, you might shout over at an official, "This is the last time you'll work for me!" or "Well, I won't have to put up with that anymore!" That's a terrible thing to say, but there's hardly a coach who's been in that situation who hasn't. It is wrong to put an official in that position, and it is wrong to put a coach in a position where he can scratch an official.

I think we should have a national organization of officials, who are assigned all over the country, rather than conference by conference. The NCAA already has taken the first step toward that by having Hank Nichols in charge of making officiating more consistent. It used to be that if you were playing out on the West Coast, you encountered one style of officiating. Up East you'd get another. When I first played up East, rebounding was like a war. Fouls were called only when a broken bone showed! But on the perimeter, you couldn't touch anybody. Now, with Hank conducting officiating clinics around the country, we're starting to see a standard style developing coast-to-coast.

There was a time when an official could belong to the association of only one conference. Now the top officials join several conferences and dole out the dates that each conference can have them. They sometimes wind up working five and six games a week. You can't do that without it affecting your judgment or becoming irritable and affecting relationships with players and coaches.

Compounding that is the increased tendency by coaches—encouraged by national television commentators—to try to "work" the officials. Guys like Dick Vitale, Billy Packer, and Al McGuire get on television and say, "See, there's Gene working the officials. Now, so-and-so better get in his two cents." Young coaches watching that get the idea that they're supposed to get on officials and ride them to better manipulate a victory.

I think college coaches should be fined for technicals just as they are in the NBA. Some coaches intentionally draw a technical foul, thinking it will gain them some advantage later on in the game. Fining the coaches—putting the money into some scholarship fund or something—would deter that. But the fund shouldn't be earmarked for some zebras' ball, or else the refs would toss around technicals like Mardi Gras beads.

When I first started coaching, I had a pretty good relationship with officials. There may have been one or two I didn't like or who didn't like me, but that's going to happen. Generally, however, I could talk to them. At an ACC tournament or Dixie Classic or whatever, the officials were invited to the hospitality affairs. Coaches and officials were in there shoulder-to-shoulder getting to know one another. I thought it was a very healthy situation.

But with the advent of big money and big pressures, all of a sudden the administrators started separating officials from coaches, creating a gap that I think is responsible for a lot of the ill feelings that exist today between the two groups. If you could just go play golf and sit down and have a beer together, much of that could be eliminated. But the big cheeses don't want that happening anymore.

We were playing in the Sugar Bowl tournament one year and there was an official there out of Dallas, Jim McDaniel. I had had some problems with Jim earlier in a game at Vanderbilt, where the teams' benches were at opposite ends of the court, opposite from the respective dressing rooms. I never could understand why they wouldn't assign each team to the end of the court closer to its dressing room.

Near the end of this game, McDaniel missed an out-of-bounds call when a Vanderbilt kid stepped out of bounds by eighteen inches. From my vantage point, I could look right down the boundary line and see it clearly. The no-call kept us from having a chance to win the game.

When the game ended, I began heading across the floor toward our dressing room. Here came the officials. I was terribly upset, so I moved right in McDaniel's path. Everytime he moved, I would move. So we eventually ended up nose-to-nose like a plate ump and a baseball manager irate over a called third strike or some other miscarriage of world justice. I bumped him, which was a definite no-no. I was warned and put on probation by the conference commissioner.

Two years later, McDaniel was working the Sugar Bowl tournament and I ran across him sitting in a hotel lounge having drinks with the coaches of Southwestern Louisiana, one of the other teams in the tournament. That really should be fine, but in the environment created by college administrators, I regarded it blatant fraternization. Administrators need to foster the concept that most coaches and officials have integrity.

One of the best officials in the country—college or pro—is Don Rutledge, who lives in Orlando. He can never work our games at Florida because he attended school there. Yet, if we made it to the Final Four and Don was assigned to that game, as he has been several times, there is nothing wrong with that. My argument all along is that if we believe Don has enough character and integrity to handle the Final Four, why doesn't he have enough character and integrity to work a regular season game?

Another is David Jones, who lives in Gainesville. He was one of the best officials in the conference, as evidenced by his 1989 elevation to the NBA, but he couldn't work our games because he lives in Gainesville. Instead, the conference spent hundreds of dollars to fly in an official from, say, Lexington or New Orleans, and put him up overnight. Those same administrators will then gather in a posh resort, beat their chests, and declare they are implementing methods for cost containment.

Red Mahelik was a college official everybody trusted. If Red made a call, you knew he believed he made the right call. He was very sincere and took his duties very seriously. When I was at The Citadel, we went to the Southern Conference tournament for the first time in school history and made it to the final, where we lost to West Virginia and Jerry West by eight points. Red blew a call early in that game.

I was up, adrenalin pumping, yelling at Red, even though I knew I shouldn't be. At the next timeout, he hustled over in his bowlegged canter with a heavy scowl on his face. I figured I was about to really get it. He dropped down on one knee in front of me and said, "Norm, I'm sorry. I blew that call."

Bless his heart. Now what was I going to say? "I'm sorry I said anything, Red."

Lou Bello, who lived in Raleigh, was the first official I knew of who brought entertainment into officiating. He'd slide in like he was stealing second base, whistling a foul. His calls were very demonstrative and his style was soon imitated by other officials. They'd play to the crowd and play to the coaches. I enjoyed those guys because they were always loose and always alert.

I first came to know Lou when I played at North Carolina State right after World War II and he was officiating locally. By the time

I got into coaching, he was officiating throughout the ACC area. Then when I moved to Florida in 1960, we bumped into one another and he asked about getting him some SEC games. I proposed him to the conference, and, naturally, they were glad to have him. We had him at a Vandy game in Florida Gym. We weren't very good, and Roy Skinner, who had played for me at Presbyterian College, was coaching at Vandy. He had a heckuva ball club, but I felt we were getting a favorable whistle in the game. You don't very often feel that way, but it was apparent to me that on close calls we were getting some breaks from Lou.

Near the end of the game, we were behind and got the benefit of a close call by Lou. We made the free throws to put the game into overtime. Near the end of overtime we were behind again, and Lou gave us another borderline call. We made the free throws and went into a second overtime.

At that point, Lou came over to our huddle and pulled me aside. He said, "Norm, you're on your own in this one!" We were. Vandy won.

I've also been on the other end when an official was leaning the other way. One incident, though, was much more than just leaning.

George Conley was one of the top basketball officials around. At one time, he was a Kentucky state representative from Ashland. His son, Larry, played at Kentucky and is now a color commentator for ESPN. George and I had one of those coach/official relationships that could best be described as stormy. Neither of us backed down, but we respected each other. I always respected him as an official, and I think he knew that I wasn't just a yapping mouth. I think he knew if I was upset, I had good reason. Sometimes, admittedly, I got too upset, but always with cause.

When I left Florida and took the coaching job at North Carolina State, George Conley was assigned to my very first game, against VMI. Frank Weedon, State's sports information director and later assistant athletic director, blew a gasket. Weedon is a nervous, excitable guy whose voice became higher pitched the more excited he became. I used to call him "Squeaky." He was tremendously loyal and insisted we couldn't have George Conley working any of our games.

When I said I didn't have any problems with George, Weedon recounted an incident the previous season during the ACC tournament, which at that time was still being held every year in Reynolds Coliseum on the State campus. Frank was assigned as the tournament manager, and one of his areas of responsibility was a little block of courtesy seats at one end of the floor for the officials who were not working the game in progress.

For one of the games, Conley brought in a woman who was not his wife to sit in the officials' area. Weedon objected, an ugly scene erupted, and Conley was forced to remove his lady friend. Upon his reluctant retreat, Conley glowered at Weedon and darkly warned, "I'll get even with you sons-of-bitches for this."

A written report of the incident was made, including corroborating statements from Clemson sports information director Bob Bradley, ACC referee supervisor Footsie Knight, and Wolfpack football quarterback Jim Donnan, all of whom witnessed Conley's tirade. Donnan, now head coach at Marshall, was one of several football players who helped Weedon with the tournament. He had been the first to balk at Conley and his lady friend, but had had to summon Weedon for help. Frank knew the woman, who lived in Raleigh, but that was irrelevant. He was simply enforcing ACC policy that dictated the courtesy seats were only for the officials. No wives *or* girlfriends.

We beat VMI, 67–58, but we were so bad you couldn't tell anything about the officiating. Then on January 7 Conley worked another of our games, a real barn burner at Maryland.

Conley's head suddenly appeared in our huddle. "This is a final warning," he said. "If I hear one more thing out of your bench, that's going to be the end of the game. I've had it."

I was stunned. To my knowledge, we hadn't had anything but the normal chatter. "Get the hell out of here!" I snorted. "I'm busy. I don't know what you're talking about."

When the players broke and returned to the floor, I asked an assistant, Charlie Bryant, what the hell all that was about. "I don't know, Norm," Charlie said, shaking his head. He was as bewildered as I was.

The game rolled down to a little more than a minute to go, and George made an unbelievably bad call. It wasn't even close. One of our players, Nick Trifunovich, was dribbling and was rammed from behind by a Maryland player. Nick went down, the ball went out of bounds, and possession was awarded to Maryland. Arguments ensued, and I was hit with two technicals. After Maryland's Jay McMillen made one of the two free throws, I shouted, "You happy now, George?"

I put my head down in disgust. The next thing I know, Charlie was shaking my arm and shouting, "He called the game off!"

"What are you talking about?" I asked, looking up in time to see the officials running off the floor. I jumped up and ran after them, trying to catch them to find out what in the hell was going on. I chased them all the way to the dressing room. They let me in. "George," I wailed, "what the hell's this all about?"

He said, "I warned you. You were sitting over there shaking your fist at me. I warned you. That's it." He walked away.

The next voice I remembered was Weedon's, and it was now in full soprano. "I told you. I told you not to let Conley work our games. I told you it was gonna happen."

The next morning, my president, Dr. John Caldwell, called me in and was on my case. This was embarrassing. National news. Game called with a minute to go.

I explained to him that I didn't know for sure why Conley had called the game. We had filmed the game, so we looked at the film with Dr. Caldwell and all agreed that he blew the call. It was filmed from the opposite side of the court from the bench areas, so my coaches and I were clearly visible when Conley called the game. None of us were doing anything. However, sitting on the end of the scorer's table was Frank Weedon who made a sarcastic gesture—not an obscene gesture—as if to say, "Okay, George, you got us back."

That's when Conley called the game and ran off the floor.

Thank goodness we filmed the game from the side of the court facing us.

Dr. Caldwell also had the written report on the incident at the ACC tournament the previous year. He said, "We just forget about it. This is one where we bite the bullet and go on. But we will never have George Conley work one of our games again."

He issued this public comment on the matter, which appeared the next day in the Raleigh paper: "I have reviewed thoroughly with coach Norman Sloan last night's episode at the Maryland–North Carolina State basketball game. It is neither possible nor necessary that I attempt in this statement to review all that transpired in the game situation Saturday night. Coach Sloan is an honorable and dedicated coach and a man of high standards. On the basis of my knowledge of the situation at present, I do not find that his conduct was in any way unusual or reprehensible."

I would learn to value and appreciate having the school president stand up for me when the slings and arrows were flying.

Or, during a fad embraced by Georgia fans: rolls of toilet paper.

After I returned to Florida, there was a year when we were having problems around the country with students throwing cups and streamers and other objects on the floor after the home team made its first basket. It became a real problem, and there was some discussion about making it an automatic technical foul.

At Georgia, the drill was to rain toilet paper onto the floor during introductions and after the first Bulldog basket. It became a community project. Somebody in town was contributing boxes of toilet tissue that were available at the door. As they came in the building, students would pick up a roll of toilet paper. Just prior to this particular game, we discussed whether to stick them with a technical immediately or give the benefit of a warning. My understanding from the conference office was that the decision was to open the game with a technical foul if the toilet paper came down during introductions.

I called the SEC office for John Guthrie, supervisor of the basketball officials, and he told me he would be at the game and give the officials specific instructions. An announcement would be made prior to the introductions, warning that the first roll of toilet paper to hit the floor would result in an automatic technical foul against Georgia. The introductions occurred, the toilet paper hit the floor, and all that happened was a warning.

I was upset. Now Georgia coach Hugh Durham got on the public address system with his high, squeaky voice and told the crowd that if they threw any more toilet paper on the floor it would cost Georgia a technical foul. He told them it was okay to have thrown it one time, but now it had to stop. Heck, he was virtually patting them on the back for their spirit. I knew the toilet paper would come down after that. Sure enough, after the first Bulldog basket, there was a deluge. In some of the rolls, students had put rocks and other items to give it a little weight. I don't think they meant to hurt anyone, but it was dangerous nonetheless.

The game was stopped, and we shot a technical. So we were off and running on a controversial note. Our games with Georgia were known to careen along at the very edge of control to start with. We had several forgettable incidents, including one fight that was totally out of control.

We lost this particular game, which didn't help my mood any.

They had assigned a campus policeman to walk on the court with me at the start of the game and off the court at the end. A fairly small guy, he told me he was to walk with me and protect me from objects that might be thrown from the stands. I had never much been in favor of that sort of thing. I understand the school's concern, but I feel you just incite the situation when you make a show of a bodyguard.

At the start, a few things were thrown, but nothing serious. However, at the end of the game, fans were gathered above the exit to the lockers, pelting us with cups and obscenities. I turned angrily to the campus cop and demanded: "Aren't you gonna do anything about that?"

He said there was nothing he could do.

"What?" I screeched. "Then why the hell are you here?"

With that, he got mad at me for my indignant attitude and started telling me if I would take care of myself, he would take care of the fans.

"No, you're not taking care of anything!" I snapped.

By now, we had reached the hallway, barking at one another about his performance as a peacekeeper. In the heat of the moment, I uttered the magic indictment.

"You're a gutless little fucker, aren't you?" I challenged.

It was not exactly the job evaluation he wanted to hear, and he jumped up in my face, shaking his finger and telling me I couldn't talk to him that way. By now we had reached the door of our dressing room, and I came right back at him. "You better get out of my face," I stormed, "or I'm gonna pinch your head off."

He came totally unglued. He jerked his handcuffs out and came at me screaming, "He's mine! He's mine!"

I just pushed him aside and stepped past a couple of our players into the locker room. When I stepped through the door, Kenny McClary, who was six feet, six inches, and 230 pounds and Dwayne Schintzius, seven feet, two inches, and 270 pounds, filled the doorway. The little campus cop continued screaming and kept poking between the players trying to grab me.

Guthrie arrived, saw this ugly scene unfolding, and rounded up the little cop's sergeant. John somehow managed to restore order, assuring everyone wearing any type of uniform that I would behave and get on the bus without further incident. The sergeant ordered my "bodyguard" to back off, but the little guy hung around, screaming and beating his handcuffs on the wall. He wanted so badly to put those handcuffs on me and throw me in jail.

Later, when we came out of the locker room and headed to the bus, he was still rattling his handcuffs. He walked along beside me, glaring and popping the handcuffs in one hand.

Some of my friends had a lot of fun with the whole escapade. At our team banquet at the end of the season, one of the "awards" was a pair of engraved handcuffs mounted on a plaque.

Coping with a changing media was even more difficult for me than dealing with the striped shirts. What I would tell a young coach now is that he should be completely open and honest with the media, and then have thick skin. He would have to understand that his candor may gain him some compassion and empathy with some segments of the media, but it won't entitle him to a cheerleading press. I came to understand that only in the final few years of my career, and I had some problems because of it.

This is one of the areas where I'll admit my advancing age was a hurdle. I wasn't too old to adjust to players and I wasn't too old to adjust to the changes in the game, but I don't think I ever made a good adjustment to the changes in the media.

I've told Joan that if I had it to do over again, the biggest thing I would change in my professional life would be my relationship with the press. The successful people work at it. I wouldn't be dishonest, but I wouldn't be as combative, wouldn't challenge reporters at press conferences. It wasn't necessary to do that and, admittedly, showed a lack of control. Before a game, I was fine, but I started becoming more and more combative as a game went on. I enjoyed it, too. I openly confess that I enjoyed competing. But when the game ended and you're supposed to be a different person, I was still combative. The juices were still flowing, and I had a difficult time turning that off before the postgame press conferences.

I worked alongside Dean Smith for years. Super coach, super image. But he was one of the biggest phonies I ever encountered when it came to dealing with the media. He was overly image-conscious, although I can look back and see there were some advantages to that. I might handle it differently, knowing what I know now, although I would have a certain amount of internal conflict about where to draw that line between candor and playing a public role.

Dean was very effective with his act. He turned everything to his advantage. If a problem broke at North Carolina State or some other ACC school in, say, academics, you could bet your bottom dollar the next week there would be something coming out of Chapel Hill extolling the positive academic aspects of Dean Smith's program at North Carolina. You could count on it. As a result, he not only reaped the benefit of the positive publicity, but he put the rival school on the defensive, creating a contrast with his exemplary program.

UCLA coaching legend John Wooden was interesting in this area. I got to know John well, and he was uncommonly sensitive about the press. Nell, his wife, couldn't handle it. She could not cope with a negative article and would literally become bedridden at times by coverage of John's program.

I always thought John was covered very favorably. The western media seemed to be the last affected by the Woodward and Bernstein syndrome, and by the time the California sports journalism developed that cynical and investigative tinge, John had retired. He received good press, yet was paranoid about media coverage.

As the media changed, so did college athletics. When I was at Florida the first time, the papers in Tampa and Orlando wouldn't even carry the box scores of our basketball games. There was no thought of sending a staff member to cover the games. Now just about every major paper in the state will have a beat writer—sometimes also a columnist—assigned to the games in Gainesville. That makes dollars. The media and the road to the Final Four have played a big part in creating the interest and the big bucks that are there.

The flip side is that it can make life tough for the coaches and the Dwayne Schintziuses of the world—tough for those people who stub their toes along the way. When you have that many people covering a story, there's competition and pressure to break stories. I came to realize those guys had as tough a schedule as I had; they're competing with each other on a daily basis.

If somebody would explain all this to developing young coaches, it would help them. I didn't have anyone to do that for me. I went through that transition and wasn't smart enough to recognize it until it had already taken place. When did the "balanced story" become journalistic law, requiring that even upbeat stories contain criticism? If I had a hard time dealing with that, you can imagine how it frustrates young players. They have a very difficult time regularly reading critical things about themselves and their teams.

There was a long time when I would joke that the newspaper is only good for wrapping yesterday's fish. Well, that's not true. The printed word affects people. "I read it in the paper," people will offer as evidence of some wild claim. In most minds, that attaches proof to almost anything.

I'm not down on the media, but in some ways I just think that both the print and electronic media come up short. On the print side, there are too many young guys who don't do their homework. As a result, they don't know their butts from third base about basketball.

This may stun a lot of people, but I don't think Dick Vitale is good for college basketball. I think he has used college basketball. I think he has used college basketball and his flamboyant style to create a guru image for himself and his wallet. There's just too much hype involved in television coverage of games, and Vitale is at the forefront of that.

The change in the media that was toughest for me to embrace was in the early eighties when so many sportswriters tried to become amateur investigators. I happened to catch Frank Deford, editor of *The National*, on one of the network morning shows when his sports daily began publication. He described the makeup of his staff and emphasized that he would have "some of the best investigative people in the business." Frank went on to explain that investigative reporting is a very important part of every sports page.

When there's something to investigate, I would agree. Usually, however, it's a little like appointing a grievance committee that has to find some grievance to justify its existence. I would imagine that investigative reporters believe they'd better get their rumps out there and dredge up something that will permit editors to stamp their feet indignantly and say, "Ahah! We caught you red-handed!"

One Florida paper came up with some old expense accounts and reported that I had billed the athletic department several hundred dollars for pistachio nuts. The story ran under dark headlines and was picked up by the wire services. It appeared in a North Carolina paper under the headline: "Sloan in Trouble Again."

What the investigative reporter failed to unearth was the deep, dark secret that the pistachio nuts were in gift packs that we sent out annually at Christmas to sponsors of our television show and other promotional efforts. The pistachio caper became a joke around our office.

I used to discuss this at press conferences, often without enough diplomacy. I'd tell reporters that if they weren't so busy turning over rocks trying to find worms, they would better understand and appreciate what was happening on the court. The Worm Brigade.

I think Watergate influenced so many things in this country, not least of which was the sports page. Swept up by this craze more than most was the *St. Petersburg Times*, which dispatched not just one, but two investigative reporters to concentrate on Florida athletics in addition to its regular sportswriters. Talk about a grievance committee in spades! That was the *Times*, whose people fed on every rumor from players who quit or spent time on the bench, often badgering them and attempting to intimidate them with tactics I associate more with the CIA or KGB than sports journalism.

One day I received a call from Lolita McClary, wife of one of our players at Florida. She has a distinctive accent that I recognized right away. In hushed tones, she said, "Coach, don't say a word. Just listen." Then she did whatever it is you do on today's phone systems to bring an extra party into a telephone conversation. (I never have grasped all the extra little tricks that are available from Ma Bell these days.) For the next thirty minutes, I listened in shock as a reporter with the *St. Petersburg Times* attempted to get confirmation from Kenny McClary on a bizarre assortment of wild allegations of drug abuse, slush funds, and recruiting violations. The reporter ranted and cursed and threatened, saying he knew all about all these improprieties and advising that it would be better on Kenny if he came clean.

"Man, where are you gettin' all this crazy shit?" Kenny would say. But each time Kenny insisted the allegations were off base, the guy would turn it up another notch, even to the point of saying he would help Kenny "get even with Sloan." As mentioned in an earlier chapter, McClary was disgruntled for a period of time over his playing status as a senior. Thus, he became a prime target for the Worm Brigade.

There was obviously some collaboration between the *Times* and a *Time* magazine reporter named Ted Gup, who began using the same high-handed tactics and asking about many of the same wild rumors. One dealt with a former player named Ronnie Williams who was recruited in 1980, the year I returned to Florida from North Carolina State.

Ronnie Williams played at St. John's Prep in Wisconsin under Coach Gary Richert, who later coached in Florida at St. Leo's, a small college just north of the Tampa–St. Petersburg area.

Marquette was interested in Ronnie, but he seemed to like the idea that it could be his show at Florida. That appealed to him. And indeed, Ronnie set Florida's career scoring record, although it later was broken by Vernon Maxwell. But he didn't take care of himself, failed to make the NBA partly because he was overweight, and has been playing professionally in Europe the past several years.

On the night of February 1, 1989, Richert called to say he had just finished a remarkable and stormy conversation with Ted Gup, the *Time* reporter formerly with the *Washington Post*. Richert said Gup alleged that my assistant, Monte Towe, and I had handed over two briefcases filled with money—one to Richert and one to Ronnie—at the time we signed him. Richert said Gup charged that we also had given money to Ronnie's mother and that we got the St. Leo job for Richert, put him on our schedule, and gave him ten thousand dollars out of gate receipts each time we played.

The whole thing was utterly ridiculous. In the first place, we were one of the few schools recruiting Ronnie Williams. We had nothing to do with Richert getting the job at St. Leo. And we had absolutely no access to gate receipts at Florida basketball games.

Richert said he found the charges so absurd that he initially joked about it, but after realizing that Gup apparently was serious, he emphatically denied all of it. In a heated exchange, he demanded to know Gup's source of these allegations. He said Gup refused to divulge his "very reliable source."

The next morning, February 2, I called George Solomon, the sports editor of the *Washington Post*. George was the basketball publicist at Florida when I was there the first time. I asked him about Gup, and he confirmed Gup had worked at the *Post*. "He's a good man, Norm," said Solomon.

"He may be, but he's gone off the deep end on this," I said, and proceeded to tell him about Gup's wild charges to Richert.

The next day, February 3, I managed to reach Ted Gup.

"Ted? Norman Sloan," I said.

"Yeah, yeah," he said, upbeat, like he was glad to hear from an old fraternity brother. "How're you doing, Norm?"

"I understand that I'm supposed to know you," I said.

"Oh, oh. . . . Who told you that?"

"Gary Richert did. He said you told him you and I knew each other well, and you've been after my ass a long, long time."

"Why, that s.o.b.! That's not true."

"Well, what's going on?" I asked.

"Oh, you mind talking? You mind if I record this?"

"I wish you would," I said.

A moment or two passed and he said, "We have it on good authority that Ronnie Williams has told some people you gave Gary Richert ten thousand dollars and gave Ronnie ten thousand to sign at Florida."

I told him that was baloney and asked him who his "good authority" was. Of course he wouldn't say. I told him to get his good authority, and I'd get Williams and Richert and we would all sit down and talk about it. He declined. I told him he was making serious charges, and I didn't appreciate it.

"Well, let me tell you, Norm," Gup said, "Richert admitted these things. He said you gave him ten thousand dollars and that he and Ronnie went out and bought cocaine and had a big party."

"Bullshit!" I retorted "Where you coming from with all that?"

"I'm just telling you, Norm. I don't care what the guy told you. He told us that."

So I got back with Richert that night, calling him from a pay phone in the lobby of the Orlando Arena. The arena was celebrating its opening week, and Joan and I were there attending a concert featuring Kenny Rogers and Dolly Parton. Our Florida team would play Stanford in a nationally televised game the next afternoon in Orlando Arena, and Ted Gup's fishing expedition hardly had me in the focused frame of mind you'd prefer for big games.

I told Richert what Gup had said about Gary "confirming" the cash to him and Ronnie Williams.

"Yeah! Hell, yeah!" snorted Richert. "The sonofabitch was saying all these crazy things, and finally I got disgusted and told him, 'Yeah, that's right. We each got ten thousand dollars apiece and went out and bought cocaine and had a helluva party. Is that what you want to hear?'"

So then Gup, who knew better, tried to use that as a wedge to get me to admit that something rotten really did happen.

Richert added that Gup had called him back and berated him for sharing their first phone conversation with me. Richert said Gup again charged that Richert had accepted money for players and that he was going to print it no matter what Gary said. Gary said he then informed Gup their next communication would have to be through attorneys.

Richert thinks Gup also talked to the *St. Petersburg Times*, resulting in the *Times*"s Tom Zucco showing up at Gary's house with more of the same questions. Gary said they nearly came to blows before he ran Zucco out.

In my final conversation with Gup, he said he had checked his notes and found that he had been mistaken, that Richert "did not implicate you, Monte, or Florida in any way."

Finally, I figured we had to protect ourselves. On Monday, February 6, I briefed Norm Carlson, Florida's sports information director, who confirmed with *Time* magazine that Gup was preparing a story on college basketball recruiting. Carlson suggested we call Richert and get on tape his account of what had happened. We did that, and I added my own five-page memo of everything I could recall from the wild week of Gup-gate.

The *Time* story ran in the magazine's April 3 issue and made no mention of Florida. Mostly it dealt with Jerry Tarkanian and UNLV. Another wonderful week of dealing with the Worm Brigade.

Coping with new techniques in the electronic media can be equally exasperating. Upon my return to Florida, that first team in 1980 wasn't very good, even with Ronnie Williams. But the one team we could beat was Auburn. We beat them twice, home and home. We got to the SEC tournament in Birmingham, and who do we draw but Auburn.

We were up by two with about a minute to go, and during a timeout I was telling our guys to play good, sound, tough defense. "But the one thing I don't want is for any of you to let somebody drive by you. Keep them on the outside, and if they make a shot from out there we'll live with that. But don't let anyone inside for a cheapie."

We had a player named Mike Milligan from Long Island, the main recruit that my predecessor, John Lotz, brought in the previous year. Auburn inbounded, and Milligan's man stepped right by him for a layup to tie the game. I went bananas.

We went back up by two with less than a minute, and Auburn called time. Here came our guys to the sideline, and I was still livid.

Little did I realize that Joe Dean's television crew had a boom microphone dangling over our huddle. In a most animated fashion, I began going over the same things I had just stressed in the earlier timeout. ". . . AND DO YOU SUPPOSE," I screamed, "WE

CAN KEEP THEM FROM MAKIN' ANY MORE FUCKIN' LAYUPS!!??"

The game ended. We won, 50–48, and were overjoyed. We went to a restaurant called Michael's, had a big steak, and went back to the hotel happy. The next morning, I had breakfast set up with one of our top alumni in that area, a heart surgeon.

He could tell there were no holes in my elation, so he eventually said, "Y'all haven't heard about the television flap?"

"No, what do you mean?"

"Ooooooh," he said. "I think there's something I need to tell you."

He proceeded to explain that my X-rated admonishment in that last timeout huddle the previous evening was picked up loud and clear by the regional network televising the tournament.

Ouch.

Florida's athletic director was Bill Carr, a rather strait-laced guy. But Bill was fine. He was a little cool about it, but nothing serious. Bill was a football center at Florida, so he had been in the heat and understood that something other than the king's English is occasionally employed in tense moments of athletic combat.

About halfway through the next week, I happened to be talking to Bill. He was pleasantly surprised that he hadn't received a single letter of complaint about my television ad-lib in Birmingham. I had received two. One was a nice, supportive note from one of our fans. The other was from a lady in Talladega, Alabama.

She started off telling me what an awful thing I had done. She said little boys and little girls who are looking up to coaches and athletes as role models were likely watching the telecast. They heard this profanity. Eloquently, she went on and on, and I began to feel lower and lower.

Then I get to the last sentence. "And besides all that," she wrote, "it was a horseshit, fucking thing to do."

I howled. My secretary, Sharon Sullivan, had already read the letter and was standing in the doorway, waiting for me to get to the punchline.

CHAPTER 13

Storm Clouds at Seven-Feet-Two

From the moment we first began scouting him in high school, we could tell that Dwayne Schintzius, the seven-foot, two-inch, man-child, would be a difficult but rewarding project. Tethered to those awesome physical tools and delicate skills were a terrible self-image and a stubborn streak as wide as a foul lane.

But I never imagined a relationship that would bottom out in the tiny bathroom aboard the University of Florida's thirty-passenger airplane, the two of us wedged into the tiny compartment, me angrily grabbing a handful of his notorious "lobster cut" and shaking his head until he bolted for the safety of the cabin. This came near the end of Dwayne's stormy sophomore season at Florida, just hours after he had refused to re-enter a Southeastern Conference tournament game against Georgia in a crucial moment during the final seconds.

Our most difficult season with Dwayne had begun with a large, unflattering spread on him in *Sports Illustrated* at the outset of his 1987–88 sophomore year. The profile was an offshoot of an incident the previous spring that vaulted him into national attention as an antihero. We had advanced to the NCAA Sweet Sixteen at the Meadowlands to play Syracuse. The game offered a juicy matchup of Schintzius and Syracuse's outstanding center, Rony Seikaly, a seven-foot junior who would later become a star with the NBA's Miami Heat.

The matchup became even more compelling after Dwayne's

brash and ill-advised comments in a press conference the day before the game. Dwayne was coming off a big performance (twenty-one points, six assists) against Purdue's fine center Melvin McCants in subregional play a few days earlier and was full of himself when he was led into an interview room in the bowels of Brendan Byrne Arena to face about a hundred sportswriters. I probably shouldn't have taken an immature freshman to a press conference of that scope, but he was the person the media wanted to talk to. I failed to coach him to be careful about what he said.

When Dwayne starts talking, even he is never sure what will come out. Instead of cutting his losses, Dwayne has the knack of complicating a problem, as evidenced by his assorted bizarre utterances that contributed to his spectacular and costly tumble in the 1990 NBA draft.

I don't think he meant to come off with such braggadocio that day in the Meadowlands, but he began saying what he expected to happen in the game the next day and overstated what he was going to do with Seikaly. The next morning the New York papers tabbed him as the Mouth of the South. This ridicule developed a thyroid condition after Seikaly blew him away in the game that night, outscoring Dwayne, 33–6. Syracuse sent us packing, 87–81, and Dwayne had secured his role as a national target that would only be expanded by the *Sports Illustrated* profile the next fall.

I can't tell you how much more difficult that article made him to deal with. He became completely defensive, reaching the point in practice that if I'd push him hard, he'd start gagging and acting like he was hyperventilating. He'd make horrible sounds. One thing I learned a long time ago in coaching is that when a player says he is sick or in pain, you can't ignore it. You can't take the chance. But in my mind I knew it was mostly an act, so the entire year was a tough situation. I think Dwayne wasn't playing as well as he thought he needed to play in respect to all the publicity he was getting. It came to a head in the SEC tournament semifinal game against Georgia in LSU's Assembly Center.

It was a close game. Dwayne was having a hard time, and Georgia center Alec Kessler was getting the best of the battle. At six-eleven, Kessler is a tough cookie. When he flipped Dwayne a couple of elbows, Dwayne got all fired up and began screaming at an official, calling him the "m——f——" word as he ran by. The ref hit Dwayne with a technical.

I took Dwayne out of the game. He was still in a rage. I guess one of the biggest mistakes I've made over the years is when a player was emotionally upset, I made him come sit by me. I probably should have let them go sit on the end of the bench, where they wanted to go, and cool off. But I made them sit by me so I could talk to them while their mistakes were fresh in my mind and theirs.

At first Dwayne ran down and grabbed a seat near the end of the bench. I made him move up next to me. He was angry and embarrassed. I chastized him about cursing the official and asked him a question—I can't recall about what—and he wouldn't respond. A player who refuses to communicate is one of the most difficult things to deal with for a coach. I'm trying to communicate, and he just sits there and freezes up. That's what Dwayne did. We were struggling late in a conference tournament game, so I took the attitude of "to heck with him" and went on with the players we had on the floor.

Then we reached the desperate situation in the final seconds where we were two points down and shooting one free throw. Obviously, our only chance was to miss the shot intentionally and hope to put the rebound back in to force an overtime. This calls for deploying your tallest players on the lane, so I turned to Dwayne and told him to go in for so-and-so. He just looked at me. I told him again, and he just sat there. So we went with the players on the floor.

Georgia got the rebound to seal its 72–70 victory, and in the postgame press conference I was asked why I hadn't put Schintzius back in the game for that last free throw. I said I had tried, but Dwayne refused. The story crackled nationwide.

What I didn't know was that my top assistant, Monte Towe, was so upset with Dwayne, he took off his sportcoat and threw it at him in the locker room, a career first for Monte. So Dwayne had been duly put on notice that he had committed a definite no-no and responded by going into his best act of innocence.

On the school plane, a twin-engine Fairchild F–27, the first row of seats faces the rear. I always took one of them. Dwayne always sat on the first row facing forward because there was a generous space there that afforded him maximum leg room. When we lifted off from Baton Rouge that Friday night shortly after losing to Georgia, Dwayne turned on his act. He had his legs crossed and alternately whistled and sucked orange juice, trying to show me just how nonchalant he could be in the wake of what had just happened.

We had been in the air about forty-five minutes before I decided

I'd had a snoot full of his innocent airs. I stood up, leaned over him, and said, "I want to talk to you—NOW. Come with me—NOW."

I walked him to the toilet at the front of the plane, and we both went inside. I closed the door. You can imagine the scene with two of us inside an airplane restroom, with one of us seven feet, two inches and 270 pounds. It was, well, close quarters. He plopped down on the toilet, and I was wedged to one side between his knees and lavatory, hunched over. I started in on him. Funny, but I can't recall ever attending a coaching clinic covering the proper techniques for chewing out a seven-footer in an airplane head.

"I have taken all I'm going to take from you!" I began. "I have tried to be considerate. I have tried to be helpful. The entire coaching staff has. Now you've embarrassed us on a national scale. You not only embarrassed yourself and your family, but you've embarrassed me and our entire program. You do realize, I hope, that I will be criticized if I don't do something drastic to you because of this. You've put me in a bind now."

I went down a laundry list of ridiculous antics he had perpetrated all season.

He blinked and recoiled with a scowl. "Well, what have I done wrong?" he had the audacity to ask.

He had that long, gooky hair, and I reached out and grabbed a handful of it and shook him. "For starters," I screamed, my eyes now narrowed to turkey buzzard slits, "your goddammed hair!"

With that, he went to pieces. He jumped up, pushed past me with a thump, and scurried back to his seat where he sobbed uncontrollably the remainder of the flight. When we landed in Gainesville, he forced his way off the plane before anyone else and announced he was through with this bleeping team. He refused even to board the waiting team bus for the five-mile ride to the campus. At that time, it was fine with me.

Monte had the presence of mind to tell Phil Weber, one of the assistants, to ease alongside Dwayne on the shoulder of the road and talk him into his car. Weber's instructions were to take Dwayne to Monte's house, where Dwayne's car was parked, and keep him there until Monte arrived. When Monte arrived, he discovered the somewhat slapstick scene of Phil's 300ZX parked crossways in the driveway, blocking Dwayne's old Chevy.

At 2:00 A.M. the three of them hashed it all out on the front lawn, Monte finally extracting promises from Dwayne that he wouldn't do anything foolish and, particularly, wouldn't leave town. After all, despite the loss to Georgia, we were scheduled to open the NCAA tournament the next weekend. With that, Monte instructed Weber to move his car and let Dwayne out.

Monte said, "It was either that, or we were going to have to come up with some wild insurance claim to get Phil's 300ZX replaced. One way or another, Dwayne was driving out of there, even if it was through Phil's car." Allowed to drive away, Dwayne promptly broke his promises; he left town. He made the two-hour drive home to Brandon, but not to his parents' home.

I called Ken and Linda Schintzius to clue them into this latest adventure with their son. They called back the next morning to say they had not seen Dwayne. They called back Saturday afternoon and still no Dwayne. What he had done was drive to Brandon before dawn Saturday, and he was staying with a buddy of his. He finally surfaced at his parents' house on Sunday, and Ken called to tell me Dwayne was there and they were having a family conference. This was on Pick 'Em Day for the NCAA tournament, and we found out we would travel to Salt Lake City to meet St. John's, with or without our troubled center. Ken said they'd let me know what transpired out of the family conference.

Sunday night, Ken called and said he thought everything was going to be all right, though a couple of things could be a little sticky. They were going to bring Dwayne back to the campus on Monday. We'd have a meeting and go from there.

Ken and Linda brought Dwayne to my office, and we quickly cut through a lot of things with Dwayne's admission that he had been wrong in many of his actions, including his refusal to go back into the Georgia game. The big point was his hair.

"I am not going to cut my hair," he said. "If you try to force me into changing my hair style, then I'll go somewhere else."

I looked at Ken.

"This is what we spent most of our time on yesterday," he said. "He's absolutely adamant that he is not going to change his hair style."

I told them that made it kind of simple for me, since I wasn't that hung up on hair styles. "I don't like your hair style," I told Dwayne. "I think it's untidy and unbecoming, but that's me. You obviously see it in a different light. I'm going to ask you to do this: if we talk to you and say it needs to be a little neater, that you need to trim it up some, let's don't have a big argument about that. Because I've given more than my mile."

They called it the lobster cut, and it became his signature. Kids began imitating it.

So Dwayne came back on the team and was easy to work with in preparation for Salt Lake City. Out at the tournament, he was a delight, though not particularly productive (eight points, five rebounds) in our opening-round victory over St. John's, 62–59. He came back with seventeen points and nine rebounds in the next game, but we were eliminated by the very fine Glen Rice-Rumeal Robinson Michigan team that would win the national title a year later.

In the days before we left for Salt Lake City, Dwayne began to hang around my office, wanting to talk more. He wasn't about to say he was sorry, but we'd sit down and we'd talk. At one point, he shook his head and said, "You know, Coach, sometimes I can be a real shithead."

I laughed and told him we all are at times and assured him that was normal. He was feeling apologetic and didn't know how to handle it. That was as close as he could come to an actual apology. Instead of saying, "I'm sorry," he admitted that he could be a "shithead."

I thought Dwayne Schintzius had finally turned the corner.

Throughout Dwayne's junior and senior years at Brandon [Florida] High School, we recruited him hard. Monte made it almost a personal mission, and, as a result, he and Dwayne developed a special relationship that remains intact today despite countless brushfires.

Dwayne and his father, a sergeant in the Hillsborough County Sheriff's Department, were very receptive to us from the start. However, the Brandon coach, Frank Vining, was very much opposed to us recruiting Dwayne and represented the first hurdle we had to clear. Vining didn't like Florida and was enamored with Kentucky. He gave us a difficult time.

Dwayne had problems in his relationship with Vining. Naturally, we took his side. After all, we were trying to get next to Dwayne, so every problem he had with Vining, we more or less blamed the coach. That's one of the distasteful facets of recruiting.

After we signed Dwayne and had to start working with him ourselves, I had a lot more sympathy for what Vining went through. Dwayne was a very difficult young man to coach. He couldn't stand criticism at all and was very moody as a practice player. We saw that in Dwayne when he was in high school, but we always managed to find some reason that he was dogging it that day in practice.

The gulf between us and Vining grew so wide that when Dwayne indicated he wanted to sign with Florida, the coach did everything he could to block it. Finally, we asked for a joint meeting with Vining and the school principal, Charles Nelson, who had been a student at Wake Forest when I was playing at North Carolina State.

I promptly laid out the problem, that the coach was trying to block our efforts to recruit Dwayne to Florida. Vining vehemently denied it at first. I pointed out certain instances where he had said Dwayne belonged at Kentucky where the program is more advanced than Florida's and he would have another big man to practice against. He said Florida would never have a big man.

As I ticked off the various things he had said, I could see he was getting angry. Finally, he jumped up and shook his finger at me and said, "Who are you in basketball? What have you ever accomplished?"

I just sat there. He went on to verify that he was very much opposed to us. He said, "Sure, the kid will be much better off at Kentucky." He turned back to me and shook his finger again. "You don't fuckin' scare me," he said.

That was all Nelson needed to see. Before we left the room, he made very clear to Vining that the matter of where Dwayne would go to college was out of his domain. We didn't have any more trouble from Vining, although the situation between Dwayne and him was terrible for the rest of that season.

Hurdle number two was Ken Schintzius's own growing fascination with Kentucky, which was being expertly fueled by Joe Hall's assistant, Leonard Hamilton, now the Miami Hurricanes' head coach. Ken Schintzius was soon blown away by Kentucky and Hamilton. Kentucky talked about flying them up to Kentucky in a private jet, and Leonard told Ken he could just let them know anytime he wanted to fly up and see Dwayne play at Kentucky. I'm not going to say it would have happened, but Ken envisioned himself sitting there in that plush executive jet, wearing a blue coat, sipping those free drinks, and having a big time going to the games.

He started giving us the arguments about why Dwayne should consider Kentucky.

As everyone found out, Dwayne dances to his own tune. He may be wrong at times, but Dwayne Schintzius calls the shots in his life. And he had his mind made up that he was going to Florida.

In sitting with Joe Hall and Leonard Hamilton at Kentucky, Dwayne heard all the reasons why he should come to Kentucky: championships, postseason tournaments, and more. He interrupted and asked, "Hasn't Florida beaten you the last two times you played?"

Hall shuffled uncomfortably and said, yeah, but look at the overall record. "No, there's a change going on," Dwayne said, holding his ground. "And I could be a part of it if I become a Gator." He told them that right there in Joe's office.

Dwayne was a Gator at heart, and he had made up his mind. Joe later told me that at that point he knew that Dwayne was solidly committed to going to Florida. That's one thing I appreciated about Dwayne. All along, he wanted to be at Florida. He wasn't worried that we were in a building mode; he wasn't worried about a lack of tradition. He wanted to be at Florida and to be one of the guys who helped Florida become a winner. That helped me a lot through that first year with Dwayne. I had to go back many times and draw upon that knowledge.

Dwayne would blow up, yell and scream at us, and stalk off the floor. I'd send him to the dressing room, and he'd go there on his own. He was a very difficult person to coach, but he had a great year for a freshman.

Before enrolling, Dwayne played in several national high school all-star games that summer, and Monte tagged along to protect our interest. Even though a kid has signed with you, there follows an extended period of time when the NCAA allows no contact with the recruit. It's a rule that has never made sense to me, and we were scared to death of it. Monte followed him to California and to Las Vegas, and he would just sit in the stands. He couldn't say anything to Dwayne, but by his presence he was telling him, "I'm here. I care about you." The junkets gave Monte a chance to observe Dwayne under circumstances away from that uneasy relationship with his high school coach, and Monte started telling me about halfway through this tour that Dwayne was very hardheaded, uncommonly sensitive to criticism, and not a willing worker. Having played for me, Monte knew he was talking to a coach who was liberal with the criticism and worked players hard.

"He is going to be worth all the trouble he will cause," Monte told me, "but he is going to cause a lot of it."

There was, but I don't want to suggest that I regret having Dwayne on our team. My relationship with Dwayne Schintzius was a challenge, but a delightful one that took an upturn right from the moment he burst out of that airplane restroom sobbing.

Following Dwayne's sophomore year, he went to summer school at Florida, even though he didn't have to. Monte and I—especially Monte—spent a lot of time with Dwayne that summer. He moved in with Monte, renting a bedroom in Monte's house for one hundred fifty dollars a month. We had to get in touch with the NCAA to find out how much rent he would have to pay, because we knew that would run up a red flag immediately.

Monte says, "For the first time, Dwayne really started enjoying who he was. He had a lot of individual attention that summer, and he realized these people really cared about him."

Monte would get up early and run with him. They played golf, tennis, spent a lot of time together. I'd spend time with him too, and by the start of his junior year, we had constructed—brick by brick—a good working relationship. I'm not going to say it was perfect, but we knew when to be a little considerate of him, and he knew he had to show some consideration for us. All in all, I thought that during his junior year we had a very good relationship. Had we been allowed to stay, I think it would have been an excellent senior year, too.

Even with all the progress we made that summer when Dwayne lived in Monte's house, he virtually wiped it all out with one foolish act with a tennis racket. Before the season began, he went out with his friend, Rob, whom he had stayed with when he ran off threatening to quit near the end of the previous season. The Schintziuses never approved of the relationship, but he was Dwayne's friend. These big guys don't usually have many friends.

Rob came to Gainesville, and they were out far too late drinking at a bar called the Animal House. They got into a confrontation with some other kids, and somebody threw a beer can at Dwayne's old car. It was an old Chevy coupe, the same one he had during his last two years in high school. It broke down all the time and wasn't much, but you didn't throw beer cans at it. When Rob jumped out to defend the honor of the old Chevy, Dwayne got out to help, only to discover they were badly outnumbered. So Dwayne reached in the back of his car and grabbed the most menacing weapon he could find—a tennis racket. It must have been an awesome sight, to have someone seven feet, two inches, tall coming at you swinging a tennis racket.

Just when we thought we had the ship on course.

As a result of the incident, I suspended him for the first three games of his approaching junior season. At the urging of the dean of student affairs, the student affairs disciplinary panel extended the suspension through the early-season Alaskan Shootout, even though the assault charges were dropped. That gave Dwayne further cause to feel he was being singled out. We had spent that whole summer working with him, and with one foolish incident the cloud had returned. Everywhere we went from the opening game on, when Dwayne was introduced, a shower of tennis balls hit the floor.

I thought the situation helped Dwayne mature greatly. We discussed everything he was going to be confronted with during the season, and he handled it beautifully. He never lost his cool. A couple of times he'd scoop up a tennis ball and feign that he was going to rifle it back at courtside fans. The people would duck and flinch, and Dwayne would laugh, reach down, and roll the ball gently toward the sideline.

The thing that really helped him turn it in his favor was a game at Vanderbilt. We were leading until the closing seconds, when Vandy went ahead. We got a breakaway layup that would have put the game into overtime. Renaldo Garcia spurted free, but Chatman missed him with the pass and the ball went out of bounds with two or three seconds left in the game. As Vandy was getting ready to inbound the ball, ten of the most beautiful tennis balls I've ever seen in my life came bounding onto the court. One of the refs, John Clougherty, bless his heart, had the guts *at* Vanderbilt to call the technical foul on the crowd. We sent Schintzius to the line to shoot two technicals. With the place going bonkers, he netted both of them. Neither one touched the rim. He scored seven points in the overtime, leading us to an 81–78 victory. Advantage, Mr. Schintzius.

I don't think many people understand what it's like to be seven-feet, two inches, and everywhere you go you're an oddity. There's nothing normal about the way you're treated. Tom Burleson, another seven-footer I coached along the way, used to tell me after he matured how difficult it was that everywhere you went somebody would look up and say something stupid. Just this past summer, Tommy, a former NBA player now out in the business world making his own way, took me to lunch one day at a barbecue place in North Carolina. A cute little waitress stopped in her tracks, looked up, and started to say something. Tommy answered the question before it was asked. "I'm seven-foot-four," he said.

In high school, Schintzius wouldn't even go into a public place and eat with his family, preferring to opt for the drive-through windows. It was a big day for Ken and Linda when they came to Gainesville one Sunday during Dwayne's freshman season, and he suggested they go into a restaurant for lunch. They couldn't wait to tell me how happy they were that he had reached a point that he would eat in public.

Wilt Chamberlain had his idiosyncrasies in dealing with the public, and Bill Russell would never sign autographs. Dwayne did some silly things. If he was in a particluarly bad mood, he would answer the constant flip question "How's the weather up there?" by spitting. "It's raining," he'd say.

When those stories circulate, they don't endear you to people. I have gone into coliseums with Dwayne and with Tom Burleson, and I've heard the demeaning comments people make. I wanted to go up in the stands after them myself, and I marveled that Tom and Dwayne could just go on and play. It becomes so personal and so rude that it takes tremendous self-control to be able to turn the other cheek.

Dwayne has a long neck. His explanation to me when I questioned him about his hair style was, "I care what I look like. Coach, I have a very long, ugly neck. With this hair style, it covers my neck up." It was an important thing to him.

He always saw himself as awkward and unattractive. I told Joan all these things when we were recruiting Dwayne, and she had a chance to join me on a visit to his home when he was there. When we left, Joan said, "I find him very attractive. I think he's a very personable young man." He is, but he doesn't see himself that way.

We had him in our basketball camp one summer when Burleson came down to help us. In truth, we brought Tom in principally to help Dwayne. It was before Dwayne's senior year in high school, and I'll never forget when those two guys met. I think it was the first time that Dwayne ever looked somebody eyeball-to-eyeball.

He instantly had an attraction and affinity for Tom, who was great in this situation. They'd go upstairs and work, one-on-one. We videotaped one of these sessions, and it was awesome to see the two big guys going at it. Dwayne just looked fabulous.

We figured he would be carried away with the tape. We sat him down, and after we watched the tape with him, I asked what he thought. "I thought I looked like a geek," he snorted.

You see, Dwayne could never see himself as the attractive, personable individual he is. So he did unattractive things. He'd come slouching in, instead of erect and sharp.

When he does stand erect and dress up, he really is an impressive-looking guy, but he fights this terrible self-image. Again, I don't know that I wouldn't have been fighting the same thing if I had gone through life with people asking me how the weather was up there.

Within weeks after his refusal to re-enter the Georgia game made national news, Joan and I went to the Final Four in Kansas City. It was the year Kansas won the tournament. Curt Gowdy, the old announcer, is a good friend, dating back to when he used to do voice-overs for us at North Carolina State. We were all on a bus going to Kemper Arena and Curt struck up a conversation. "What is it with this big guy of yours?" he asked, putting Dwayne down by the tone of his question. I told him Dwayne was all right, that he just had a self-image problem stemming from his size.

Inside the coliseum, here came Gowdy again, almost running. "Listen, I was just talking to Bob Kurland. He would be tickled to talk to Schintzius for you and thinks he can help him. Being a seven-footer himself, he seems to know what you were talking about with Dwayne and his self-image. Bob said he went through the same thing."

I had played against Kurland when I was in the service and he was at what was then Oklahoma A&M, now Oklahoma State. Bob was one of college basketball's first big-name seven-footers. We talked there at the arena, and, sure enough, Kurland went out of his way to spend a night in Gainesville not long after that so he could meet with Schintzius.

Dwayne and he talked for about four hours in the Gator Club room. When they came out, Bob and I were getting ready to go to lunch. I had no thought about inviting Dwayne to go with us because that had simply been something he didn't do. But Kurland turned to Dwayne and said, "Hey, big guy, wanna have lunch with us?"

Dwayne eagerly accepted but asked to be given twenty minutes. He showered, shaved, put on some neat clothes, and was ready to go. I thought, "Good, Lord, what has this guy accomplished in four hours?"

So Bob and I and our wives and Dwayne went to lunch there in the athletic dining hall. When it was over and Dwayne said his good-byes, Bob and I walked back over to the basketball offices. "What in the name of heaven did you say to Dwayne?" I asked. "Obviously it's had an effect on him already."

Bob said it was very simple. "All I told him was, 'Hey, we're giants. Why are you worried about these other people? They'd like to be like us. They're jealous. They're just average people, and we're giants.'" Apparently that struck a chord with Dwayne. You can imagine how I felt. We had spent all summer working with him, and Bob Kurland comes in and works this fantastic feat. Then Dwayne went out and in one misadventure with a tennis racket threw the whole process back to square one.

We also sought the assistance of a university-connected psychiatrist, Dr. Ross McElroy, to help Dwayne in dealing with his self-image and to help me in dealing with Dwayne. I saw Dr. McElroy twice in formal sessions and occasionally called him for input on handling day-to-day situations that arose. Dwayne saw him maybe a dozen times, but resisted. He said the visits weren't accomplishing anything, and I had to agree. For one thing, doctor-patient confidentiality got in the way. Dr. McElroy wasn't at liberty to share a lot of things with me that might have been helpful. We curtailed the visits, but at least Dwayne knew we were all in this canoe together.

I think that maybe people who know this background can understand why Dwayne was so upset when the Halloween Massacre rolled around in his senior year and it was announced that we were no longer going to be his coaches. He had developed a confidence in us, and we understood each other. It was a devastating thing to him. I think the same was true for Livingston Chatman. As I detailed in an earlier chapter, it took two years of working with Chatman to break down his black-white barrier.

People looking in from the outside might criticize me and say that I lost control. But to me it was just good coaching. We worked out relationships. It's easy to have a terminal decision: "You go your way and I'll go my way." That doesn't solve anything. It took me a long time to see that in this business.

But we worked it out. With Livingston and Dwayne as leaders on the ball club, we won the SEC championship in 1989 and were looking at the 1989–90 club as a team with a chance to go to the Sweet Sixteen. And who knows what might happen when you get that far?

But 1989–90 became a disaster. Don DeVoe came in as interim coach and was insensitive to all that had gone into molding Chatman and Schintzius. I don't mean to come down on DeVoe, because Arnsparger had created an impossible situation for him, one which Arnsparger made even worse by prodding DeVoe into making Dwayne's hair style an issue. Chatman and Schintzius both left the team, and a potential Final Four team floundered to a shameful 7–21 record, losing a school-record fourteen consecutive games at one point.

On the one hand, I admired Dwayne. Knowing how much was at stake, he took a stand and risked it all. But I think he was wrong. He should have stuck it out and played because he had accomplished so much. By quitting, he put himself in a position of starting all over again. He practically wiped out three years of positives and put everything on the line for the one week of the Orlando All-Star Classic, sort of an NBA audition for top college seniors a month before the league draft.

It was during this time, just before and after he quit the team, that Dwayne became cozy with an overzealous booster named Bobby McKibbin, who was in the construction business. It was a relationship that would cause Dwayne and the university further embarrassment.

First, when Dwayne quit, he accepted an expensive new car purchased by McKibbin on the condition that Dwayne would pay him back upon becoming an NBA pro. Also, he began running around at night with McKibbin, drinking and—uncovered later by a Florida Department of Law Enforcement (FDLE) sting operation—hiring prostitutes from a Gainesville escort service. According to findings of the FDLE made public in the summer of 1991, McKibbin arranged for and paid for the prostitutes. He and Dwayne would have sex with them in a shared motel room or in McKibbin's condo.

When the scandal broke, Dwayne admitted the actions and offered this lame, lamentable explanation: he didn't always have sex with the prostitutes, sometimes thinking of his fiancée and just "laying there, kissing." When Dwayne Schintzius opened his mouth, there was no telling what would come out.

Some reporters made an energetic attempt to hold the school and/or me accountable for these liaisons, making thinly veiled assertions that McKibbin was acting as a representative of the basketball program. Don DeVoe fanned those ideas by claiming that McKibbin had "carte blanche" status during my coaching reign. Those suggestions are utterly ridiculous.

McKibbin did make a few trips with us, and occasionally he came in our dressing room after games, but so did a lot of fans. He hardly ever came into our office, and he certainly had nothing whatsoever to do with our recruiting.

I first noticed him seated in the stands at one of our practices about two years after I had gone back to Florida for the second time. He was hard to miss. He wore work clothes and drove a pickup truck. He told Monte he hadn't missed a Gator game in seventeen years and was described to me as a guy who was just a big Gator basketball fan and loved to be around the team. But he was not a mover and shaker in the booster organizations. I don't even know if he was a member of Gator Boosters.

I'm confident that while I was at Florida, McKibbin had no special relationship with the coaching staff or with any of our players, certainly not with Schintzius. Dwayne was a loner the whole time he was there, but obviously Dwayne and Bobby became close about the time Dwayne left the team, and Monte started putting pressure on Dwayne about how he was handling himself. Until we were fired, Monte rode herd over Dwayne. Even after he and I were forced out, Monte did everything he could to get Dwayne to do the right things.

DeVoe and Arnsparger accused Monte of being a party to Dwayne's quitting the team, but the truth was exactly the opposite. Monte busted his chops to get Dwayne to rejoin the team. I never talked to Dwayne during this time, but I talked to his daddy once after he quit. I urged Ken Schintzius to do everything he could to get his son to go back to the team.

Dwayne's midseason resignation—against Monte's constant advice—not only scuttled the Gators, but Dwayne's own standing with the NBA. Marty Blake, the famed NBA chief scout, had told us Dwayne would have been drafted about fourth or fifth the previous year had he chosen to go pro after his junior season. But after sitting out the last half of his senior season and reporting to Orlando at 293 pounds—some 20 pounds over his college playing weight—he was woefully ineffective in the Classic. Dwayne's draft projections began to cough and sputter, and the villagers below ran for cover.

NBA officials remained intrigued by Dwayne's abilities, and many were tempted to take a flyer on him, despite the anti-Schintzius public sentiment that rapidly spread. One of those officials was Orlando Magic general manager Pat Williams. I called him right after Dwayne quit the team to put in a good word on Dwayne's behalf. I knew Pat would be upset, and at first he was very critical: what a stupid mistake that was, it cost him a lot of money, and so forth. Then he said an interesting thing to me. "What are you going to tell the other [NBA] teams when they call you?" he asked. I got the impression Pat wanted to talk himself into taking Dwayne. It was my sense that his talk about other players was a smoke screen. Before the All-Star Classic, I think he was trying to lead every other team to believe that he was down on Schintzius, but if Dwayne had done anything at all in the Classic, the Magic would have used their number four pick to take him, if he were still available.

"Do you think he'd cut his hair for us?" Pat asked.

"Are you kidding?" I replied. "You're the ones who sign the paycheck."

Some coaches were even questioning Dwayne's basic basketball talents, but they were wrong. He has plenty of talent, a great center body, great hands, a great shooting touch, and the strength of an ox. His poor work habits are a legitimate rap. He loves to work in the weight room, but when it comes to practicing basketball, you really have to motivate him. That's a realistic concern.

The killing blow came in the final days before the draft, and, typically, it came from Dwayne's own tongue. He told a *Miami Herald* reporter he had not been candid during his series of individual interviews with NBA coaches and scouts, instead telling them "what they wanted to hear." The next sound heard was Dwayne's name being peeled, once and for all, from a lot of drafting boards. San Antonio saved Dwayne from the embarrassment of falling completely out of the first round by taking him with the twenty-fourth pick.

I think Dwayne Schintzius is a young man with a fabulous career ahead of him in the NBA. But he has a lot of growing up to do.

Later in the summer, at a San Antonio rookie and free agent camp, a story broke quoting Dwayne as saying that Gainesville was possessed by demons that caused a lot of unusual problems with the athletic programs at Florida. Monte asked Dwayne why on earth he would tell a reporter something like that. "Aw, Coach," Dwayne said impishly, "I didn't think he would print it."

Dwayne Schintzius has the physical tools to be an outstanding NBA player. He is very fortuante that he is with a coach like Larry Brown who is understanding and willing to work with him. Dwayne needs that kind of personal attention. Nothing would give me greater pleasure than to see Dwayne Schintzius become a success in the NBA.

CHAPTER 14

Rating My Fellow Asylum Inmates

In this chapter, I will attempt to rank what I think are the top jobs, programs, and coaches currently in college basketball. Venturing into such dangerous waters is, at best, a subjective exercise leaving one open to all sorts of charges of bias and politics.

But after thirty-eight years competing with America's college programs and coaches on the court and in the prospects' living rooms, I think I'm better qualified to formulate such rankings than those who often hastily scribble out the ballots that shape most of the lists you've seen. My experience also provides an understanding of the various factors that are truly important in permitting certain programs and certain coaches to sustain their success.

I've always felt that coaching should be evaluated based on success with mediocre talent. Dean Smith is a fine coach, but he is a superb recruiter. Bob Knight now deals with exceptional players at Indiana, but I give him credit for the job he did with mediocre talent when he coached at Army. He had some success there with ordinary players.

When I first went to Florida, perhaps more so than any other time in my career, I felt I exhibited the kind of coaching that results in winning games. For the most part, though, I think the players win games. The thing that makes a job a great job, a program an elite program, and a coach an eminent coach, is superior talent. You are not going to be considered a great coach unless you have the best players, and the closer you are to having great talent, the better your chances of winning are.

But I had a measure of early success at Florida with mediocre teams. One year we were picked tenth in the league and came in second. It bothered me that none of the reporters picked up on that; my pride was wounded. About the same time, Don DeVoe was picked as the best coach in the SEC; about three years later, he was picked as the worst coach in the league. Don DeVoe didn't change; the relative talent level of his players changed.

Coaching today involves dealing with big money, an aggressive press, better players, and an explosion of competitive programs. It's a whole new ball game, and I really don't think it is proper to go back and try to rate coaches from earlier, simpler times.

I could name a few whom I did get to know and believe could have made it in most any era. Coach Adolph Rupp and Coach Everett Case didn't coach in the modern era, but they could have made it. They could recruit. John Wooden's time did lap over into what I consider the big-money era, and he proved he could deal with it, too.

For a situation to be superior, the school has to have a commitment. I don't care what kind of location you have or what kind of tradition is in place, if the school doesn't have a commitment, you can have only flashes of success at best. At one time, schools like Long Island University, CCNY, and NYU had high-profile, prestigious programs and were the best jobs. Those schools decided—and I'm not saying they're wrong—that having an outstanding basketball program wasn't one of their priorities. It was like letting the air out of those programs.

When I was being courted to go back to Florida, I told Bill Carr and Dr. Robert Marston that if I did return, I wanted to compete with Kentucky basketball, not Florida football. "Can you tell me," I asked them, "that your commitment is going to be such that we will have a chance to compete with Kentucky in basketball?" They said it was, and I took the job. However, I now see things happening at Florida that indicate the school is reverting to the old days of King Football. Keep in mind that Steve Spurrier played at Florida under that same philosophy. I don't blame Steve. He was weaned on that kind of thinking.

Lon Kruger had been hired two weeks when Steve appeared on a television program and said he heard Kruger was a good coach but admitted he hadn't met him. That isn't healthy. In the first place, if Bill Arnsparger knew what he was doing, he would have created a function where everybody would have met Lonnie.

That makes me think back to the first time I went to Florida in the dark ages. I was there two weeks before anybody showed me where my office was. Now they're going to have to overcome that all over again. And Bill Arnsparger doesn't have the perception to see that these things are important. He just doesn't understand.

But Florida should be a top job. They should be great in all sports, like a UCLA or a Texas. I don't think Mississippi State will ever be a top-flight job. I think it's a marvel what they've done with the basektball program at Clemson, although it may be more of a tribute to the ACC than anything. They're not selling Clemson; they're selling, "Hey, you want to play against North Carolina and Duke and be on television?"

Next, if you are going to develop a program that pays for itself and maybe generates money for other sports in your athletic program, you need a facility to attract prospects and you need tradition. For a long time I thought we had no tradition at Florida, but I was wrong. You can have a tradition of success and interest, or you can have a tradition of no success and no interest. Either way, you do have tradition. You either have a positive one or a negative one.

I thought we were doing an excellent job at Florida in changing the tradition from negative to positive, where you could stay so many straight years in the NCAA tournament, or have twenty-win seasons—all those things that define tradition. We were developing fan interest and selling out our season tickets, and a lot of good things were happening. But the situation is different now, and the school will have to climb that hill again and overcome the chaos and self-destruction of the recent past.

A winning program has to have loyal fans. Every kid who ever visits Kentucky comes back and says, "I didn't have any idea that people can be so wrapped up in a sport as they are in Lexington." North Carolina and North Carolina State have that. It's important when you bring a recruit in that you can introduce him to a lot of people who are fanatics about your sport and your program.

The local media are an important ingredient in all the good jobs and good programs. I'm not saying the media have to be a band of cheerleaders; I don't think there are many places like that left. But the media have to be knowledgeable and interested in basketball. The media in Florida helped make it a poor environment for basketball when I returned to Florida in 1980. It has improved considerably since then.

I once argued with the *Gainesville Sun* sports columnist Jack Hairston, charging that he did not appreciate or reflect the level that Florida basketball had reached. I argued that college basketball had become—even in Florida—one of the premier sports and that the NCAA tournament had become one of sports' premier events. "Nah," he argued, "I write what the people want to read about."

"No, I don't agree with that," I countered. "You create their interest."

He asked me what I thought the solution was, and—typical of me to overstate the case—I said, "A few timely funerals." It really ticked him off. To some degree, I was probably right. Some people are never going to change their attitudes, and you have to wait until somebody else comes in with a different perspective. However, Jack has become a very good basketball writer.

I think some people have failed to get the most—or even close to the most—out of their situations. I think Notre Dame is one of the best jobs in the country, at least it should be one of the strongest. It has the unmatched ability to recruit a very large, special-interest group. Every Catholic kid in America has to think seriously about Notre Dame if he is an outstanding or highly sought-after athlete. But I think Digger Phelps has done the least with the best opportunity of any coach I've known in my coaching career. It certainly came as no surprise to me that Notre Dame offered no resistance to his "resignation" after the '91 season. A real sore spot with me over the years has been coaches who beat themselves on the chest and talk about how pure and good they are for the game. Digger Phelps is one who did that. Aside from that, I don't have any personal ax to grind with Digger, but I think his failure to capitalize on Notre Dame's immense potential is a fact. He had the same opportunity that Lou Holtz has made the most of in football.

Notre Dame is an international school. The Fighting Irish have alumni all over the world—powerful alumni. They have a superior reputation academically and, as an independent, have the opportunity to structure their schedule. I always thought Al McGuire was a master of that at Marquette. He balanced his schedule, slid the right people in, had the right opponents before big games and after big games, things like that. When you're in a conference, you can't do that.

At Florida, for instance, we often had to play Kentucky, Vandy, and Tennessee in succession on the road. It wasn't until the 1988–89 season that for the first time—ever—Florida won all three of those games in one season.

First, the top jobs, meaning programs where a head coach is operating with huge, built-in advantages because of geography, tradition, or the other factors I've mentioned. This list I will offer alphabetically:

Arizona
Duke
Illinois
Indiana
Kansas
Kentucky
Louisville
LSU
Nevada-Las Vegas
North Carolina
Notre Dame
Oklahoma
St. John's
Syracuse
UCLA

Randomly there are some of the reasons why.

North Carolina. Dean Smith has done a masterful job of using his former players and emphasizing the ones who have gone into the NBA or into coaching. He utilizes their help in recruiting.

Kentucky. For the same reasons. Commitment, fan interest, television exposure.

Indiana. Ditto. The Hoosiers are rich in all those things.

Duke. A relative newcomer to this division. I think Mike Krzyzewski has shown enough consistency that he has built Duke into one of the best jobs in the country. I think now if Mike left Duke, somebody could come in and pick up the reins and maintain Duke as one of the top programs. By building Duke's basketball reputation to the level of the academic reputation the school already enjoys, Krzyzewski has created a situation in which he or his successor will annually have a shot at the truly top student-athletes in the country, even more so than, say, Stanford, which also enjoys a high academic profile.

Arizona is another newcomer. Lute Olsen is now able to cull and screen and be selective with his recruits. Arizona is an example of a school that had its potential realized through the efforts of an outstanding coach. Sometimes a top-flight program makes it a great job; sometimes you become a great program because you've done a top-flight job. The latter is the case with Lute and Arizona.

Nevada-Las Vegas. Jerry Tarkanian created a superior program out of what was neither a good job nor a good program. But it would take a special personality to follow Jerry and maintain his momentum.

Ditto for *Oklahoma.* I think only Billy Tubbs could have done that at Oklahoma. They've had outstanding basketball coaches at Oklahoma, but none of them raised the program to the level that Billy has. There aren't very many basketball players in Oklahoma or in the surrounding states, so Billy works the junior college circuit. It was a good move, and he will continue to be successful doing that.

UCLA. This has long been one of the best jobs and best programs. What's been interesting to me is that I've seen a lot of these programs blossom during the early part of my coaching career. Some of them survived the advent of television and big money and "The Road To" the Final Four. When John Wooden retired, UCLA had trouble staying in the top echelon. I coached against John in the Final Four in his next-to-last year, and we took home a mere seventy-five thousand dollars for winning a national championship. The whole ballgame changed just after John left, and his successors couldn't deal with it. They couldn't deal with the pressure that television and the rest of the media created for that job. They had some good people there—Gene Bartow, Larry Brown, and others. They've gone on to success in other programs. UCLA has a chance to come back, though probably never to the position of dominance the Bruins once enjoyed. Yet, I guarantee there are supporters out there who are not going to be satisfied until that condition exists again. They've been through it, and they remember how it felt and believe it can be done again. It can't. There are just too many other good programs now to do what John Wooden did.

When we beat UCLA and won the title in 1974, a reporter asked if I thought we were starting a new dynasty. Hell, no. We just won one championship, and we weren't going to have a dynasty at North Carolina State. Perhaps we had established the momentum to have a good program every year. But dynasty? No way.

Kansas. The Jayhawks are rich with tradition. This has been one of the best jobs—and programs—for a long time. They have fallen on some hard times, but I would still consider Kansas one of the top jobs in the country because the commitment and the fan interest are still there.

St. John's. Because of its location more than anything else, St. John's is one of the top jobs and programs, year in and year out. They are *the* school in metro New York still trying and still committed to being nationally ranked and winning a national championship. The fire still burns at St. John's. Lou Carnesecca has done a great job of taking advantage of the great wealth of talent that lives within a subway ride.

Louisville. I don't understand Louisville. When I first heard of Louisville, Peck Hickman was the coach there, and they were one of the best programs in the country. They've continued to maintain a lofty reputation and rankings. Yet, Louisville is not one of the most attractive cities around, and the university is basically a "city college," right downtown. It does not have a pretty campus, and the school is never mentioned in the academic league with the Dukes and the Stanfords. I'm sure it's a good school—don't misunderstand me—but just another urban college. But they have developed a tradition and a fan following and have maintained a good flow of talent through the program. I give Denny Crum a lot of credit for that.

Syracuse. This is one of the top programs in the country now because of the emergence of the Big East as a showcase league. Georgetown would have broken through without the Big East, but I don't think Syracuse would have. I believe the television exposure and the rising prestige of the Big East have helped to create a recruiting appeal for Syracuse.

Illinois. The school I *really* don't understand is Illinois. This is a school in close proximity to a world of talent. It's a world-class university with superior facilities and great tradition. Lou Henson has begun to convert that potential in recent years, but just what the current troubles with the NCAA will do to their momentum remains to be seen.

LSU. Dale Brown has built this into one of the top jobs. Joe Dean and others who played there B.D. (Before Dale) will tell you this was always a great program, but that wasn't really true before Dale Brown. They have superb facilities and fan interest. Pete Maravich got some of this going, but LSU really wasn't a winner until

Dale completed the transition from budding potential into a winning, respected program. I think someone could now come in after Dale and keep it going.

There's a dose of fate involving LSU that touched my life. Press Maravich, Pete's father, became Everett Case's successor at North Carolina State in 1965. Two years later, because Pete couldn't get in at State, Press left and took the job at LSU, taking Pete with him and creating the vacancy at State that I filled. That act provided the spark that ignited LSU basketball and also had no small effect on the life of one Norman Sloan.

Now the envelopes, please, for the best programs. A lot of these are going to be the same. These are the places where the people in the program have truly capitalized on the school's natural advantages and commitment or have overcome the disadvantages to create a winning situation. Most conspicuous by its absence on this list will be Notre Dame, which is a top job but hasn't become a top program.

Again, alphabetically:

Arizona
Duke
Georgetown
Indiana
Kentucky
Louisville
LSU
North Carolina
St. John's
Syracuse
UNLV

UNLV's Jerry Tarkanian and Georgetown's John Thompson are the two guys who have done the best job of building programs and turning schools into great jobs. They have done it at two exactly opposite kinds of schools.

Georgetown is a classic example of how one individual can take a situation that wasn't a great job and build a superior program out of it. But I think if John Thompson leaves, Georgetown goes back to the shadows. John Thompson *is* the Georgetown job and program. Being in the middle of a huge pool of black talent and being a role model or symbol with the black population, John can do things another coach wouldn't dare. It's a white school, affluent, with high academic standards—everything John's basketball players aren't. You have to give John and Georgetown credit for creating an academic program in which these players can function.

I can't call UCLA one of the best programs right now. They're starting to come back, but they've been out of it for quite some time. Georgia Tech could be a possible breakthrough. Tech could become both one of the top programs and one of the elite jobs in the country, but they haven't been consistent. Because they are in Atlanta and have a good national reputation, they enjoy an advantage in recruiting. But Bobby Cremins is going to have to be more consistent than he has been.

Now the envelope you've been waiting for: the top coaches. I have put them in the order of how I look at them, based on the job they've done at the program where they work. It's not that some are better coaches than others, in terms of taking five guys and doing something unique with them. It isn't just a matter of knowing X's and O's. It includes recruiting talented players and getting the effort out of those players. Not every coach can do that.

My Baker's Dozen current best coaches list:

1. Jerry Tarkanian, UNLV
2. Dean Smith, North Carolina
3. John Thompson, Georgetown
4. Lute Olsen, Arizona
5. Bobby Knight, Indiana
6. Jim Boeheim, Syracuse
7. Denny Crum, Louisville
8. Lou Henson, Illinois
9. Mike Krzyzewski, Duke
10. Lou Carnesecca, St. John's
11. Dale Brown, LSU
12. Nolan Richardson, Arkansas
13. Lefty Driesell, James Madison

Jerry Tarkanian has recruited effectively for UNLV. A lot of these recruits could not have gotten in at other schools, and other coaches weren't anxious to work with some of them. But Jerry has built one of the toughest and best programs in the country, not only in terms of victories but also in terms of consistency. And he has done it with the NCAA nipping at his heels all the way. I don't understand how he has withstood the constant barrage from the NCAA and the endless references to his program as "outlaw" and "illegal." I don't know how he has taken all of that. I don't think I could have done it. The short time that I had to live with all of that negative publicity and innuendo really ate away at me. I was thrilled to death for Tark to win the national title in 1990.

What gets overlooked is how Tark has helped more kids than those few who have gotten in trouble, and that applies to a lot of coaches. Take Schintzius and Maxwell, for instance. They did a lot of things that resulted in bad publicity, but can you imagine what might have happened to them if it hadn't been for the amount of time we coaches invested in them. Tark's kids sat in a hottub with the wrong guy, and they hanged Tark out to dry. What got overlooked was that those kids who tended to use poor judgment were also saved a lot of times by Tark. I think coaches do a world of good that goes unnoticed, and I'm afraid Tark will be remembered for little, if any, of that.

At press time for this book, Tark had agreed to coach the 1991-92 season, then retire.

Dean Smith does a masterful job. I have a high regard for him. He is a program builder. People like Dick Vitale give Dean credit for being a great coach, and I interpret that as meaning on-the-floor coaching. Dean is good; he doesn't mess up his players. But I do think North Carolina could have won more national championships than it has if he would have turned individuals loose. When we went head-to-head in recruiting, one of the knocks that he would put on me was that I ran a "star program" at North Carolina State. "We have a *team* concept," he would boast. Well, when James Worthy goes through your program averaging sixteen points a game or Michael Jordan averaging sixteen or seventeen points a game, I have to wonder. If those guys had been up there averaging thirty points a game like they were capable of, I think Dean would have won more national titles.

To Dean's credit, he hasn't had many kids quit or transfer, and he has built tremendous depth. If he has fifteen kids on scholarship, he's going to have fifteen outstanding players. To my way of thinking, Dean Smith is the best recruiter in the business. Over the years—even back when UCLA was dominating—Dean Smith had more of the great players than UCLA had. But in my opinion, Dean's system kept them from being UCLA.

On the other hand, if he had leaned more toward the so-called "star" system, he would have had some players leave his program, and he may not have been able to recruit others.

Dean has been able to keep a lot of talent happy, and he has been consistent. He has won only one national title, but he's been up there with twenty-win seasons—first or second in the conference—seemingly every year.

On the whole, John Thompson does a superb job, although I have a problem with one of his pet tactics. All coaches use their affiliation with national teams—the Olympic team, Pan-Am team, whatever—as a recruiting tool, a wedge. John made it a sledgehammer.

When we were recruiting Thurl Bailey at North Carolina State, John told Thurl that if he didn't sign with Georgetown, he would personally see to it that Thurl wouldn't represent this country on any national teams. Thurl never even got a chance to try out for any of the national teams, and he was a great player. He still plays for the Utah Jazz.

Lute Olsen has done a grand job at Arizona, turning it into a school that every top player in the West seriously considers. They're an attractive school. They have facilities, and they have been winning. You have to give Lute credit for that.

Bobby Knight doesn't want to be called Bobby any longer, sort of like when Lefty Driesell wanted to be called Charles. It didn't work, and he finally gave up. Bobby may get upset about it, but he's still "Bobby" to me. I don't mean any disrespect, but he's been Bobby all of his life, and suddenly he thinks that isn't proper and wants to be called Bob.

You're going to get along fine with Bobby Knight until you recruit against him and beat him, until you compete against him and beat him, or if you ever have the audacity to challenge him on any of his regular pronouncements.

I am fortunate in that I have a wonderful marriage. I married a marvelous woman, a tough lady whom I respect immensely. I would no more demean her in public than I would sprinkle salt and pepper on Michael Jordan's sneakers and try to eat them.

We had breakfast with Bobby and his first wife in the coffee shop of one of the big Las Vegas hotels while we were at the Pizza Hut Classic in the midseventies. Joan and I came away from that breakfast with queasy stomachs. Bobby had demeaned his wife over breakfast, talking down to her and about her in front of her so viciously that both of us were stunned.

Later, we were playing in the Hoosier Classic right after Florida's football team had been put on probation. There was Bobby's wife—the same gal we had felt so sorry for in Las Vegas—sitting up there screaming at Vernon Maxwell and cursing like a sailor. Shortly after that the Knights were divorced.

I was on a clinic with Bobby in Louisville at a time when women's athletics and Title IX was just starting to gain momentum. Several women coaches were sitting in the audience. Before that time, you just didn't see any women at coaching clinics.

Bobby couldn't deal with that. He started off, first of all, by jumping on the women and belittling the Title IX movement. He said they wanted the same money without the same pressure that men's programs were under. "I think if you're going to get the same money that we do," he told them from the podium, "you ought to get your ass fired just like the men do."

He told three of the foulest jokes I have ever heard in my life, even making a point of doing it because of the women in the audience. He told them that if they were going to come with the men, they'd have to be treated like the men. I think what he did was unbecoming and unnecessary.

Bobby and I got into a tiff that was completely my fault. At the 1987 trials at the Olympic Training Center in Colorado Springs for our various national teams, Vernon Maxwell did not make the first cut-down for either the Pan-Am Games or the World University Games. When asked about it by a reporter, I noted that two of Bobby Knight's players—one a nondescript junior college player—were invited to the World University tryouts that his bosom pal Mike Krzyzewski was holding at Duke. I also said that there are more ways to cheat than giving a kid illegal aid. You can also cheat by promising a kid a tryout or promising a kid a place on one of these national teams if he signs with a certain coach.

Little did I know the reason Vernon didn't make the team was that he had flunked a drug test. When I made my statement, Bobby angrily called Bill Arnsparger, told him about Maxwell's drug test, and threatened to go public with it, breaking the confidentiality that is supposed to exist around Olympic drug tests.

I called Bobby, and he wasn't in. He called back. It was summertime, and we had a young part-time worker named Amy Tyner in the office. Amy took the call and told him I was at our beach condo in Daytona Beach. He asked for the number, and she said she couldn't give it out. She offered to call me and advise that

Bobby was trying to reach me. Typical Bobby, he began showering her with profanity.

After a moment, Amy broke in and said, "You know, Mr. Knight, my mother raised me a lot better than your mother raised you. I can tell by your language."

When we hooked up, I apologized to Bobby for reading into the player selections something that apparently wasn't there. I even followed with a letter of apology, explaining that I didn't know about Maxwell's failed drug test.

When I was forced to retire at Florida, Bobby was quoted as saying college basketball was "better off without people like Sloan."

Bobby likes anybody he can beat or browbeat. He doesn't like anyone who will stand up to him and yell back. I think Bobby is an excellent basketball coach, but he is a bully. I don't like those who try to dominate people, but I would like to think I would never say the game would be better off without Bobby Knight. I don't know that you should say that about anybody in any profession. Everybody with enough ability to stick around for any length of time makes a contribution of some sort.

Though we had a good relationship at first, Bobby and I started falling apart when we beat him in head-to-head recruiting for a big kid named Glenn Sudhop, a seven-foot, two-inch, center out of South Bend, Indiana. When we signed Sudhop at North Carolina State in 1975, Bobby started accusing me of all kinds of recruiting irregularities.

The truth was that Sudhop didn't go with Bobby Knight because he didn't think he could take Bobby's kind of pressure. As it turned out, he couldn't take it from me, either. Glenn and I didn't have the best of relationships at State because he didn't want to work hard. I used to tell him he was going to wind up as the tallest used-car salesman in South Bend. I was wrong. He wound up as the tallest milling machine operator at International Harvester.

Bobby has always done a fine job wherever he has been. He was a good selection for the Indiana job. I was one of the people who interviewed for that job the year Bobby did. I always considered Indiana to be one of the best jobs in the country because of the great basketball tradition in the state, the pool of talent, and the school's commitment. Also, football wasn't a threat like it was at Ohio State or Michigan. At Indiana, Bobby Knight is the Bull Gator.

That's part of why I think Billy Tubbs has done such an outstanding job at Oklahoma. He went into a school with a smothering football atmosphere and got the job done. Tark and Dean didn't have to overcome football at their schools.

Knight does as good a job as anybody I know of demanding and getting intensity every minute a player is on the floor. That's why he has had some unhappy players who left from time to time. But the ones left behind always played hard, and that will win for anybody. He does an excellent recruiting job, but you can do that when you have fine facilities and fan interest and success.

Jim Boeheim does a super job at Syracuse. He has taken a situation that was average and turned it into a program that, year in and year out, is one of the best in the country.

Denny Crum has done that at Louisville, and Lou Henson has done it everywhere he has been.

Duke has had some fine teams in the past, but Mike Krzyzewski has given them consistency at the top level. Lou Carnesecca has done the same thing for St. John's.

I don't know why I wrestled with putting Dale Brown on this list, perhaps because I've been so close to him in the same league. You tend to look more closely at a guy's warts when you know him so well, but I think Dale has done a super job. He can recruit, and his kids play hard.

Nolan Richardson hasn't been around long enough to make a lot of lists like this, but I think Nolan is one of the best coaches in the business. I think you will see that he will have consistent success at Arkansas, even though it is not one of the most attractive programs in the country. He does all the things I like to see—he presses, runs, and forces an up-tempo game.

Lefty Driesell. There isn't a finer basketball coach around than Lefty. His teams were always tough to play against, and I thought he was good for the game. It's a shame that he became the first victim of the recent trend of school presidents who react to public cricitism, knee-jerk style, to show that they are cleaning up something. Lefty was a victim of Lenny Bias's tragic death, which touched off a widespread probe of drug use in basketball and gave Dr. John Slaughter, the University of Maryland president, the self-perceived need to run a coach up the gallows to prove to his peers that he was controlling athletics. Lefty was no more responsible for the tragedy of Lenny Bias than Lenny's own parents were.

Lefty is one of those guys I can relate to. I feel I have not received the recognition from the media that my numbers merited, and I think Lefty was in the same canoe, perhaps because he was outspoken, controversial, foot-stomping intense. Dean Smith was cool and composed. When there's a Lefty vs. Dean or a Norm vs. Dean, the media gravitate to Dean. He comes out looking like the good guy, and we come out looking like the crazy guys.

Yet, Lefty Driesell had some of the best insights in the game. To my knowledge, he was the first coach ever to say that the NCAA tournament should include every Division I school. We were at an ACC conference meeting when the floor was thrown open to new business and Lefty proposed that the ACC sponsor a move to have every school in the NCAA postseason tournament. We all laughed like hell. We thought he was kidding, but he was right. One day it will probably come to that. If they don't, somebody will have to come up with an equitable way of sharing the wealth. Lefty's idea was to have sixty-four sectionals, and from that you would have sixty-four teams to begin the next week moving toward the Sweet Sixteen and Final Four.

Then you wouldn't have to send, say, Maryland to Seattle or Oregon State to Atlanta and miss all that class time. The NCAA and college presidents contradict themselves all over the place when they talk about going to classes and cutting the regular-season schedule back to keep kids from missing school work. At the end of the season, they find no problem with sending teams criss-crossing the country, dropping out of class for two weeks to play on the opposite coast. In 1989 Seton Hall went to the West Coast for the Sweet Sixteen and stayed; they never came back until after the Final Four. The students missed two solid weeks of classes. Alabama did a similar thing this past year.

The NCAA is trying to balance each regional and create intersectional games to benefit the television ratings. That isn't right. It puts a bigger strain on the student-athlete, and for no other reason than to ensure that the school can make more money. This is hypocritical, and I said so when I was coaching. Lefty was the first to have the foresight to say we should invite every team to the tournament, and the situation will be inequitable until we do that.

But this is where Lefty and Norm typically got in trouble. In his own unique way, Lefty added, "And by God, I'm damned sick and tired of people throwing in my face how many times Dean's been to the NCAA tournament and I haven't."

This was in an ACC coaches' meeting with Dean sitting right

there, which was not always a given. Number one, Dean wasn't ever on time. He was always late, and he would receive three phone calls that would require him to leave the meeting every time. He was just busier than the rest of us. I don't know who was calling him, whether it was one of his staff members or his wife, but he would have three phone calls. We all laughed about it. Lefty even challenged him on it. Lefty was a mess. Dean mumbled and sort of laughed it off.

Anyway, Lefty had made what I thought was an insightful and intelligent observation about the NCAA tournament. Then he screwed it up as far as public perception was concerned by throwing the other honest expression in there about Dean. It came off as sour grapes and self-serving.

I didn't include Rick Pitino on my top coaches list, and I'm sure many readers will want to know why. I just don't think Pitino has been a college coach long enough to establish that he is one of the best. He had one good year at Providence, but he never did have a good year at Boston University. And he has had one year at Kentucky. Understand that I think he will be a fine college basketball coach, but he hasn't done it yet. He has one of the best jobs in the country, so he should become one of the top coaches. He's going to have good talent, year after year.

Any discussion of coaches must also touch on their shaping of the rules. Since I started in this business as a college player, there have been many changes in the rules. Most of them have been for the better. The widening of the lane from the old "key" was a good one.

But there are a large number of coaches whose egos are so big that they think they control the game with what I call a myth: the game plan. You can have a game plan in basketball, but the other team gets possession every time you score and most of the time when you don't. It's up and down the floor so fast your game plan doesn't really exist.

Some coaches act like they don't want to give up their sliver of control over the game. That's why they don't like fast breaks and twenty-four-second clocks. Their attitude is that "now you've thrown the game into the hands of the players, and we're no longer setting up and running my plays." I know I've been guilty of that at times. When the game turns into a fire drill and the score is going south, I'd stand up and holler, "Three! Would you puh-leeeze run number three?!" So they run it, and they score, and you say, "See? I tried to tell you. If you'll just run the plays, we'll win this thing."

I've been in the game long enough now to admit this is a fallacy. In my first head job at Presbyterian College, I didn't know the first thing about zoning because my college coach didn't recognize zoning. We ran the same offense against our opponents whether they were man-to-man or zone. The term *zone* was never mentioned; we pressed and ran. Coach Case was a fast-breaking, full-court press coach, which was the ideal way to run the game.

I got to thinking about that and realized I knew very little about zones. I figured I'd better go to a clinic and listen to one of the name coaches talk about attacking a zone defense. So I decided to go hear Adolph Rupp at Kentucky and talked to my athletic director about going. We didn't have any money in the budget for that, so I got in my little blue Studebaker and paid my own way to drive from Clinton, South Carolina, to Lexington, Kentucky, for the three-day clinic. I think the fee was twenty-five dollars, and my room and meals were about that each day. That was a lot of money to me at the time. On the third day, when Coach Rupp concluded, he still had not said a word about zone attack.

Traditionally, at the end of a clinic the young coaches gather around the clinic speaker for the thrill of talking to a famous coach or, perhaps, to ask a specific question. I was there in the little knot of guys surrounding Coach Rupp, and when I got in my shot, I introduced myself and explained that I had come expressly to hear him talk about zone attack.

"Well, I tell you, son," he drawled in that distinctive nasal twang, "we kinda just get in the gaps and shoot it and slap at it if we miss." That was it. Well, it upset me no end because I had paid all this money to go hear him, and that was the sum total about zone attack I got out of the trip.

But if you asked me now at the end of my thirty-eight years of coaching experience what is my basic philosophy on zone attack, I'd say, "Get in the gaps, shoot, and slap at it if you miss." My point is that Rupp was also a guy at the end of his career who understood that a coach doesn't have that much control over a basketball game. There are just a few basic things you can do: press and run, get down in a gap and cause two defensive players to commit so there will be an open man, throw the ball around, and take a shot; and if you miss, try to get the rebound. That's how simple the game is, but I guess there will always be some coaches who think they can choreograph a basketball game like a Broadway musical.

Yet, even though we're into the modern era of basketball and have all these guys with all this size and talent, we're still standing around holding the ball, watching Ralph Sampson against all that collection of North Carolina stars, standing around doing nothing. There became pressure to at least put in the forty-five-second clock. The coaches kept it from going in for awhile, because their fear of giving up control of the game—ego.

The game clock has been a good thing, but I'd like to see it become a thirty-second clock. The biggest problem we have in college basketball is that the game is too slow and takes too long to be completed. We don't handle the out-of-bounds play properly. When I was on the coaches' rules recommendation committee, I advocated the international rule that doesn't require the officials to handle the ball on an out-of-bounds or turnover.

If a team travels, the team that gains possession grabs the ball and throws it in, and away you go. As the rule stands, every time there is a change of possession, the official has to handle the ball, usually after stopping to make sure the defensive team is ready.

Good old American ego gets involved. It's our game, by God. We invented it, and we're not going to let Europe tell us what kind of rules to use. Well, I like the international rule on inbounding, I like their thirty-second clock, and I like their three-point line, which is nine inches longer than our college line.

We did the right thing in putting in the three-point shot, but there was no way we were going to copy the international line. Ours was going to be different, by golly.

CHAPTER 15

In Retrospect

Obviously I've had a lot of time since late 1989 to think about my coaching career, things I've done right, and things I've done wrong. I've also had time to think about college sports in general and about the roles coaches, administrators, sportswriters, and the NCAA play in the good and bad of it all. Those subjects are at the heart of what this book is all about, and I have deliberately chosen to put them near the end so that you, the reader, will know why I have come to my conclusions. You may agree; you may disagree. But I think I owe it to myself and to you to tell it the way ole Stormin' Norman sees it.

Very few people know what it's really like to coach in the pressure cooker of big-time college sports. Opening up that world has been another of my objectives. It's easy to make wild assumptions about what recruiting and competing and promoting are like. The reality, as I hope you have seen, is quite different.

If I had my whole career to replay, right at the top of the list would be to work harder at creating the proper perception of me and my program. Perception, I have learned, is everything. Far too often, facts are incidental. The coaches who are successful year-in and year-out are bathed in glowing reports.

In Rick Pitino's book about his first year at Kentucky, there is an interesting story about his hiring. When Rick was an assistant at Hawaii, that school landed on the NCAA carpet over recruiting infractions. One of the central kids was a player whom Rick had recruited. When Rick was hired, Kentucky had just run Eddie Sutton out of town after not really proving that Eddie himself had violated any rules. As far as I know, Sutton violated as few rules as anyone I've known at Kentucky.

When Pitino and his wife were on campus for their interview, C. M. Newton, the Kentucky athletic director, was tipped that a story was going to break the next morning about the Hawaiian blotch on Rick's record. C. M. canceled the meeting set with Pitino the next day, saying he had to first go see the president about "that darned Hawaiian thing."

But after huddling with Newton, Dr. David Roselle, University of Kentucky president, contacted Pitino to say, "You're the man. We know you're clean. We know you'll run a clean program." In other words, Kentucky wanted Pitino, so they created the perception they wanted: that he had done nothing wrong at Hawaii.

And maybe he didn't. If they hadn't really wanted him, however, they would have talked about how they couldn't hire anyone with a cloud hanging over his head. But the sun was shining because Dr. Roselle *said* it was.

We can put this under the heading of hypocrisy. Kentucky needed a guy like Pitino. They needed his charisma and coaching record, and they were willing to fight down any questions about his ethics or the NCAA rap sheet.

Yet there was at least as much of a cloud over his head as was billowing over my Florida assistant coaches, Monte Towe and Kenny McCraney. Both were fired when I was forced out and they have been batted down at every turn when attempting to find other coaching jobs.

The perception I created for myself was poor, in part because I made a minimal attempt to bridle my emotions. I see that now as a mistake. After having had time to think over my career, I believe a coach must swallow and keep a calm demeanor, even when justified in throwing a tantrum. I was always very combative in games, and I think a lot of officials misunderstood my behavior. A lot of coaches are combative for show, but whenever I got up and yelled and screamed at the officials, it was because I was angry with them. It was honest expression, and my emotions during a game were always raw.

Dr. Wayne Reitz, Florida's president during my first years at the University of Florida, once called me in to discuss my sideline behavior. He said, "Norm, you're doing a great job and I think a lot of your wife and family. But you need to calm down on the sidelines. You're a little too active. Put a seatbelt on or something."

Two days later, we were playing Tennessee in a tough game in cozy old Alligator Alley, when George Conley, the famous ref, made a terrible call. After George and I had words, I stormed back to the bench where I put a toe into a basketball that was lying on the floor right in front of me. Had they been watching, I'm sure I would have gotten a tryout with any NFL team! The ball shot right at Dr. Reitz, who was sitting about ten rows up in the stands. I thought I was history for sure, but he never said anything about my uncanny field goal.

If I was upset at a player, it made no difference to me that fifteen thousand people were in the building. The player and I had a special relationship. We had a problem, and we were going to solve that problem right then. That was just the way I always operated.

When I went to press interviews after games, I made a lot of statements to reporters that were ill-advised. I'd come out after a loss with that look on my face that means I'm taking everything personally. My wife, Joan, would try to protect me. She would come down to the press conferences, and if I continued to discuss the game with a reporter in the hallway in combative terms, she'd sidle up, gently take my arm, and pleasantly say, "C'mon, Norm, it's time to go."

What she was really saying was, "Hey, motor mouth, you're getting yourself in trouble again."

Dr. Bob Marston, president at Florida when I began my second term there as head coach in 1980, was a classic example of a college president who really didn't know what was going on in the athletic program and didn't care until the media focused on him. Toward the end of his regime, we had a telephone scandal in the fall of 1982. Several basketball and football players were using the athletic department's number to run up long-distance calls, obviously an NCAA violation. The coaches did not know they were doing it.

Lorenzo Hampton, later a running back for the Miami Dolphins, was at the forefront of this particular scandal. The basketball team was preparing to play in the Great Alaska Shootout in Anchorage, and most of my starters were implicated. Hampton got a lawyer and managed to get the hearing postponed until the football season was over. As a result, the student judiciary committee put the players on conduct probation, meaning they couldn't represent the school in any extracurricular activity for one semester. Since football season was over, the football players involved laughed all the way back to the dorm.

But my players' punishment was going to be meaningful because our season was just beginning. If the probation was levied for the fall semester, our guys would miss the seven or eight games before the Christmas break. And if it was imposed for the second semester, they would miss the entire conference schedule. I thought that was terribly inequitable and expressed that sentiment to Dr. Marston. My contention was that there had to be a better way to handle this for the basketball players than to knock them all out of so much of the season.

That was about the time some Florida State football players were involved in the theft of television sets from a Maas Brothers department store in Tallahassee, and there was widespread criticism of what was being perceived as lenient handling of that situation by Florida State. President Marston went on record vowing behavior like that would certainly never go unpunished at the University of Florida. I had no problem with that. I was in favor of some punishment for the phone abuse. "But don't you see," I pleaded with Marston, "how this is inequitable between football and basketball?"

It was a losing fight. He was only concerned that public opinion had come down heavy on Florida State in the wake of the Maas Brothers caper, and he insisted that at Florida we would punish its athletes. And he did. But he punished only the basketball players. The only compromise he made was that we lost our guilty players just for the three games in the Alaska Shootout and not for the entire pre-Christmas schedule.

My criticism isn't that Marston did the wrong thing. My criticism is that his actions were largely a reaction to the media. This is what is happening today. The media have put college presidents and boards into such a position that they feel they have to step in and personally do something to show the public they're in charge. The result is that when the media gets to rumbling, college presidents display an awful lot of hypocrisy.

Of all the people who can't cope with media criticism, college presidents lead the list. Bob Marston absolutely unraveled if something negative was said or written about him or his reign.

College presidents need to stand up and accept some responsibility when there's a problem in the athletic department. They're part of the university, and they need to have some input all along, not just by grandstanding in a crisis. College presidents need to come out and say, "I approve of letting these marginal students play ball at my school." Or, "I don't approve of this." But don't sit there silent until the graduation rates scrape bottom, then flog the coach or call a press conference to self-righteously denounce a deplorable situation.

I started coaching in 1951 at Presbyterian College and have never coached at anything but the college level. Since then many changes have taken place.

I went through integration and the changes it spawned in terms of personal relationships and style of play. I've gone through the first wave of drug horrors. I've experienced dramatic changes in the way college sports are covered by the media. I've seen the infusion of big money in college basketball and the ugly impact it has wrought.

At the 1990 NCAA convention, executive director Dick Shultz said, "I don't think we have any major problems in college athletics. But what we do have is a bad perception." So the NCAA is attempting to change its image rather than taking steps to correct the basic problems. It's a cosmetic approach, and it puts a lot of people in a bind. We now have an exercise in public relations, not the corrective surgery that is needed.

The first incision should be made in that group of rules that are denying student-athletes the right to accept or earn expense money like a regular student. For those whose families qualify for financial need, there is some federal money available through what is called a Pell Grant, up to about two thousand dollars a year.

For a long time, the NCAA wouldn't even allow scholarship athletes to have any of that money. Plus, they took away the old fifteen-dollar-a-month laundry money and ruled out the opportunity for athletes to work or sell programs. I never could understand why any of this was a problem for the NCAA. Finally, the NCAA started allowing players to take up to one hundred dollars a semester, then one hundred fifty dollars a semester, out of the Pell Grant. Shortly after that, Tates Locke, then the coach at Clemson, asked me if I had all of our kids fill out the Pell Grant forms. "You ought to check into that," he said. "At Clemson last year we made about $150,000 off the Pell Grants."

"What are you talking about?"

"Well, you can only give the kids a few hundred dollars," Locke answered, "and the athletic department keeps the rest of the money."

So we started having players fill out the forms. As is the case with most anything like this, you realize there are some problems with making it work right. The money went directly to the players, and the ones who qualified for the Pell Grants received a check for one thousand dollars per semester. They were required to give back to the school the amount over the hundred or hundred and fifty dollars the NCAA allowed them to keep. As can be expected when you put a thousand dollars in a kid's hands, you might get it back and you might not.

So the NCAA declared a Pell Grant recipient would be ineligible until he coughed up the money. Last-semester seniors would just laugh at you. Their eligibility was over anyway.

Because the Pell Grant proved to be a significant source of revenue for college administrators, the smaller schools squashed any proposal for the athlete to retain more of his Pell Grant money. To me, this seems a scandal of the highest order: schools taking federal money right out of these kids' pockets. I'm surprised that the media and the politicians have never gotten more into the injustice of the Pell Grant money.

In recent years I came to realize that the student-athletes have not been getting a fair and equitable scholarship. The Pell Grant was an opportunity to give those in need some extra money when they could prove they deserved it, yet the NCAA membership voted it down left and right.

Colleges need to find a way to show some loyalty to coaches and provide them greater security. That would go a long way toward solving the problem of cheating. I remember after Tates Locke got into all the NCAA trouble at Clemson, he told me, "It wasn't a tough decision for me. I had to go get some players, because if I didn't start winning, I was out." Other coaches on the hot seat stayed within the rules and got fired. Good things were said about them, but they were out of a job.

Presidents and coaches need to sit down and talk about these things, but these issues are typically handled on the floor of the NCAA convention. Two things people should never have to see being made are sausage and NCAA regulations. You grab a mike and spout into it, then somebody across the floor grabs a mike and spouts back. Nothing meaningful gets accomplished. It's a circus.

In a small group, we can sit across a table—coaches, presidents, and the NCAA—and dissect the problem. Don't you see, NCAA, this is how big money for schools and none for the athletes inspire cheating? Don't you see, Mr. Presidents, that we're admitting a lot of kids who don't belong in college?

Unfortunately, we're all acting like it isn't taking place.

Instead, when school presidents meet, they talk about cutting scholarships, cutting the season, cutting back on the schedule. That doesn't solve a thing. We have yet to address the real problems or come up with real solutions. The presidents have slapped a Band-Aid on a toe to fix a broken leg.

Cutting back on the length of the season does not help athletes with their schoolwork. Pete Carrill, the Princeton coach, made the astute observation that players do a better job academically during the season that they do out of season. You talk to any coach—basketball, football, baseball, whatever—and he or she will tell you that is a hard fact because the players use their time effectively in those structured weeks and months. They're practicing time management.

The number of games is not a problem; being away from school too much *is* a problem. During Christmas vacation, between semesters, or in early January before the winter quarter begins are good times for taking long trips, and the students' classwork is not affected negatively.

At one time I was in favor of freshman eligibility, but at the end of my career I became very much against it. Freshmen *should* be allowed to practice. Basketball is a very important part of their lives, and to take it away from them totally would not be a good idea, psychologically and for other reasons. They should have four years of eligibility after their freshman year because more than 90 percent of incoming college students take five or more years to graduate. Under the current setup, most athletes finish their eligibility after their first four years. They played during the toughest year of their college adjustment—their freshman year—and the best year—the fifth—finds them no longer eligible to compete. Holding all freshmen out would solve the Proposition 48 and Proposition 42 problems that have been so disturbing to John Thompson and others. This change just makes a lot of sense anyway; the NCAA allows you five years to complete your eligibility.

At the 1990 Nike summer camp, which annually assembles 120 top high school senior basketball players on the Princeton campus, some interesting data came out of the testing that is part of the camp. The players participate in games in the afternoon. In the mornings they are tested and attend courses designed to help them with entrance exams.

Out of the group, ten campers had a third-grade reading level and thirty had a reading level below the sixth grade. The NCAA is making a lot of money from the national tournament. They should take some of that money, poll some people to find out who the top two hundred prospects are when they are sophomores, then put these kids into a meaningful program for two months each summer to help them prepare for college. And once they are enrolled in school, they should receive some sort of allowance so they can better compete on the social level and feel like they belong.

Another improvement would be the elimination of athletic dorms. This is another area where I've become not only older but wiser. I used to be 100 percent in favor of athletic dorms, but I came to realize they contribute to a lot of the problems in college athletics.

Rob Harden came to Gainesville as a freshman recruit in 1981. His father, Al, was an ex-coach who had become a rep for Converse shoes. Young Rob, a promising five-foot, ten-inch, guard, picked Florida over Oklahoma and Purdue. His younger brother, Roger, said at the time that he, too, wanted to go to Florida, so we had a very happy young man on our hands when he showed up. He moved into the athletic dorm for his freshman year and hadn't been there two months when I received a phone call from Al Harden one night. His opening comment was, "There's trouble in paradise."

He was calling to tell me that Rob, who had been raised in an all-white environment, had just phoned home and apparently had a problem with some of the black players. I looked into it, and you might say that was true. Some dorm yapping had escalated to the point that Rob announced, "When my brother Roger gets here, we'll handle you niggers."

With that, George Jackson, a six-foot, six-inch, 210-pound black, scooped up Rob and dangled him upside-down out over a stairwell three stories high. I'm told that for a few moments Rob Harden became even whiter than normal! I tell that not to embarrass Rob, who I hope has learned to choose his words more carefully when conversing with large black males, but as an example of the kind of *Animal House* atmosphere that is fostered in too many athletic dorms.

Dean Smith has always maintained a philosophy that he didn't want an athletic dorm at North Carolina, so his kids lived in a portion of what they call Granville Towers, above-average student housing. My son, Michael, lived in Granville when he was a student at Carolina. The cafeteria was on the first floor, and the basketball players ate there just like all the rest of the students. I think that's an ideal setup. I've seen too many problems in dorms and dining rooms that are restricted only to athletes. Athletes see only other athletes the majority of their lives, and I think it is a healthy thing for them to mingle with other students. A lot of problems could be avoided, and the student-athletes would get a better overall educational experience.

Duke coach Mike Krzyzewski uses a very effective tactic in recruiting that wouldn't work just anywhere. When many of his recruits are in for their official visit, rather than putting them up in a hotel or a dorm room, Mike will have the player stay in his house, have dinner with his family, and interact with his own children in an effort to (a) make the kid feel more at home and (b) expose any character flaw that Mike doesn't want to discover *after* the kid is already under scholarship. That kind of relationship impresses the kind of true student-athlete that he can recruit at Duke.

If Krzyzewski were to recruit kids out of South Raleigh or South Anywhere—the ghetto kids—it would be very different. The athletes would be very uncomfortable in his house. Most kids under consideration at Duke are from middle- to upper-class homes where there is financial security and it is assumed that they will go to college and get a degree. Those kids are comfortable in Mike's home and are impressed that he can show them a "family" touch.

But if you took, say, Vernon Maxwell, whom I recruited at Florida, and kept him in your house over the weekend, he'd go bonkers. He'd feel oppressed and want to get out and away from you. He wouldn't feel comfortable eating with you.

This is where the system is letting the kids down. We don't put them in an environment where they can learn the social graces. Instead, we warehouse them in athletic dorms, and they don't get to see how the rest of the student body lives.

Big money came to college basketball in a sudden gusher. At Presbyterian in 1951, my starting salary was $3,450. Joan and I opened a soft ice cream business and ran the college canteen to make ends meet. Fifteen years later, I was up to only $10,000 a year at the end of my first term at Florida.

The next year, I made that much in a month from my basketball camp at North Carolina State. Shoe contracts have blossomed to the point that some coaches rake in six-figure fees. I stayed away from the latter because I didn't feel they were right. The coach says, "You gotta wear these Converse shoes, son, because I've got a big contract with Converse. Hundred thou a year." Chris Jackson, the fine guard at LSU, turned up on the front of *Sports Illustrated* wearing Nike shoes. Dale Brown, the LSU coach, has a contract with Converse. Converse went crazy. If you're a youngster and you're coming through that system, you're not going to like it.

In 1982 the Atlantic Coast Conference signed what at the time was the biggest television contract in the nation. Each school received about two million dollars a year; overnight, salaries went from fifty thousand to one hundred thousand dollars. There's big money out there for basketball coaches now. Florida gave my replacement, Lon Kruger, a fifty thousand-dollar loan that he doesn't have to repay if he stays there the full five years of the contract. Heck, that was what I fought for when I made the jump from North Carolina State back to Florida in 1980; now they're giving that much away as a perk. Plus, they gave him a twenty-five-thousand-dollar-a-year annuity. I'm not complaining about that. It's just what is happening to coaches' salaries. It may seem out of line until you take into consideration there's little security and lots of pressure.

The big money has made it a war. We won the national championship at North Carolina State in 1974 and took home a check for seventy-five thousand dollars. In 1989, every game we played in the NCAA tournament earned our team nearly a quarter of a million. We played one game and made almost three times as much as North Carolina State did for winning the national championship in 1974. The Final Four teams in 1990 each collected $1.4 million.

Schools foolishly start building part of that into their budgets. The administration says, "Shoot, you ought to be one of the best sixty-four teams in the country, don't you think, Norm?" They budget it and spend it, and then if you don't land a bid, it's like they lost that money. There's a lot of pressure on coaches to get into the NCAA tournament.

When you're involved in anything on a day-to-day basis, you hardly notice most changes. It's like a man and his receding hairline. He looks in the mirror every day but doesn't notice his hair loss because it takes place in such minute steps. To someone who sees him only once every few years, the change is more dramatic and apparent.

But since I have been out of coaching, more and more the word that keeps surfacing is *hypocrisy,* especially as it relates to the treatment of athletes. The people running college athletics seem to be working so hard to make sure the athletes are given the bare minimum. My attitude was always that we should be giving them the most we can give them—I mean from an NCAA rules point of view right down to an athletic director's decision on whether to give them fifteen dollars for postgame meal money or twenty dollars.

My attitude was that if we were in New York for a game, we should give them twenty dollars; we should find a reason to give these kids the most we can give them. But the athletic departments seem to be almost unanimous in believing that we should give players as little as we can. I've never understood that philosophy.

Yet the same administrators hire promotions people and do all they can to maximize revenue, then do everything possible to minimize the amount given to the kids whose sweat and talent generate those funds. That philosophy is being embraced by college presidents, coaches, and athletic directors who are all making big money, taking exotic trips, and staying in lavish hotels with food and drink paid for by the school. (Have you ever heard of the Southeastern Conference or an NCAA body gathering at a Holiday Inn? Or—heaven forbid—utilizing campus facilities that are just sitting there free of charge?) The administrators don't want to change the status quo. To tinker with the formula might mean giving up their lavish suite at the Hyatt Regency or their charter plane. It's so phony and hypocritical, it's ridiculous!

Academics is another area that reeks of hypocrisy. The same people who call for higher graduation rates are often the very eggheads who make the decisions about postseason play. They assign an East Coast team to a West Regional, yanking the athletes out of class for weeks at a time, all on the premise that the tournament matchups will be better and more equitable. Or worse, to assure good television ratings, which is the real reason behind these decisions. As long as the big bucks roll in, there is little consideration for how many extra days a student will have to miss a biology or English class.

Recently there have been some advocates for moratoriums on games scheduled during exam periods. Well, certainly you shouldn't play games during exams, but coaches don't have total control of schedules. Television now organizes games for us. During my last three years at Florida, each season television organized one game for us with a team of their choosing; and the television chose the place and the time.

For instance, in my last year, CBS put together our game against Stanford in the middle of our Southeastern Conference schedule, on a Saturday in Orlando. We had to push our previously scheduled game with Ole Miss back to Sunday. So after we played Stanford in Orlando on Saturday, we had to go back to Gainesville to play Ole Miss the next afternoon. Ole Miss had been there all weekend practicing and waiting for us. It was all done for the money and exposure that our program would reap.

Bobby Knight has been outspoken against uncommonly late starting times to accommodate television. He's right. ESPN wants you on during prime time, so they insist on a 9:30 start. As a result, the visiting players don't get back in their own dorm rooms until 3:00 A.M. Do you really expect these kids to get up and make their eight o'clock class that morning and be able to compete against students who made 1200 on their entrance exams and had a full night's sleep?

We spend a lot of time talking about doing something for the student-athlete. What we actually wind up doing is more for the benefit of television and the mad scramble to balance budgets bloated by salaries and lavish perks for the adults. Administrators are enjoying luxurious offices, big salaries, cars, and other perks, and the kids see it quite clearly. So here's this kid whose lifestyle hasn't changed, but the coaches and administrators are doing quite well for themselves. Do you really expect him to compete in the classroom and have respect for the "ethical" standards we set for him?

University of Tennessee athletic director Doug Dickey says the problem with giving the players, say, a hundred dollars a month is that they will go out and spend two hundred and create a whole new set of problems. To some extent, that would be true. That gets into money management. But under the current system, you don't have the opportunity to talk to players about money management or for them to learn about it. I don't buy Doug's argument at all. We all have a certain amount of money to operate on, and if we spend more than that, we're making a serious mistake. There's nothing at all wrong with a kid learning that lesson in college. Most nonathletes have that opportunity.

Needless to say, I was more than a little amused at the irony of Dickey's sentiments when I read of his own money making efforts at the University of Tennessee. When Tennessee laws forbidding state employees to sell Shacklee products to the athletic department training table, he set up a former Tennessee football player as a distributor. An internal audit later revealed this legal conflict of interest, and he repaid his profits in the form of (presumably) tax deductable contributions to the athletic department.

Dr. Thomas Hearn, president of Wake Forest, points to the Pell Grant money as the way the system provides for kids who are financially disadvantaged. But kids can't start receiving Pell Grant money until six months after they enroll in school, often longer than that. Applications get bogged down in red tape, waiting for an IRS report or for some other forms that establish the family's financial need. I've known it to drag out for more than a year. But even then the kid doesn't perceive that you're doing something for him. That *you* are. Not the federal government, *you*. Kids will say, "I'm entitled to the Pell Grant money whether I played basketball or not. Now, what are you going to do for me for playing basketball?"

If you buy Hearn's argument, then make it legal to loan incoming freshmen some money until the Pell Grant checks start coming in. The kids still have to have some money for getting to school in the first place and getting set up in their dorms.

I can see more clearly now why student-athletes have so many reasons to be bitter, to feel they're being exploited. I now know where they're coming from when they say they were treated like a piece of meat. It really wasn't that bad, but they feel they were cheated while millions of dollars were available to help them if the schools really cared.

This is not to say that an underprivileged young athlete cannot fight through problems and make the most of his college opportunity, but it takes a special young person with determination and character. A special young man like Clyde Austin comes to mind.

Clyde was a young black player from Richmond, Virginia, with two brothers and a sister at home. His father was deceased. When I first met Clyde and his mother, I noticed that her walk was a little hesitant and she had some difficulty talking. It seems that her live-in boyfriend had come in at 5:30 one morning in a drunken stupor, put a pistol to her head, and blasted her. She still carried the bullet in her head and gradually lost her ability to walk and talk.

Clyde, a high school sophomore at the time, was awakened by the shot and ran into her bedroom. The boyfriend dropped the pistol and ran. When Clyde saw the gruesome scene, his mother bleeding from the skull and lying apparently dead, he scooped up the pistol and chased the guy several blocks with every intention of avenging his mother. Fortunately Clyde's chase failed.

When Clyde signed with us at North Carolina State, the Austins were financially destitute. His mother very quickly reached the point that she became confined to a wheelchair and could not work. Once on campus, Clyde began dating a State coed, Pat, whose family had money. With Pat's help, and with some social aid that he arranged himself, Clyde brought his brothers and sister to Raleigh, rented an apartment that he shared with them, and had his mother put into a Raleigh nursing home. As a college freshman basketball player, he had taken all of this responsibility. It was awesome.

He never once came in and asked me or anyone else for help. He took care of all the social work and all the red tape. To me, what he was doing was one of the sweetest stories of college athletics. He was a credit to himself and to college basketball.

Then one day in his senior year—the season of 1978-79—someone called and told me that the next day the Raleigh *News and Observer* would break a story that Clyde Austin had bought a Cadillac. As it turned out, he had.

That next morning on the front page—not the front page of sports, but *the* front page—was a photo of Clyde and his big Cadillac. I guess it was about as big a Cadillac as you could find. Clyde and Pat got the money together, made the down payment, and bought the car. I brought him in and started reaming him about it, explaining what the appearance was. An insecure young man easily led to tears, he disarmed me with one statement. "Coach," he said, "on Sunday when Pat and my brothers and sister and I get in that car and drive around, I feel like I'm somebody. The rest of the week, I don't feel like I'm anything."

It said volumes about the kind of hell that kid was living in during the week in class. He didn't feel like he was equal. He saw the affluence of the other kids in their clothes and heard their talk of fun things—things that were impossible for a college student bearing the responsibilities of a family and an invalid mother.

Clyde's car was thoroughly investigated by the NCAA, the university, and just about every newspaper in North Carolina. There was never any indication that he had gotten one dime of outside help from Wolfpack boosters or anyone else. Clyde's story has continued to blossom with sweetness. After a brief tryout in the NBA, he joined the Harlem Globetrotters and was captain of the 'Trotters for years. He became a lay preacher, started a little business, and completed requirements for his college degree in the summer of 1990.

But for every Clyde Austin there have been hundreds chewed up by the system and spit out as frustrated, bitter failures. Let's be honest: we're talking about a group of young men and women, most from low socioeconomic backgrounds. We ought to be helping these kids. I'm not talking about a blank check. I'm talking about basic needs.

As freshmen, their confirmation is changing. Some are getting three meals a day, often for the first time. They're working out in the weight room. They're filling out, and they're going to have to buy clothes. They become campus celebrities. And they don't have a dime in their pockets. These kids need money, and the coach begins to worry about things like fixing games, selling drugs, or signing early with an agent for under-the-table payoffs. The system is encouraging those violations of the rules, making these kids very vulnerable to temptation.

I hear the argument that the poor kids and the marginal students are better off for just having been in the college environment for four years whether they can graduate or not. That's a lie! You don't put someone in an environment where he fails every day and expect it to be a good experience. That's why some of these kids we're forcing into college athletics don't want to go to class: they can't compete there. We found out a long time ago that group tutoring often doesn't work. There are kids who don't want to demonstrate, even in front of teammates, that the subject matter is beyond their grasp. So they sit there and are disruptive or don't participate at all.

Bringing kids into school who don't belong there is not entirely the coach's fault. It's unrealistic to simply say, "go get better people." The coach has to get people who can win, or he will be fired and people will say, "Gee, nice man. Did a good job, graduated a lot of kids, but he just didn't win enough."

When Jimmy Valvano was being blasted about the low graduation rates at North Carolina State, part of the poor profile included a player I had signed named Craig Watts. Craig wanted to study engineering, and Dr. Larry Monteith, dean of the school of engineering, was helpful in recruiting him.

When I left, Monteith became chancellor, and one of his public criticisms was, "How could it be that Jimmy Valvano didn't graduate Craig Watts?" Heck, Monteith probably had as much to do with recruiting Watts as I did, yet he wasn't critical of the engineering school. Instead he criticized Jimmy Valvano.

In recent months, there has been a public disclosure of graduation rates of various college athletic programs that shows what all of us in the business have known all along. Graduation rates are low for athletes at schools where the overall graduation rate is low. If you coach at Notre Dame, you're going to have high graduation rates; if you coach at Louisville you are not. And there is precious little that a coach at either place can do about it.

As a coach, I didn't admit players to the school and I didn't teach players in the classroom. Somebody once asked Wimp Sanderson, the very fine coach at Alabama, what percentage of his players graduated. He said, "All of those that *want* to and *can*."

He's right.

When I was at Florida from 1960 to 1966, every player we had in our program who stayed for his full four years of eligibility graduated. They got their degrees. Every one of them. We're not talking about 52 percent or 65 percent. Twenty-five percent of them even went on to get graduate degrees.

Then, all of a sudden we stopped having standards, unless you consider Proposition 48 a standard. Proposition 48 means you have a 2.0 high school grade-point average in a core curriculum—a C average—and 700 on the SAT entrance boards. Does anybody honestly think that a 700, 2.0 has a chance to graduate from a decent university? We're kidding ourselves.

If you're going to take people who aren't any better prepared than that, you owe it to them to have an academic program in which they can succeed. Don't ask those kids to compete with students who are going to be doctors and lawyers and those who have 3.4 averages and score 1200 on their boards.

It doesn't fit. It won't work.

Then they pin the coach up against a wall and say, "What percentage of your players graduated?" At Florida, one of the last things they did before gunning me down in the Halloween Massacre was to give me a thousand-dollar bonus because more than 50 percent of my incoming freshmen class of 1983 graduated. Is that ludicrous?

I notice now in Steve Spurrier's new contract as Florida's football coach—and in the contracts of many other coaches—there is a big bonus if a certain percentage of the players graduate. I thought encouraging athletes to keep up their class work was a part of our job. I didn't know you had to have *bonuses* to get that done. I'm not blaming Steve. But it is ridiculous for a school to take the attitude that if they give the coach some money, he'll probably get a higher percentage of graduates. It doesn't work that way. It won't happen.

The NCAA just signed a billion-dollar contract to televise the postseason basketball tournament. Richard Shultz, current executive director of the NCAA and a man of great intelligence, says: "Now we have to be creative on how to distribute that money." Creative? They won't give one nickel of it to the student-athlete, I promise you. Not one nickel.

When the recent point-shaving allegations erupted at North Carolina State, Charles Shackelford tried to justify that he had taken money from an agent by saying, "I was young and I was poor." Well, that's the profile of so many of today's college basketball stars. What's new about that?

They feel like they have been cheated. They are saying, in effect, "I didn't get any of that billion dollars. We players are entitled to some of that."

The system is wrong. We're using college athletes unfairly. Too often they come in with poor self-images to start with, particularly in academics and often in social areas. Then we inflict further damage to that self-image while they're there.

We aren't treating them fairly, and they know it. They aren't treating themselves fairly, either. They make some mistakes; they're young adults. They're not helpless little children. We need to treat them fairly, then hold them responsible. I think that can happen.

I think we ought to give them a chance to pay their way back and forth from home to school, to buy some clothes,and to have some spending money. Then see if we're faced with the problems that are confronting collegiate basketball and football today.

When Dr. Marshall Criser first took over as president at Florida, I went in to talk with him. *He* didn't hire me, so I thought it would be a good idea to sit down with him and explain how I saw my job and, in turn, listen to his perception of my job. We got into the issue of the unfair scholarship and the fact we were taking kids that didn't belong in a university.

I explained that I was trying to walk a middle ground, taking some kids that are good students but average athletes, and some kids that are good athletes but academic risks. We put them in a bag, shook it up, and hoped we could come out looking pretty decent. I explained that could cause some pain. I said there are some options.

"One, we could be like Vanderbilt," I said.

"Oh, my God!" he exclaimed. "I hope we don't have to be like Vanderbilt!"

Well, what's *wrong* with being like Vanderbilt?

Academically, all presidents want to be like Vanderbilt. But as far as their won-lost record in football is concerned, nobody wants to be like them.

Something is going to have to give. And I put the responsibility squarely in the lap of the college presidents. Something can be done about the deplorable situation in big-time college sports today. But it will take hard work, integrity, compassion, and courage.

And everybody will have to cut the hypocrisy.

Epilogue

Where I fit among that group of coaches is for someone else to determine. I had my moments in the sun, and I feel I made my contributions to the coaching profession and to a sport that remains dear to me. The enjoyment derived from putting this book together, reliving my interactions with those coaches and all others along the way, has been a bonus my wife and I hadn't expected. We are a very close family, and, next to them, the biggest thing in my life has been college basketball. The game has enabled us to do so many things together. I am a little concerned that I have been too hard on myself here, perhaps leaving the unfortunate impression that we had more bad times than good. That's not true. The bad times—the tough times—were there, and they stung. But the joyous, warm, happy moments were by far in the majority.

I think the pressures of being in the public eye on a day-to-day basis probably helped make ours a closer family than if I had been in a more private profession. Often we circled the wagons and drew strength from one another. Something would occur that caused me to take a rap, and my family would come to my support in wonderful, bonding conversations around the dinner table.

Perhaps the most dramatic example of that was when our son, Michael, was so distraught by taunts and criticisms aimed at dear ole dad by his school chums at North Carolina that he asked permission to transfer "home" to North Carolina State. Michael had gone to Carolina on a Morehead scholarship, a generous academic grant that provides money for transportation, clothes, and other ordinary living expenses in addition to room, board, and school costs. I have often used the Morehead as an example of what an athletic scholarship should entail.

As you know, State and Carolina are bitter rivals, fostering constant barbs thrown from both camps. At Chapel Hill, Norman Sloan—Morehead scholar Michael Sloan's father—was a hated enemy ranking on the popularity index somewhere between a kindergarten arsonist and a Scud missile.

I had told him how tough it would be for him to live behind enemy lines, but he insisted he could handle it. He managed it for one year, but the slander and needling began to take their toll during his sophomore year. One Monday near the end of that basketball season, my secretary, Frances Lewis, advised she had scheduled an appointment for me on Wednesday with one Michael Sloan.

I promptly called him, but Michael insisted on waiting until Wednesday to discuss this thunderclap matter. You can imagine the things that ran through my mind. It was a tough two days for Joan and me.

At last, seated across the desk from me, he nervously began, "Dad, I'm very unhappy and want to transfer. I want to come back to North Carolina State."

First off, I was greatly relieved this was not going to be an announcement of legal, academic, or domestic transgressions. He went into all the harassment: at 2:00 A.M. after our game with them, some student would leave an order for two dozen eggs and a gallon of milk on his door. (We were the ag school, you see, and Carolina was the country club set.) It was tough hearing disgusting comments about his mother and me. I reminded him that he and I and his mother had talked about the unique difficulties at great lengths and that I felt very strongly that once he had chosen a school he should stick with it. I was pretty tough and holding my own until Michael threw one below the belt for the clincher.

With great agony and anguish in his voice, he said, "Dad, I can't imagine being a graduate of North Carolina."

"Son," I blurted, "you come on home!"

He transferred to State, and we had two wonderful years together. He became manager on the team, traveling with us, and we had a lot of quality time together we wouldn't have had otherwise.

Joan and I made many friends—dear, lifelong friends from all socio-economic strata—all because of basketball.

In my mind, the exercise here was to offer an overview of how sociological changes—drugs, integration, money, and television—

affect college athletics, with supporting anecdotes. Ironically, I may have done what I've so often accused sportswriters of doing, going overboard in an attempt to balance the story.

But my thirty-eight-year journey through college coaching was a richly rewarding experience. In the fall of 1990 Joan and I were having lunch in Athens, Greece, looking up at the Acropolis. I laughed and said, "You know, when you and I were in high school, I didn't even know what the Acropolis was. Now we're having lunch at the base of it."

Basketball was what enabled that to happen.

After we won the NCAA championship in 1974, we took a seventeen-day tour of the Orient. I was able to take my family behind the Iron Curtain. All because of basketball.

So I surely don't want to leave the impression that my coaching career was a downer or an embittering experience. On the whole, it has been a fantastic, uplifting adventure. At the end, we were depressed and hurt. As I exited, I had some bitter feelings, but doing this book has been the tonic to overcome those feelings. It reminded us of all the good times, making us realize that the darker moments were but momentary missteps along the way. Going back to visit with players like David Thompson and Tommy Burleson and Hawkeye Whitney and Rick Anheuser were nostalgic replays of golden, struggling times and heartening updates on their lives. Being reminded of the players from all the way back at Presbyterian College who would show up at Florida once a year to applaud their old coach is salve for any fractured ego. Those kinds of things were some of the real pluses to being in this business.

Sure, the game has its warts and misfits, and there will always exist the need for the kinds of corrections I indicated. But college basketball remains a marvelous vehicle that provided this old trouper with an unforgettable ride. For that I am eternally grateful.